THE LONG TRAIL

KIPLING ROUND THE WORLD

For my children and grandchildren, with love

THE LONG TRAIL

KIPLING ROUND THE WORLD

MERYL MACDONALD

*For John and Mary
with best wishes
Meryl Macdonald
29-7-2000*

TIDEWAY HOUSE

Copyright © Meryl Macdonald 1999
First published in 1999 by Tideway House
P O Box 26, Bristol, BS9 1YH
email: mmb@tidewayhouse.freeserve.co.uk

Distributed by Gazelle Book Services Limited
Falcon House, Queen Square
Lancaster, England LA1 1RN

British Library Cataloguing in Publication Data
A catalogue record for this book is available from the British Library

ISBN 0-9536324-0-7

Typeset by Amolibros, Watchet, Somerset
This book production has been managed by Amolibros
Printed and bound by Professional Book Supplies, Oxford, England

Contents

List of Illustrations   vii

Acknowledgements   ix

List of Abbreviations   xi

Introduction   xiii

INDUCTION 1865-1882

Chapter One   '...if only he would *work*'.   1

COMPRESSION 1882-1892

Chapter Two   'Subversive pamphleteer' to Special Correspondent   27

Chapter Three   *From Sea to Sea*: a Globe-trotter returns   43

Chapter Four   London: fame – and fever   68

EXPLOSION 1892-1914

Chapter Five   Home-building, but '...gypsies by birth.'   87

Chapter Six   'We must begin again...' in England   112

Chapter Seven   East or West? '...A divided mind.'   129

Chapter Eight   '...the discovery of England' on four wheels   139

Chapter Nine   Haunted landscapes; a Viking galley 'beyond the world's end'   154

Chapter Ten   Letters to the children – but meddling in politics   174

Chapter Eleven	War Correspondent on land and sea; '...a short life'	193
Chapter Twelve	Motor tours: pilgrimage and pleasure	209
Chapter Thirteen	Bateman's 'enormously empty'; the long trail ends	226
Epitaph		247
Index of Kipling's Works		249
General Index		253

List of Illustrations

Illustrations 1-21 appear after page 70 and illustrations 22-34 after page 166.

1   James Macdonald (1761-1833), born Ballinamallard, Enniskillen;
     Rudyard Kipling's great-grandfather.

2   George Browne Macdonald(1805-1868); Rudyard Kipling's
     grandfather.

3   Hannah Macdonald (1809-1875); Rudyard Kipling's
     grandmother.

4   Frederic W Macdonald (1842-1928); Rudyard Kipling's uncle.

5   Alice Kipling (1837-1910), Rudyard's mother.

6   Ruddy, not yet six when he was left at the 'House of Desolation'.

7   The United Services College at Westward Ho!

8   Young Kipling in the centre of a group of USC boys.

9   India: the young journalist in Simla.

10   'Trix' Kipling (1868-1948); Rudyard Kipling's sister.

11   The last leg of Kipling's voyage Home in 1889 was in
     the *City of Berlin*.

12   John Lockwood Kipling (1837-1911). His genial wisdom
     prompted a niece to call him the 'enquire within'.

13   Father and son trying out ideas for JLK's *Beast and Man in India*.

14   The beloved Josephine in the nursery at Naulakha.

15   Josephine and nurse at Naulakha.

16   'In the Neolithic Age' depicted for cousin Florence at Rock
     House.

17   Carrie with Nip and Tuck and the cockney coachman at Naulakha.

18 Arundell House, 'the hired girls' school' in Tisbury where they spent the summer of 1894.

19 Rock House, near Torquay.

20 North End House, Rottingdean.

21 Rudyard and Carrie rented The Elms for five years.

22 Elsie, John and Josephine (London 1898).

23 ss *Majestic*, in which the Kiplings made the ill-fated voyage to New York.

24 Bateman's. Its feng-shui was good.

25 Bateman's front door.

26 Outward bound for the Cape on the *Walmer Castle*.

27 How Rudyard altered the Animal's head in a copy of *Just So Stories*.

28 Fourteenth century misericord at Chichester Cathedral.

29 King George V meets his speech-writer on a visit to the War Cemeteries.

30 With cousin Stan Baldwin at Kipling's installation as Rector of St Andrew's University.

31 The new Rector signing autographs.

32 A peaceful vista in the garden at Bateman's.

33 Rudyard in later life, happy to be 'dominated' by Aberdeens.

34 Rudyard Kipling in his study at Bateman's.

Acknowledgements

I acknowledge with thanks the permission of A P Watt Ltd on behalf of the National Trust for Places of Historic Interest or Natural Beauty to quote from published and unpublished material by Rudyard Kipling and members of his family; also for their permission to quote from *Early Verse by Rudyard Kipling* 1879-1889 edited by Andrew Rutherford; and for their permission on behalf of The National Trust for Places of Historic Interest or Natural Beauty and Professor Morton Cohen to quote from *Rudyard Kipling to Rider Haggard, The Record of a Friendship* edited by Morton Cohen. I acknowledge with thanks the permission of Macmillan Ltd to quote extracts from *The Letters of Rudyard Kipling*, Volumes 1-3, edited by Thomas Pinney and published by The Macmillan Press Ltd (Rudyard Kipling's letters © 1990 and 1996 by the National Trust for Places of Historic Interest or Natural Beauty.)

I am indebted to the authors/executors for their kind permission to quote extracts from the following:

> Miss Ann Cornford: *Cope Cornford Papers*
> Earl Baldwin: *The Macdonald Sisters* and Hannah Macdonald's Diary
> Miss Lorraine Price: *Price Papers*
> Miss Serena Thirkell: *Three Houses*
> George Webb: *Kipling's Japan*
> Birmingham Museums and Art Gallery: *Millership Papers*

My grateful thanks to Professor Tom Pinney for taking the trouble to read my typescript, thus avoiding some egregious errors on my part. (Any errors remaining in the text are mine alone.) My grateful thanks also to Bet Inglis of the Kipling Archive at Sussex University, for her ever ready assistance and enthusiasm over the years; and to John Burt, her predecessor. And a special 'thank you' to all my friends in the Kipling Society for their interest and support: in particular Professor Carrington, Rosalind Kennedy, Ronald King, Lisa Lewis, John Shearman and George Webb; to Betty Sutherland for her hospitality at Bateman's; to Lady Helen Hardinge and Mrs.George Lanchester who each made me welcome and kindly answered my enquiries; to Joan Holmes for her hospitality and expert knowledge of Westward Ho! and the USC; to Frank Morley and Howard C Rice Jnr for their interest and assistance; and to Dorchester Library's County Librarian who helpfully introduced me to the *First* Edition of *Grose's Dictionary of the Vulgar Tongue*.

Ever since I first thought of writing about Rudyard Kipling's interest in 'things mechanical' I have sought information far and wide on early motor cars and ships. Almost without exception I have received courteous and helpful replies to my endless queries. I record with gratitude the following:

Peter Brockes (National Motor Museum, Beaulieu); Stewart Daniels (Rolls-Royce Enthusiasts' Club's historian) whose invaluable technical knowledge was put at my disposal; John Fasal; Ian Luckett (Jaguar Cars, Coventry); Michael Over; Richard Westcott (BL Heritage Ltd); and the National Maritime Museum Library for its extensive researches on my behalf.

My researches into early motoring history for Chapter Eight led me to an invaluable source of information: *A History of the First 75 Years of the Automobile Association 1905-1980* by Hugh Barty-King, published by the AA, 1980.

Not all of my letters of enquiry have elicited a response. Any errors or omissions in the above as a consequence will be rectified in future editions.

Finally, a warm vote of thanks and appreciation to Jane Tatam, my painstaking consultant, whose expert guidance throughout the publishing process has brought to fruition what had previously seemed impossible.

Illustrations

No 6 is courtesy of Miss Helen Macdonald; Nos 9, 22, 29, 34 are reproduced by permission of the National Trust; Nos 11 and 23 courtesy of National Maritime Museum, London; Nos 14, 15, 17 are from the Collection of Howard C Rice, Jr; Nos 20 and 21 are courtesy of Michael Smith; No 28 is courtesy of the Dean and Chapter of Chichester Cathedral; Nos 30 and 31 are courtesy of St Andrews University Library; No 33 is courtesy of Mrs Mary Ley.

All other illustrations are the author's.

List of Abbreviations

AK	Alice Kipling.
Birkenhead	*Rudyard Kipling*, Lord Birkenhead
BoW	*A Book of Words*
B-r B	*Barrack-room Ballads.*
Carrington	*Rudyard Kipling, His Life and Work*, Charles Carrington
CK	Carrie Kipling.
CMG	*Civil & Military Gazette.*
EB-J	Edward Burne-Jones.
EM	Edith Macdonald
EP	Edith Plowden.
FWM	Frederic William Macdonald.
GB-J	Georgiana Burne-Jones.
GBM	George Browne Macdonald.
HM	Henry (Harry) Macdonald.
HRH	Henry Rider Haggard.
JK	John Kipling.
JLK	John Lockwood Kipling.
KJ	Kipling Journal.
KP	Kipling Papers.
LCC	Leslie Cope Cornford.
Letters, Vol,	*Letters of RK*, Volumes 1-3, Edited by Thomas Pinney.
LoT	*Letters of Travel.*
MB-J	Margaret Burne-Jones (Mackail).
OBK	*O Beloved Kids*, ed Elliot Gilbert.
Orel	*Kipling, Interviews & Recollections*, Vols 1 & 2, ed Harold Orel.
PP	Price Papers.
SB	Stanley Baldwin.
SoM	*Something of Myself.*
USCC	*United Services College Chronicle.*
Wilson	Angus Wilson, *The Strange Ride of Rudyard Kipling.*

Introduction

Six months' short of his seventieth birthday, Rudyard Kipling confessed to having always wanted to build or buy a 400-ton brig and sail her round the world.

'Never did. Now, I suppose it's too late,' he told the American graduate who had driven down from Oxford to meet him. But it was not too late for a turn round the Bateman's pond in the *Queen Mary*, his six-foot skiff with hand-cranked paddle wheels.

'You can be the engine-room,' Kipling told his visitor, 'I'll be the passenger-list.' The young man was so overcome with nerves at meeting the famous author that he cranked too hard and broke the paddle-wheel. They were marooned in the middle of the pond.

Kipling laughed and the ice was broken. While they waited to be rescued he talked of many things, putting his 'engine-room' at ease. He spoke of ambition – and of secondary ambitions, like his brig. The more you had, he said, the more fully you lived. It was as if he sensed what was troubling his visitor that day: the difficult decision he had to make about his future. Indeed the young man, being so young, was looking for something – a word or a sign – that might indicate which path he should choose: whether to take up the offer of a safe but dull teaching post – or devote his time to writing and finding publication.

'Do the things you really want to do if you possibly can,' said Kipling. 'Don't wait for circumstances to be exactly right. You'll find that they never are.'

The young man had found the answer he was seeking; as later he found publication.[1]

For someone whose life had been regularly punctuated by long sea voyages from the age of two – until in old age he complained he never wanted to board another boat – the building of a brig seems an odd ambition to have cherished over the eventful years. And yet the fact that he wrote so many stories, poems and essays about the sea seems to indicate that it had a particular significance for him. Why was this, when, with Methodist ministers for grandfathers on both sides of his family, he had no obvious maritime or naval connections?

What about those early voyages from the land of his birth (India) to the land of his people (England) where he went to school: could they have been instrumental in turning the key of Davy Jones' locker, as it were, in his fertile imagination? Certainly by the time he left his North Devon school and once again sailed 'The Exiles' Line'[2] for India he had already made the voyage three times; four if you count his parents' honeymoon trip to Bombay when he first managed to make his presence felt aboard ship by putting the pregnant Alice Kipling off sea-travel for the rest of her life. That it might have had the opposite effect on the embryonic poet did not, however, manifest itself when the sixteen-year-old Ruddy, seasick and alone, reluctantly left England, his sweetheart and all thoughts of university behind him – called home by his parents to do a man's work in India.

It would be nearly seven years before he saw the sea again and there is little evidence to suggest that he missed it. But he was overjoyed to be in his father's house once more, and threw himself into the work that had been found for him on the local newspaper. He wrote exclusively about his adopted country and people; 'mine own people' he called them, so closely did he identify – and empathise – with them. ('Mine Own People' was his original choice of title for *Life's Handicap*, his first volume of short stories after leaving India, until he discovered to his chagrin that a book bearing the same title was already in print – and by a female writer too.) India was in his blood, although not in the biological sense, as has sometimes been implied, and for the first few years in the sub-continent he had no thought of returning home. Not, that is, unless Flo Garrard[3] should ask him to return.

After four years in India he wrote: 'Would you be astonished if I told you that I look forward to nothing but an Indian journalist's career? Why should I? My home's out here; my people are out here; all the friends that I know are out here and all the interests I have are out here. Why should I go home? Any fool can put up rhymes and the market is full of boys who could undersell me as soon as I put foot in it...Besides I was brought out of the stockyard on trust. Bitted, mouthed and broken...on spec. Very well. I shall begin to pay for my breaking in a few years. Then it will take some time to refund that expenditure...'[4]

When three years later, a combination of soaring ambition and deteriorating health prompted him to leave India, he took ship for England the long way round, writing travel pieces *en route* for his newspaper, whose manager's parting words had been nothing if not a challenge to the young journalist. 'Take it from me you'll never be worth more than four hundred rupees a month to anyone,'[5] when he was actually earning seven hundred at the time. That rankled.

This was the voyage that made Kipling, of necessity, a travel writer; and by default, a globe-trotter. He sailed on six different vessels – all but one, screw-driven, three-masted schooners from the homely

'Mutton-mail'[6] out of Calcutta, to the luxury flagship *City of Berlin* out of New York. He became acquainted with the sea in all its moods and with passengers in all theirs: that breed of globe-trotter who '...sitting in my chair, discussed India with the unbridled arrogance of five weeks on a Cook's ticket. He was from England and had dropped his manners in the Suez Canal.'[7] The habit was catching, for Kipling's own manners plummeted into the Pacific at the sight of San Francisco harbour, and were to remain volatile throughout his travels in America. Moreover, whether he liked globe-trotters or not (mostly not), he found he had become one himself, from helmet to deck shoes.

His biographers tend to accept Kipling and the Sea as a phase in English Literature, no more, no less: the brilliant journalist exploiting to the full what literally flowed past his elbow during those long and often tedious voyages. When we read his vivid descriptions of the sea we can almost feel the spume on our face, the lift and wallow of the deck beneath our feet – almost feel seasick with him. And when he describes the inner workings of a marine engine we are astounded at the technical knowledge of this man who had never shown the slightest interest in things mechanical at school, or used his hands to advantage except when wielding a pen.

Kipling's unfailing knack of culling the life-stories of 'nameless men on steamers and trains round the world'[8] provided him with many of his plots. And he rarely needed to take notes. He argued that if a thing did not stay in his memory it was hardly worth the writing out.[9]

Someone who knew him well once said that his mind was like the leaves of a book, which could be quickly turned to suit the company he was in. Aboard ship, for instance, he had a chameleon-like ability for adapting to his surroundings which made him indistinguishable from, say, the engineer who was convinced he was another engineer – because he spoke their language; or the commercial traveller who could have sworn he was one of them, because he spoke theirs. With his intense interest in other people's obsessions – whether deep sea cables or domestic cookers, ('once a journalist, always and forever a journalist') he could seal off any personal unhappiness in a water-tight compartment – most of the time. Only when he was ill and overworking would it seep out and temporarily submerge him.

In the years to come he made several long sea-voyages and had many homes. But unlike the average globe-trotter he was often a prey to melancholy, of longing for his previous home across the sea: for North Devon when he was in India ('Exiles are we – yet, through our dreams/ Old scenes and faces glide,/ So that the city's murmur seems/ The voice of Northam tide.');[10] for India when he was in London living near the Thames, (he would recognise the rig of an East-bound schooner and long to be on her. 'She'll lift the Southern Cross in a week – lucky old tub – oh, lucky old tub!');[11] and for America when he was back in England after four of the happiest years of his life in Vermont; those honeymoon years of early marriage, home-building and child-rearing, of starting to put down roots.

The Welsh have a word for it: *hiraeth*. It is an overwhelming yearning tinged with melancholy that is entirely Celtic, and not always understood by the more phlegmatic Anglo-Saxon. It often overcame Kipling when he was within sight or sound of water, and it acted on his imagination like a spark in a combustion chamber.

But the question still remains why Kipling, with no nautical connections apart from a hotchpotch of sweet and sour childhood memories, should write so compellingly about the sea; beyond, I believe, the call of journalistic duty. Was it perhaps that the man who has been called – among other things – the Poet of Empire looked upon the oceans of the world as the main arteries of that empire, carrying the life-blood of men and materials between the pink-shaded areas on the map? But if that were the case, why did he not stay up on the bridge to survey 'our dominion over palm and pine',[12] instead of getting involved below decks with the engineers *and* their engines?

Let us take a look at his parental background: Yorkshire farming stock on his father's side, Celtic on his mother's, Alice Macdonald; and with Methodist ministers on both sides. No Captains Courageous in sight; not even a Petty Officer Pyecroft. Like others before me I, too, had accepted this lack of sea-going forebears in our family. Until the day I went on a small pilgrimage to see for myself where generations of our Highland ancestors had lived and died.

I found myself in Skye, off the west coast of Scotland. And there, as I stood gazing out to sea from the ruins of Duntulm Castle, one of the many cliff-top strongholds of the Macdonalds, *and feeling strangely melancholy myself,* the truth hit me between the eyes. Our Gaelic ancestors had been sea-faring men, more at home on the water than on the land. They had to be: the sea was their life-blood, their only means of communication. When Gillebride and his son, Somerled, sailed across from Ireland almost nine hundred years ago to repossess their lands from the Vikings, much of the western mainland of Scotland and all the islands from Man to Orkneys were in the hands of the invaders from the north. It took three hundred years, many sea battles – and some judicious intermarrying with the enemy – before the Vikings were persuaded to leave the Western Isles for good. It was the heroic Somerled, half Scots and half Norse, descendant of Clan Cholla and the kings of Dalriada, who in the space of forty years became King of the Isles (Rex Insularum), commanding a huge fleet of galleys in defence of his sea kingdom. And it was Somerled, with the help of a little galley-boat diplomacy, who persuaded the Norwegian King of Man to let him marry his daughter, Ragnhilda. (Their grandson Donald would become the progenitor of Clan Donald.) Somerled's attitude towards both Scottish and Norse Kings was beautifully impartial: he would pay lip service to either while they left him and his people to live in peace and by their own Celtic laws. But let either king try to impose feudal serfdom on the independent men of the Isles and his galleys would be launched, three men to each oar...anything between 60 and 160 galleys would accompany him to a hosting. And Somerled won all his battles.

(As the convoy of small boats rounded the distant point on the Sound of Sleat, it was easy to pick out the galley from where I stood on Isleornsay jetty. Tiny though she looked – she was only forty feet long and open to the elements – her russet sail and honey-coloured hull stood out against the dark mass of hills and silver-grey water. The sail was furled and the oars manned as she approached the shore where a reception committee of Highland chiefs and misty-eyed spectators awaited her. To the skirl of pipes the *Aileach* skimmed over the shingle almost to the feet of the Macdonald High Chief and his Cupbearer who handed a ceremonial quaich of whiskey to each crewman. It was a moving and heart-warming 'home-coming'.

Dreamed of and planned, built and manned by the combined efforts and faith of Irish and Scots descendants of the great Somerled, the *Aileach* {a replica sixteenth century sixteen-oar Highland galley} had sailed from north-west Ireland in the summer of 1991, threading her way delicately through the unpredictable waters of the Western Isles, bound for Stornoway. Not since the days of the Lords of the Isles had such a vessel made the passage.

During the six weeks' voyage she survived a Force Nine gale and a broken mast. The graceful swan-necked birlinn, the familiar of our sea-going ancestors, had proved her sea-worthiness beyond any doubt; and her crew that the spirit of Somerled was still alive in the Highlands and Islands.)[13]

At its zenith Clan Donald was the most powerful of all the clans. 'In their time was great peace and welth (sic) in the Isles thro the ministration of justice.'[14] Its territory ranged over five hundred islands and included parts of the Scottish mainland and north-east Ireland, some twenty-five thousand square miles in all. Fifty cliff-top castles guarded a kingdom which was united by the sea, so that a fleet of ships was a necessity as much as a show of strength. What Somerled learned about shipbuilding from the Vikings he had artfully adapted to the needs of his own people, so that the Highland galleys or birlinns were smaller and more manoeuvrable than the invaders' long-ships. In them the chiefs went to war or to woo; in both activities their prowess was formidable, their objectives the same: to ensure the clan's perpetuity through the male line. Somerled's son Reginald founded and endowed the abbey on Iona and built the nunnery there. His sister Beatrice became its first prioress.

'It is no joy without Clan Donald,/ it is no strength to be without them;/ the best race in the round world:/ to them belongs every goodly man.'[15]

And the not so goodly. First and foremost the chiefs were warriors, occupied in what one of the clan's own historians called 'the congenial employment of robbery on the high seas'.[16] Ashore they begat sons with equal fervour, either by handfasting (which in Celtic law did not mean illegitimacy) or by a series of wives; or both. From which nests of half-brothers fratricide was not uncommon. As the chiefs' possessions and wealth increased, so too did the intricacies of succession. Whether the inheritance of the chiefship should be by Celtic or feudal law often depended upon whose side the last chief had favoured. At the time of Robert the Bruce two of Donald's grandsons, Alasdair and Angus Og, who in turn inherited the Lordship, fought on opposite sides. Angus Og led five thousand (some historians say ten) Highlanders to the field of Bannockburn and was instrumental in the defeat of the English.

But being Celts they were poets and dreamers too and a strong religious streak lay hidden within the wildest of them – even though it might not surface until late in their lives. The eponymous Donald was one such chief. The time came when Donald felt the need to make the long pilgrimage to Rome. His remorse at his misdeeds was so great that he took no fewer than seven priests with him. Afterwards he richly endowed the abbey at Saddell in Kintyre which his grandfather had founded and spent the last years of his life within its walls, in repentance.

It is interesting to reflect that to this day the Norse king's Black Galley is depicted on the clan's crest, against its mast the red eagle of the Earls of Ross – the result of another fortuitous alliance in the fifteenth century when the eighth Lord of the Isles married the earl's daughter; their son subsequently claiming the title to add to his own. (By this time the Macdonald Chief had been demoted to Dominus Insularum, a title considered less of a threat to the mainland Kings.) But inevitably it had to happen: the tenth Lord of the Isles was wrong-footed between Scottish and English kingdoms and forfeited both titles. The Crown claimed the Lordship and today Prince Charles is its holder. By the seventeenth century the clan chiefs were forbidden to keep more than six retainers in their castles and only one galley of sixteen or eighteen oars; at least, in theory.

Of the many branches of Clan Donald descended from Somerled, only three of the Scottish branches have chiefs today, of which Sleat is one. And it is from one of Sleat's sixteenth century cadet branches (younger sons of the Chief) that Rudyard Kipling's mother, Alice Macdonald was descended.

It was not all war-making between the Islands; many of our Sleat ancestors were poets and scholars, one at least was a notable historian while a certain Donald of Sleat was a poet *and* cattle-dealer in the seventeenth century. The less cerebral among them occupied their spare time cattle-stealing from their neighbours, the Norse-descended MacLeods, on what seems to have been a *quid pro quo* basis.

By this time the clan chiefs were sending their eldest sons to school and university on the 'continent', as they used to call the mainland. The younger sons combined to engage a tutor, who might be a student of divinity on vacation, to teach them and their families English and the Classics. It is said that during the eighteenth century 'the gentry of the Isles' were probably the best educated in the world. 'Young ladies could quote Latin and Greek and gentlemen composed poetry in the tongue of Horace rather than that of Ossian.' [17]

And then came the Jacobite Rising, Culloden and the Highland Clearances, the abolition of the clans and the ensuing mass emigration of families driven from land which had been theirs for centuries. From Sleat in Skye, John Macdonald, Jacobite, son of the fifth Macdonald of Ostaig, took ship with his wife for the New World. The ship was blown off course and put into Belfast, where for some reason they decided to go no further. The two expatriates settled in Fermanagh where their son James was born, in poverty, in 1761. Was it a coincidence that they chose to live in the county from which, six hundred years earlier, Somerled and his father had picked two hundred fighting men to sail with them (from Malinbeg) to re-possess their lands? Or was it an inherent desire to return to the supposed birthplace of their ancestor – also expatriate born?

This then was Rudyard Kipling's Celtic inheritance, for James Macdonald was his maternal great-grandfather. Kipling admitted to knowing little about his ancestors but thought it was 'more or less' established that his mother's family came from Skye. 'Our Methodist forebears, I fancy, took more account of a man's religious convictions than his ancestry. One hears a good deal about their eloquence and piety and but little of their cattle-lifting fathers.'[18] Or, he might have added, their roving, sea-going ancestors; either of which would have held more appeal for him – as a teller of tales – than his 'godly ancestry'.[19] Instead, and for reasons which I believe had much to do with his innate reticence and in deference to his father's Yorkshire stock, Kipling kept to himself what he knew about his mother's forebears. Doing so gave him all the freedom he needed to write about galleys and sea-faring Vikings as often as he wished, without being accused of ancestor-worship. (In fact the question has been posed more than once: was Kipling a Viking? But the questioners were looking towards his Yorkshire ancestry and the fact that his surname was of Norse extraction. And it may be that there was Viking blood on the Kipling side too.) As for the ubiquitous galleys, symbol of Clan Donald's four hundred years of sovereignty over the western seas: where would Kipling have been without them? He used them in stories and ballads, in adventure and allegory: Viking, Greek and Roman galleys – but never Celtic. Even here he distanced himself from anything remotely connected with his Highland ancestors.

But he was uncomfortably aware of the Celtic gift of second sight. While disclaiming it in himself – unconvincingly, but with good reason – it was present in several of the Macdonalds, including his mother and sister. ('Table-turning'[20] in their father's house had been one of the more unusual talents of Alice and her younger sisters. As the large circular table spun round and round with the girls excitedly running round after it, one of them was sent to fetch Papa from his study, as instructed, to witness the performance. The astonished minister jumped on the table, thinking to stop its gyrations, but it continued to spin round under his weight. History does not record whether the matter was raised with the Lord during family prayers that evening.)

Kipling could see the damaging effect on his sister when she became deeply involved in certain forms of spiritualism, and turned his back on any suggestion of communication with the dead after losing his son. 'And nothing has changed of the sorrow in store/ For such as go down on the road to En-dor!'[21] And yet he always maintained that his best work was produced through his Daemon, an external force over which he had no power; that he himself was only the medium, the holder of the pen. When your Daemon is in charge, he would say, do not try to think consciously. Drift, wait, and obey. Undue modesty on his part – or evidence of his psychic powers? His Daemon, if so it was, had a strong sense of place. It would not function in brickyards or schoolrooms, as he discovered when writing *Puck of Pook's Hill.* But of its technical turn of mind there was not the slightest doubt. Kipling wrote two short stories, 'With the Night Mail' and 'As Easy as ABC', set in the future which would be classified as science fiction today, except that most of his fiction became fact, technological fact, within a few years – acknowledged as accurate by the men at the 'sharp end'. Indisputably, his prophetic eye saw what others could not – would not, perhaps. He prophesied the advent of two world wars years before they broke out, but his warnings in prose and in verse went unheeded by the 'Unarmed Forces', as he called politicians.

———————

But let us go back in time to pick up the story of James Macdonald, born at Ballinamallard, near Enniskillen in 1761, the first of three generations of Methodist ministers to whose influence (together with his Kipling grandfather) Rudyard would say he owed his 'pulpit streak that will come out'.[22] James' parents had joined the new Methodist Society after hearing John Wesley preach and it was at Wesley's personal invitation that James himself became an itinerant preacher at the age of twenty-three. For eleven years he 'laid the foundations of the scholarship which he cultivated to the close of life',[23] teaching himself Latin, and sufficient Greek and Hebrew that he might read the Scriptures in their original tongue while quartering his scattered parish on foot or on horseback. Throughout his life books were a consuming passion with him, a passion he was to pass on to succeeding generations.

James married a local girl, Ann Browne, and in 1795 moved to England on circuit. Their younger and only surviving son, George Browne Macdonald was schooled for the ministry from an early age, his father exhorting him, even so young as thirteen, never to be idle but to apply himself diligently to his learning. And so he did. But George was an engaging young man, handsome and sociable and with more than a touch of Irish charm about him – and for a while, when he was living and working in London, his father was anxious for his moral welfare. He need not have worried: George was safely in harness to the ministry at the tender age of twenty.

George married, as his second wife, Hannah Jones, daughter of a prosperous Manchester Methodist family. His first wife had died young and childless. So now Welsh as well as Irish was added to the Highland line: a formidable Celtic mixture. Hannah was a remarkably capable woman, as artistic (she was very musical) as she was practical – a double blessing for the strenuously busy minister whose chief earthly delights, when he was not away preaching, lay in his books and, it must be said, in the active endorsement of the primary ordinance of marriage. Hannah bore him eleven children in sixteen years. (Three died in infancy and a fourth, Caroline, from tuberculosis at fifteen; five daughters and two sons surviving.) Every third year, pregnant or not, she would pack up all her husband's 'earthly delights' and move them to wherever his next ministry might take him, according to Methodist tradition. Hannah has been called 'a very paragon of mothers'[24] and under her gentle influence her family grew up in a close, united atmosphere. One of her enduring maxims was 'Owe no man anything – not even a letter.'[25] And posterity is indebted to her letter-writing daughters for their fervent interpretation of her words. Hannah had to cope not only with the demands of round-the-clock domesticity but with an inherent Celtic melancholy exacerbated by the frequent absence from home of her beloved husband. John Kipling was to comment on the 'touch of the elegiac' in all the daughters, inherited from their mother. George, on the other hand, with his restless energy requiring little sleep, and his abhorrence of idleness was blithely oblivious to domestic problems. But he was a broad-minded and approachable father, as the table-turning episode bears out, and with an 'excellent fund of humour'[26] was a prince of story-tellers. Hannah had had the unusual advantage for those days of a private tutor, it being a tenet of Methodism to encourage education for all. Even more unusually her instruction had included Latin and musical theory. She was determined that her daughters should have at least the same opportunities, in spite of a slender purse, and set about teaching them herself from an early age. She attended classes and lectures at the local chapel to broaden her own knowledge and whenever possible a governess was employed for the girls. They all had access to their father's considerable library in which there were no glass-fronted bookcases to deter the young – and only Shakespeare was on the restricted list.

In the middle of this 'garden of girls',[27] my grandfather Frederic William was born. At an early age (eight) Fred made a profound discovery about women, complaining to his father that he could not have a bit of a quarrel with any one of his sisters without the rest descending on him. 'My boy,' said his father, 'we are in a minority in this house. We must stick together.'[28] The elder son, Harry, precociously clever and the apple of his parents' eyes, was away at school and then university for much of the time. Younger sons of the manse generally had to forego university through lack of means. At nineteen and up at Oxford Harry took life and learning very seriously; too seriously for his own good. He wrote to his father that he hoped Fred was continuing to work and 'conduct himself as becomes a cadet of the noble house of the Macdonalds of the Isles.'[29] Fred was then twelve and unmoved by any thoughts of work. But Harry earned his stripes with his sisters in the way older brothers have always done, by bringing home some of his sixth form friends from school (King Edward's School, Birmingham). Whatever Harry's motives were for introducing members of the 'minority' sex to the Macdonald household, their advent was warmly welcomed – particularly by his bright, quick-witted sisters. It was just the kind of intellectual stimulus they needed. Cormell Price (who would become Rudyard Kipling's headmaster) was one of Harry's friends;

William Fulford, to whom Alice twice became engaged was another; and the shy but witty Edward Jones (the Burne-Jones hyphen came later), upon whom the twelve-year old Georgiana's eyes rested longest, was a third.

The sisters were artistic and imaginative girls; inclined to be highly-strung and prey to fatigue or nervous prostration; inclined too to be critical of others who did not measure up to their own high standards. Alice had a quick tongue and the reputation of being something of a flirt, getting herself engaged and dis-engaged rather more frequently than might be considered proper in a minister's family; four times in all. In her youngest sister's opinion Alice 'never seemed to go on a visit without becoming engaged to some wild cad of the desert'.[30] One of her fiancés was the poet William Allingham, to whom we owe the lines: 'Up the airy mountain, Down the rushy glen'. With hindsight, we must be grateful that Alice did not climb that particular mountain. She was renowned for doing and saying the unexpected and her sisters would discuss their eldest sibling with bated breath. On one memorable occasion when she came across a treasured family relic, a lock of Wesley's hair, she threw it into the fire with the words: 'See! A hair of the dog that bit us!' She had a way with words which her son was to appreciate – and make use of – in years to come, and a turn for repartee that did her no harm in India's social circles. She also had the inestimable gift of finding out what people could do best – and then setting them to work. Whatever she put her hand to she seemed to do well, whether it was setting verse to music, helping her mother with the sewing, or later and with little knowledge of the language, teaching embroidery skills to the Indians.

But it was Georgie who was the first sister to leave home. She was not quite twenty when she married Edward Burne-Jones, then an unknown and penniless painter, after a four year engagement. They were married in Manchester Cathedral where twenty-seven years earlier (when it was still known as the Collegiate Church) her parents had been married. Soon afterwards George Macdonald's health began to fail after forty strenuous years in the ministry and it fell to Fred to give away his sisters in marriage. (Harry's bright star had faded – burnt out like a meteor – and in conjunction with a disappointment in love he had emigrated to America, to the distress of all his family.) And so when Agnes and Louisa shared a double wedding it was Fred who walked proudly up the aisle with a sister on each arm. Agnes (Aggie) married Edward Poynter, another painter on the threshold of his career who would become President of the Royal Academy. And Louisa (Louie) wed Alfred Baldwin, the youngest son of a Worcestershire iron-master; their only child, Stanley, destined to become Prime Minister of England.

Only Edith, the youngest daughter, remained unmarried – and in doing so outlived them all, including her nephew Ruddy.

There had been Kiplings in Yorkshire for generations according to parish records: farmers and cattle dealers and 'gentlemen'. John's immediate ancestors came from Lythe near the east coast, where his father, Joseph, had been born in a wall-bed at Briar Cottage (now Kipling Cottage). And it was from here that Joseph's parents had crossed the moors one day to hear John Wesley preach, with the result that they too 'turned Methody' and their cottage became the local Methodist meeting place.

Joseph entered the Ministry and married Frances Lockwood, daughter of a builder and architect from Skelton-in-Cleveland. Their first home was a small cottage in Pickering, where their son, John was born on 6th July 1837. (Lockwood was added for the first time when he signed himself John Lockwood Kipling on his three-year contract with the Bombay School of Art.) He was educated at the spartan Woodhouse Grove Academy, the Methodist boarding school for sons of the manse, where for six years boys received free schooling (and clothing) for eleven months out of the twelve, and were allowed home only once a year. The curriculum concentrated on the teaching of languages, mainly classical, and with the minimum of organised games. This was largely due to a shortage of land, the school being required to grow much of its own food, but it could explain why Kipling Senior, like his son, viewed the later public-school obsession with sport with an amused, if cynical, eye.[31] (His father-in-law to be, George Macdonald, had been educated at the same school; and it was during his schooldays there that the headmaster's niece, Maria Branwell, had married a local curate by the name of Patrick Brontë: and thus the famous Brontë sisters.) A visit to the Great Exhibition of 1851 decided John Kipling as to where his future lay and he went on to Art School in Burslem, leaving with honours. There followed an apprenticeship at a local pottery and three or four years as an architectural assistant at the South Kensington Museum, later to be known as the Victoria and Albert, where he worked on some of its rapidly-growing buildings. (The use of terracotta for external carvings was favoured by the architect under whom he worked; and it was this material that John chose to work with when illustrating some of his son's books – as we shall see.) Returning to Burslem after his father died, John rejoined the pottery as a modeller and designer. And there in 1862 he met my grandfather, the twenty-year-old Frederic Macdonald starting out on his first ministry at Burslem. ('A perilous experiment'[32] was Fred's judgement of his precociously early appointment fifty years later. And today few would disagree with him, I fancy.) Fred introduced his new friend to his family. We are told that, when John Kipling called on the Macdonalds one day, family prayers were in progress, and he entered the room as the Lesson from St John's Gospel was being read out: "There was a man sent from God, whose name was John." The timing was perfect and the Macdonalds seemed to take this as a good omen. If he had tried to arrive on cue he would have missed by a mile. It is one of life's little ironies that of Fred's five sisters, all of them imbued with the virtues of punctuality and orderliness, three of them married artists who did not know the meaning of the words; indeed John Kipling was apt to mistake time for eternity.

It was at the now famous picnic spot of Lake Rudyard in Staffordshire that John became engaged to Alice. (A mutual familiarity with Browning seemed to clinch the matter. While walking through a field together they saw a dejected old horse, prompting John to quote, pityingly: 'Thrust out past service from the devil's stud.' To which Alice promptly replied: 'He must be wicked to deserve such pain.'[33] Browning's influence on Rudyard Kipling has been traced from his schooldays, but in the nature of things this joint recital must take precedence over all others.) It was to be nearly three years before they could afford to get married, and then only when John was offered a post as teacher of architectural sculpture and design at the Bombay School of Art at 400 rupees a month (approx £36). The Assistant Director of the South Kensington Museum who recommended John called him 'one of my best boys'. The wedding took place quietly in March 1865 at St Mary Abbott Church, Kensington from the Burne-Jones' home nearby – Georgie having married her Ned five years earlier. Only a few members of the family could be present on that bitterly cold day. Hannah, mother of the bride, was unable to leave her sick husband's side, but sent a parcel of food from Wolverhampton for the wedding breakfast in Kensington Square and Fred, standing in for their father, gave his oldest sister away.

And so the mercurial, intuitive Alice marries the meditative, gentle John shortly before her twenty-eighth birthday. With scarcely a backward glance for the familiar world she is leaving behind, she sails away in the warm April sunshine towards an unknown future, to a land where only eight years previously there had been a bloody revolt against the British. And there in a little house by the sea, in a Bombay still primitive and unbuilt and with vast green spaces fringed by coconut woods, she gives birth to Joseph Rudyard on the penultimate day of the year. And almost dies. Her confinement lasted six days and nights: as long as it took for the creation of the world, she said afterwards. Surely a prophetic phrase...

The Times of India, more prosaicly, recorded the event under 'Domestic Occurrences'.

1 Arthur Gordon, Rhodes Scholar, editor, author, KJ.
2 'The Exiles' Line', *Civil & Military Gazette*, 1892.
3 The childhood sweetheart he met at Lorne Lodge, on a visit to his sister.
4 RK to Kay Robinson, Editor, *CMG*, 1886, Pinney, *Letters,* Vol 1.
5 William John Dare, manager of *The Pioneer*, Allahabad, 1889.
6 ss *Madura*, British India, screw, three-master. Built Greenock, 1873, NM Museum.
7 *From Sea to Sea,* Vol 1, 1900.
8 Preface, *Life's Handicap,* 1891.
9 *Something of Myself,* 1937.
10 'The Song of the Exiles', *United Services College Chronicle,* 1883.
11 *The Light that Failed,* 1891.
12 'Recessional', 1897.
13 The Lord of the Isles Voyage, June 1991.
14 Old saying translated from the Gaelic.
15 Translated from c. sixteenth poem.
16 A & A Macdonald, *The Clan Donald,* Vol 3, Inverness, 1896-1904.
17 *ibid.*
18 RK to Scottish friend, 1899.
19 F W Macdonald, *As a Tale that is Told*, Cassell, 1919.
20 A W Baldwin, *The Macdonald Sisters,* Peter Davies, 1960.
21 'En-dor', *The Years Between,* 1919.
22 RK to FWM after 'Recessional'.
23 FWM.
24 *The Macdonald Sisters.*
25 *ibid.*
26 FWM.
27 *ibid.*
28 *ibid.*
29 *The Macdonald Sisters.*
30 *ibid.*
31 Arthur Ankers, *The Pater,* Pond View Books, 1988.
32 FWM.
33 Browning, 'Childe Roland', *Men & Women,* 1855.

INDUCTION 1865-1882

CHAPTER ONE

'...if only he would work*'.*

Our galley chafes against the Quay,
The full tide calls us from the beach,
While far away across the sea
Is set the isle that we would reach
The haven where we fain would be...
Our galley lamps are bright with hope,
Our voices ring across the sea—
In other lands is wider scope
For all our virile energy
Let be the past, leave we the quay
With firm hands on the tiller rope.

From: 'A Voyage', 6th July 1882, Westward Ho!

Rudyard Kipling recalls his first sea-voyage, at the age of two and a bit, characteristically: '...there was a time in a ship with an immense semi-circle blocking all vision on each side of her.' It was the P & O *Ripon*, an old paddle barque, on which he and his mother sailed from Alexandria on the last leg of their journey Home from Bombay. The year was 1868 and the Suez Canal yet to be opened, so there had been the additional interest of 'a train across a desert, and a halt in it',[1] to link the two sea passages. If the *Ripon's* creaking deck timbers could have spoken, Kipling-fashion, (see 'The Ship That Found Herself') they would have had a tale or two to tell by the time she had logged her quarter of a century at sea. How she had suffered the ignominy of losing her rudder in heavy seas on her maiden voyage, obliging her to put into Torbay on her paddles; how in the Crimean War, and here she would have spoken with pride, she had been a troopship; had later taken part in two naval reviews, and in 1864 carried

General Garibaldi and his entourage to Southampton, to be met by cheering, hat-waving crowds.

It was in the April following Garibaldi's arrival that the *Ripon* had left her home port on an apparently inauspicious voyage, bearing among her passengers the newly-married John and Alice Kipling *en route* for Bombay and their new life in the sub-continent…

And now Alice and her little son were returning to England on their own to see her family: Alice to have her second baby under less hazardous conditions than her first, and the vociferous Ruddy to plague the lives of the unsuspecting Macdonald family. Aboard the *Ripon* the two-year-old had been shocked – at first – by the behaviour of the other children. Before long he was their ring-leader in throwing hats and shoes overboard; and when sartorial supplies ran out they heaved books overboard instead. It could not have been an easy voyage for the pregnant Alice who was neither a good sailor nor used to looking after her lively son single-handed. It would always be a struggle for the Kiplings to make ends meet and for many years John supplemented his pay by taking on private teaching. For the same reason both he and Alice wrote occasional pieces for the Indian papers. Both parents realised that in a few years' time they would have to leave their children in England for the sake of their health; and indeed for their education. (By the time he was five Ruddy was more fluent in the vernacular than in English, and had to be reminded to speak his mother tongue when his ayah took him in to Papa and Mama.)

Arrived in England, Alice and Ruddy went first to her parents' little three-storeyed house at Bewdley where her ailing father would die before the year was out. Ruddy, used to living in a bungalow, rampaged up and down the stairs, peering into every room. He voiced his disgust that his grandparents had 'tooken' the best rooms for themselves, and generally behaved like the spoilt child his upbringing had made him. His behaviour must have been as shocking to Alice's family as had been the other children's on the *Ripon* to Ruddy himself; with one important difference. The Macdonalds, never known for being 'a pliable breed' (as the adult Rudyard was to comment to cousin Stan), could not readily modify their opinion of him any more than they could wholeheartedly join in the fun.

In his unfinished autobiography, written in his seventieth year, Kipling recalled his impressions of that first visit Home. 'There was next a dark land, and a darker room full of cold, in one wall of which a white woman made naked fire, and I cried aloud with dread, for I had never before seen a grate.'[2] Or, he might have added, a white woman engaged in domestic work. This is the first indication we are given of the child's highly-imaginative nature which in later years would contribute to night terrors and insomnia. The potential for being hurt, psychologically and emotionally, had been signalled, but unfortunately went unrecognised when the time came to leave the children in England three years later.

In the meantime, while Ruddy wore out his grandparents by day and remorselessly kicked his Aunt Edith, whose bed he had to share, by night Alice removed herself to her sister Georgie's home for the imminent birth. Alice (always known as Trix) was born at The Grange, North End Road, Fulham after another difficult confinement. Thought at first to be still-born, she was wrapped in a shawl and placed on a chair in Ned's studio, where she almost did breathe her last, narrowly missing being sat on by a stout picture dealer waiting to see Burne-Jones – who naturally had gone out for a walk. Both mother and daughter survived their ordeals and the little family spent the next few months going the rounds of the relations: Alice to show off the new baby, Ruddy just to show off.

They stayed with Alice's brother Fred, now with an infant son of his own to show off. (He had married two years' earlier on a stipend of £100 a year and was on course to emulate his father's earthly delights in both respects.) After the visit Fred wrote to his brother Harry in America: 'Alice and her two children have been staying with us before they go back to India. The little girl is already a beauty, and we should like to steal her, but Ruddy aged three is a power and a problem with strange gifts of upsetting any household. He adores his father luckily, and I hope John will be very firm with him for dear Alice is as wax in his small fists.'[3] Fred's sister Louie Baldwin had been rather more outspoken in her comments after their visitation: 'The wretched disturbances one ill-ordered child can make is a lesson for all time to me.'[4]

It is hardly surprising, then, that once the dust had settled after the Kipling family's departure, Alice's loving but exhausted family should think twice about taking responsibility for both children throughout their schooldays. One small child in a screaming temper was bad enough (in his uncle Fred's opinion he was 'a formidable element in the home'): imagine what *two* could do, supposing Trix were to develop similar tantrums. But all were willing to share Ruddy and Trix between them, *one at a time*. Alfred and Louie Baldwin tried hard to persuade the Kipling parents to let them have Trix as a companion for their only child, Stanley, while Rudyard would have been shared between the Burne-Jones and Macdonald families. Understandably though, Alice was not prepared to have her children separated twice over: from each other as well as from their parents. And it was Alice who had the last word where the children were concerned. She would have been well aware that her son's behaviour compared unfavourably with that of his cousins, would have noticed how quickly their behaviour deteriorated under Ruddy's influence. And Alice was proud; it went against the grain to ask favours of her younger sisters, all of them by that time better-off than she was. It is possible too that she feared losing her children's love to them during the long separation. As it was, years later she was to say that she had never thought of leaving the children with her family because 'it led to complications'.[5] Perhaps she recalled her mother's rule for keeping the peace among them by forbidding positive quarrelling. 'If you want to be rude to anyone let it be to a stranger. Perhaps you will never meet again. But you have to live together and I will not allow it.'[6] Such behavioural constraints were not lightly cast aside by a Macdonald.

In the spring of 1871 all the Kipling family came Home on a long furlough. The India Office Records show that John took sick leave on half pay (about £18 a month) from April to December that year. But it may have been Alice who was in need of the sick leave, for in the hot weather of the previous year she had given birth to and lost a third child. It may also be the reason why the parents decided to leave their children in England earlier than was customary, knowing that they could not afford to bring them over again for several years. For so it was that John and Alice returned to India alone, having left Ruddy and Trix with unknown foster-parents in Southsea.

Captain and Mrs Holloway were a well-connected couple who had 'come down in the world' and who took in school-age children of Anglo-Indian parents, a common enough practice in those days. What was remarkably uncommon about the arrangement, not to say incomprehensible to most of us, was the parents' failure to confide in Ruddy, at least, before leaving them with strangers in an arid, narrow little house, the antithesis of everything they had been used to in Bombay – *without explaining why and without saying goodbye.*

It is easy to say that they acted as they did to save all four of them (but mostly themselves?) the heartbreak of an emotional farewell. Without doubt there would have been 'the mother and father of all scenes'[7] with their son. But it was an ill-judged decision that only two such highly intelligent people could have made. They seriously underestimated the traumatic effect on such an imaginative child as Rudyard; a child who had been treated like a little prince for as long as he could remember, whose life had been one long shout of joy among doting native servants, with scarcely the whisper of a 'NO' to cast a shadow in his cloudless childhood. If only they had taken him into their confidence, given him the chance to play the role of the protective older brother (a responsibility he took very seriously, even at that age), to be able to reassure his little sister that they had not been abandoned by Mama and Papa, (which is precisely what they did think at first, aided and abetted by Mrs Holloway's son Harry) because he, Ruddy, *knew better*. It might even have helped him to come to terms with the nightmare years that lay in store for him at the house called Lorne Lodge whose chilly drawing-room had a 'buried-alive smell' to his sensitive nose. The front garden was about the size of a prayer-mat where nothing grew except a dreary bank of St John's Wort sloping down to the basement window of the ill-named 'playroom', destined to become Ruddy's punishment room.

Trix was too young to understand the situation fully, and in any case was made a fuss of and treated like the daughter she never had by Mrs Holloway, so that in time she forgot about her parents and their far-away home, until Ruddy firmly reminded her of 'those days of strong light and darkness';[8] of their early morning walks to the fruit market with their ayah; their drives to the bandstand or along the bay with their brightly-dressed mother in the brougham which smelt of old leather and horses; and the studio place across the gardens where their father worked, with its mysterious oily smells and lumps of clay which Ruddy found irresistible. There was Meeta, his Hindu bearer who made toys out of oranges and Dunoo, the syce who tended his pony with the ring saddle. Of all these things he reminded Trix – and at the same time himself – as he was plunged almost overnight into a relentless régime of evangelically-based punishments that included beatings and isolation – even from his beloved sister. At night he was tormented by Harry, Mrs Holloway's twelve-year old bullying son whose attic bedroom he shared. To be fair to Alice whose 'hardness' has been alluded to by some biographers, neither she nor John had the slightest notion that their chosen foster parents were anything but good and suitable people to care for their children; as of course the Holloways were – by their own religious lights. Another important point to bear in mind about the unhappy event is that child psychology was an unknown science in those pre-Freudian days. Parents had to rely on family tradition and their own judgement in deciding what was best for their children. Alice could not, I think, be described as a motherly woman in the 'cosy' sense of the word. Few of the Macdonalds were – whether from lack of opportunity or inclination. As for John, he had been accustomed to a cheerless boarding school for eleven months of the year, and therefore may not have regarded the circumstances as being so very different from his own rigidly-disciplined schooldays. And if he had, Alice would have over-ruled him. But he admitted to being a 'timorous child'[9] sent to school much too early (at eight), that bullying was prevalent and he was unhappy there. In any event, the parents had no choice in the matter. John's life's work lay in India and his wife's place was beside him.

And so the die was cast, with what far-reaching consequences only the years to come would show. Ruddy was almost six and Trix three and a half when they were left at Southsea, and it was to be more than *five years* – literally a lifetime to Ruddy – before they saw their mother again. For Alice and John too, deprived of their children's childhood seven thousand miles away while they endured the subcontinent's fearsome climate year in and year out, it must have seemed like an eternity – particularly for Alice who never came to like living in India as John undoubtedly did. No wonder India was called the Land of Regrets for families suffering the 'long pain of tropical exile'.

Captain Holloway was kind to the little sailor-suited boy in his wife's care and took him round the dockyards and marine stores, pointed out the little training brigs standing off Southsea Castle and the timber for the navy lying in booms in Portsmouth Harbour. He had been a midshipman at the battle of Navarino and had a dry black scar on his leg to show for it, which Ruddy would gaze upon with horrified fascination. During their walks he taught the boy sea songs and filled his eager ears with tales of old naval battles so that, predictably, the child vowed to join the navy when he grew up.

But all too soon Captain Holloway died, leaving the now friendless child at the mercy of The Evangelical Woman and the Demon Boy.[10] The Woman believed, literally, in beating the Hell out of the wicked – for their own good. And this particular boy was cheeky, untidy, talkative, asked too many questions, and had heretical views on nursery procedures. *Ergo*, he was one of the wickedest small boys it had been her misfortune to look after. As punishment for some minor misdemeanour he was frequently locked up in that dark basement room where chilblains and the smell of mildew were his only companions and separation from his sister an added penance. He would fence himself about with bits of packing case to keep the rest of the world out, and then construct his own make-believe world. When his father sent him an illustrated *Robinson Crusoe* he 'set up in business alone as a trader with savages'.[11] As long as he was safely within his refuge he could weave his own pretend games for hours on end. It was an instinct that was to remain with him for the rest of his life. (Thirty years later when Edmund Gosse published a memoir of his own extraordinary evangelical childhood, *Father and Son*, Kipling would tell him that for a few boyhood years he too was under the shadow of the same 'terrific doctrine' and had the same idea of 'avoidance of [his] surroundings by "natural magic"': in his own case by discovering a charm that he used to make out of old boxes stuffed with wool and camphor scented. 'It is a strange shadow to lay on a young mind, and they that do it must be more sure of themselves than most of us...The devil of it is that that life still persists – I could give you awful instances and I have a notion that your book will undam some tides of revolt in some doubtingly Christian homes. I only hope and pray it will be so.')[12]

When Ruddy was left at Southsea by his parents he was unable to read. For some extraordinary reason Alice and John had not even started to teach him, so that before their son could read their longed-for letters from home he first had to learn how. And this, in the line of duty, 'Aunty' did for them both. (Here Trix claimed to be the first to learn. Her brother's answer to that charge, boy-like, was that she had less brain to see where it was difficult!) For Rudyard, it was the key to an undreamed-of world, and the saving grace for an unhappy child whose spirit had been finally broken when he was sent to school one day with a placard bearing the word LIAR sewn on to the back of his jacket. It had been attached so firmly that, try as she would, Trix was unable to tear it off. Many years later she recalled that terrible day when her brother had set off for school walking like an old man.

He read insatiably until Aunty, noticing his delight in the written word, made it one of his punishments to forbid it. He read all the more by stealth and bad light – and ruined his eyesight for life. (It is possible that his eyes had been damaged during his protracted birth in the unhygienic conditions prevailing in India.) He was reading extracts from Wordsworth and Tennyson, and although their names meant nothing to him, 'the words moved and pleased'. He read verses that began 'Farewell Rewards and Fairies'; he read a tale about a lion-hunter in South Africa who fell among a freemasonry of lions; and he was learning much of the Bible by heart – albeit as punishment for his 'wickedness'. Unknown to either of them The Woman was setting him a foundation course for his life's work.

The wretchedness of Ruddy's life at the hands of Aunty and her son was not revealed until he wrote 'Baa Baa Black Sheep' in Allahabad when he was twenty-two. And then it was only his parents who understood the story's implications: that the unhappy tale of an Anglo-Indian brother and sister left in the care of foster parents in England, was in part about their own children. (Interestingly, of all the critics who wrote columns and columns about the new star from the East in 1890s London, it was only Gosse in 1891, who himself had had an unforgettable evangelical childhood, who suggested there might be an element of autobiography in 'Baa Baa Black Sheep'.)

It came as a terrible shock to Alice and John reading it for the first time in the Christmas Supplement of the *Week's News*. When he had been living and working in Lahore he would often show them his work in draft form for their comments first. But not this time. Perhaps it was the only way he could tell them what those years at Southsea had really been like. But why had he never told anyone *at the time* how he was being treated? The question would be asked him over and over again, especially by Aunt Georgie in whose home he had 'entered Paradise' each Christmas and to whom he had confided many things – but nothing at all of the horrors of Southsea. Because, he said, children accept what comes to them as 'eternally established'; and, too, he had a fair idea of the penalties attached to telling tales about Aunty while still living under her roof. With Trix being treated as if she had been the woman's own daughter, might he not have been separated from his sister if he had made a fuss? Then why had he not told his parents as soon as he was able to write to them? As to that, all his letters home had been either dictated or censored by Aunty; and he had not realised that an unstamped letter would have been delivered to the addressee and not, as he feared, returned into the hands of The Woman.

I believe there was another reason for not telling, too, and it applied throughout his life. As long as he did not talk about a deeply-felt sadness or horror, he was able to lock it away in the back of his mind – at least during the day. (According to Trix they never spoke of their time at Southsea afterwards: it hurt too much.[13]) The nights were the problem. He had suffered from night terrors since childhood when on top of an over-active and *visual* imagination his eyes started playing tricks on him. At The Grange he was always afraid of what might be lurking under the bed and his cousin Margaret Burne-Jones would have to poke about with a walking stick to set his mind at rest. There was a particular reason for this, something about Uncle Ned's house that frightened him very much but which, again, was not revealed until years later.

During the 1879 Christmas holiday at The Grange, Rudyard produced a family magazine with his cousins and the Morris children. *The Scribbler* was the first outlet for his precocious talents. He met artists and poets 'who stormed in and out of this house of wonders';[14] men like Holman Hunt and William Morris (Uncle Topsy) who played games with the children, and occasionally the elderly Browning who did not. Uncle Topsy would try out his latest Icelandic tales ('to get them clear in his own mind') on a nursery audience while sitting astride the creaking rocking horse. William De Morgan allowed Ruddy to play with his painted tiles, while Uncles Ned and Topsy between them played with pieces of coloured glass and discussed the mechanics of their art, from 'the fabrication of colours, design of glass windows, the inlay of little bits, and how the lines cut each other, as they loafed in the studio…[It was] a thing to be grateful for, even though one did not comprehend it.'[15]

All his life Kipling would be fascinated by craftsmen who were experts in their own field – whatever that field might be – discussing their work.

No doubt but this fascination stemmed from those early days at The Grange when he absorbed like blotting-paper the words of great men 'talking shop'.

In the evenings Aunt Georgie would read them the *Arabian Nights* while Uncle Ned drew designs in charcoal and Ruddy lay on the sofa sucking toffee and calling his cousins 'Daughter of my Uncle' or 'O True Believer.' One whole month of Paradise it was, when the sound of his aunt playing the organ (which he was allowed to blow for her) and deep-voiced men talking and laughing together, mingled wondrously with the pungent smells of paint and turpentine. And not one of them guessed, because Ruddy did not confide in any of them, the misery he was returning to at the end of his visit, when for the first two or three nights he would cry himself to sleep in his attic bedroom.

Years later, after Uncle Ned had died and The Grange was about to be sold, Rudyard 'begged for and was given' the iron bell-pull that had let him into 'all felicity', for his own front door at Bateman's. He hoped that another generation of children pulling it might experience something of the happiness that he had felt standing on his uncle's doorstep – a small boy with a bursting carpet bag.

It has been suggested that in writing 'Baa Baa Black Sheep' Kipling exaggerated the treatment he received; that, for instance, the horrifying incident of the 'LIAR' placard was entirely fictitious; and that when he came to write his autobiography over forty years later, he confused fiction with reality. In her old age Trix (whose own memory was not always reliable) did confirm the incident, but confided to cousin Stan that 'in some ways Aunty (Mrs Holloway) saved his soul alive. He was about as spoilt as he could be when we came home in 1871.'[16]

In August the following year his grandmother, Hannah Macdonald, with one or other of her daughters, spent two weeks in lodgings at Southsea and took Ruddy and Trix out each day, either on their own or with Mrs Holloway. During that time, they said later, they had never seen or heard anything amiss, not the smallest hint of unhappiness from the children. And it was the same when Ruddy went to stay with his relations by turns. Indeed after he had spent a few days with his grandmother at Bewdley that October Hannah wrote in her diary: 'We were sorry to part with him. He is a dear, good child'.[17] The same child had left behind a very different impression on his first never-to-be-forgotten visit four and a half years' earlier. Whatever else Mrs Holloway had done, she had certainly improved Ruddy's behaviour, and consequently his family's opinion of him.

But at what a cost '...for when young lips have drunk deep of the bitter waters of Hate, Suspicion, and Despair, all the Love in the world will not wholly take away that knowledge; though it may turn darkened eyes for a while to the light, and teach Faith where no Faith was.' The authorial voice rounding off 'Baa Baa Black Sheep' appears to contradict that of *Something of Myself* looking back from his seventieth year: 'In the long run these things (his treatment at the hands of the Woman and her son)...drained me of any capacity for real, personal hate for the rest of my days. So close must any life-filling passion lie to its opposite.' Which was nearer the truth? Bearing in mind his phrase 'in the long run', I suggest there was truth in both statements. The regrettable vein of cruelty and revenge in some of Kipling's earlier work clearly indicates, I believe, that for many years he could neither forget nor forgive his treatment at Southsea. If, on his return to India, he had found John and Alice to be anything other than the delightful and loving parents they were, he could have vented his rage on them, exorcised some of the ghosts of his unhappy childhood and, perhaps, felt the better for doing so. As he put it, 'I might have found my Mother "the sort of woman I don't care for," as in one terrible case that I know; and my Father intolerable.'[18] He found neither. But deep within there remained that suppressed anger which erupted from time to time in bouts of bad temper at the office when he would throw things to relieve his feelings. One day the truth would have to come out; but not yet. It would spoil the perfect home-coming.

When Alice arrived from India, unannounced, in 1877, prompted by a worrying letter from Georgie who was concerned about her nephew's health, she found Ruddy in bed, cowering against an expected blow, half-blind and close to a nervous breakdown. The only truth we shall know for certain about his Southsea years is that they marked him for life: physically, mentally and emotionally. His eyesight was permanently damaged, so that instead of the navy (possibly) gaining an officer who was 'afflicted with the magic of the necessary word'[19] to be sinfully wasted on Duty Reports and the like, he became (among other things) the Poet of the Sea and the Voice of the Silent Service; he was prey to black depression and breakdowns when overworking and under stress; and he was emotionally vulnerable for years afterwards.

(Over forty years later, in 1920, his wife wrote in her diary: 'Rud takes me to see Lorne Lodge...where he was so misused and forlorn and desperately unhappy as a child – and talks of it all with horror.'[20])

But there must be a positive side to all things for an artist. During those unhappy years in the House of Desolation the seeds of genius were sown in its barren soil. Seeds that flourished in spite of – perhaps because of – his too-early knowledge of the heavenly and the hellish on earth. He wrote his first story, 'Will Briarts (sic) Ghost', at the age of eight and what is believed to be his earliest poem during his Southsea years: both pieces dark dramas of drownings at sea. The ghost story is about a drunken sea captain who is thrown overboard by one of his crew before their 'doomed little vessel' splits in two off the Goodwins and all are drowned. The poem concerned the loss of the *Carolina* 'bound for London Town.'[21]

> Portsmouth's dark walls stood out so bright
> Amid the flood of beaming light
> A vessel from the harbour came
> The *Carolina* was her name...

and so on to:

> ...She had sunk on a rock and then gone down
> With 300 souls bound for London Town
> She had sunk like lead with no canvas rent
> And never a spar or catline bent
> The waves sighed mid the mast of the wreck
> And fishes darted athwart the deck
> Down, down, she lies full fifty fathom down
> Does the *Carolina* bound for London Town.

From Southsea Alice took her two children to stay on a farm at the edge of Epping Forest. And there for six months Ruddy ran wild, helping with the animals, playing with gypsies, his cousin Stan who came to stay with them, and a kitten called Sprats who would sit on his shoulder and try to hook the new pair of glasses off his nose. (In the years to come the two cousins, both now household names, would reminisce together, weeping with laughter over their youthful escapades in Essex.) By the time they left the farm for London Rudyard appeared restored to a boisterously healthy eleven-year old. In town they stayed in lodgings in the semi-rural Brompton Road. No 227 was kept by an 'ivory-faced, lordly-whiskered ex-butler and his patient wife.' And it was here that the night got into his head for the first time. He would get up and wander round the silent house and slip out into the little walled garden to watch the dawn break. 'I did not know then that such night-wakings would be laid upon me through my life; or that my fortunate hour would be on the turn of sunrise, with a sou'-west breeze afoot.'[22]

His 'sorely-tried Mother' got the two children season tickets for the South Kensington Museum opposite. The building had expanded considerably since the 1860s when their father had worked there, and already three sides of the garden quadrangle were built in what had become a complex and elaborate construction programme for a unique type of museum. (It had started life as the Museum of Manufactures in 1852 and by the turn of the century after many magnificent additions, would become the Victoria & Albert. On one wall of the quadrangle may be seen a full-length portrait in terracotta of John Lockwood Kipling, complete with beard, among many other figures connected with the construction of the museum.)

Ruddy and Trix would cross the road together – there was no traffic to worry about in those days – to visit the museum. They roved at will down long, dark corridors, past ancient coaches and chariots, musical instruments and mechanical models, collections of precious stones and rings – even through doors marked 'private' where yet more treasures were being unpacked. And as children will, they soon came to regard the museum and its treasures, divided between them, as their very own. 'These experiences were a soaking in colour and design with, above all, the proper Museum smell; and it stayed with me.'[23] But I wonder if at the time he thought twice about the fact that not only his father but two of his uncles (Burne-Jones and Poynter) and one deputy uncle (Morris) had been actively involved in the decorative and design work of the museum. If he had wandered into the Green Dining Room would he have recognised the craftsmanship as Uncle Topsy's, the stained glass designs as Uncle Ned's? Being his father's son and observant, I think he would. And would he have made a point of visiting the East India Company's small store of treasures, recently acquired by the museum, which was to form the basis of the glorious Indian section today?

For another change of scene Alice took the children for a 'very black holiday' in the Potteries. There Ruddy tried his hand at making cups and plates, driving a coal cart and generally being entirely happy 'in a hundred dirty ways'.

By the end of his long holiday with his mother he had gained much priceless knowledge: that both his parents 'wrote things', that books and pictures were among the most important matters in the world, that he could read as much and ask as many questions as he chose and – he could write down whatever he thought *without being accused of 'showing off'*. He was as ready as he would ever be for his next endurance test: a spartan boarding school in far-off Devon.

Three years earlier Alice had seen an advertisement in an Indian newspaper for the newly-founded United Services Proprietary College at Westward Ho! When she read the new headmaster's name she had immediately written to him. Would the son of a gazetted officer in the Educational Department (Bombay Uncovenanted Service) be eligible for entrance or was the privilege reserved only for the Military and the

"Heaven-born" (The Indian Civil Service)? 'Our little boy – Ruddy – whom I think you saw at The Grange three years ago is now 8½ and in a couple of years' time ought to go to a good public school.'[24]

Cormell (Crom) Price had been a friend of the family since his school days with Harry Macdonald and Ned Burne-Jones. Later he became an intimate of the Pre-Raphaelite circle. What better reason, apart from its cheapness, for choosing his school for Ruddy? It offered cut-price public school education for the sons of impecunious officers serving abroad who could not afford the more traditional establishments. Its syllabus was geared towards the new army entrance examination which, since the abolition of purchased commissions (in 1871), often entailed an extra year's tuition at an expensive crammers for the more conventionally educated boy.

After their return from the Potteries Alice reported to Crom that Ruddy was eleven years old, had gone through the first four books of Euclid and twelve rules of Algebra, and was in the second book of Caesar. 'Is that pretty well for a child of his age?'[25] She enquired if it would be possible to get lodgings for herself and the children near Westward Ho! so that Ruddy could be a day scholar until such time as he should be a boarder. However this did not come to pass. No doubt Price considered that such an arrangement would not be in the new boy's best interests. But he did accompany Ruddy on the train journey down to Westward Ho! on the 16th January 1878 for the boy's first term, which must have helped to take the sting out of another parting for his new pupil.

'Into the small-boys' house at Westward Ho!...', wrote Beresford (M'Turk of *Stalky & Co*) many years later, 'there fluttered a cheery, capering, podgy, little fellow, as precocious as ever he could be. Or, rather, a broad smile appeared with a small boy behind it, carrying it about and pointing it in all directions. On persistent enquiry the name of the smile turned out to be "Kipling"...a modest name, almost diminutive, for such a broad smile and such a podgy person. Over the smile there was, strangely enough, a pair of spectacles. The two did not quite seem to go together, as in those days spectacles were regarded as a mark of extreme seriousness and crabbed age.'[26]

Even more surprising – and precocious – was the incipient moustache shadowing his upper lip. In profile the modelling of his head was almost cave-man in outline, possibly another legacy from his six-day birth, his forehead sloping back sharply from heavy brows, emphasising the strong protruding chin with its spectacular cleft. The overall impression was of a head that seemed too large for its body; and of a twelve-year-old who was practically blind without his spectacles. This earned him the nickname Giglamps, or Gigger for short, among his friends.

The first year was grim. Boys are meant to conform at boarding school and in three respects at least pupil No 264 Kipling, J R, could not. He was the only boy in the school to wear spectacles, the only boy not destined for one of the services (army, navy or Indian civil) and the only one unable to play games – all because of his eyesight. In those early days at the 'twelve bleak houses by the shore'[27] (a row of terraced villas overlooking Bideford Bay and the Pebble Ridge which had been converted into a single unit capable of accommodating 200 boys) he could neither eat nor sleep and his mother wept bitterly each time the mail brought a batch of Ruddy's unhappy letters, sometimes two or three in a day.

Within a week of the start of term Alice, who was to remain in England for another two years, wrote to Crom Price: 'Don't let Ruddy know that I have written to you – but I can't help it – the boy is very homesick...It is the roughness of the lads he seems to feel most – he doesn't grumble to me – but he is lonely and down – I was his chum you know, and he hasn't found another yet. I don't encourage the rain of letters, I discourage it – at the same time knowing that both his father and I have really an unusual twist for scribbling, and think no more of it than of talking...The lad has a great deal that is feminine in his nature, and a little sympathy from any quarter will reconcile him to his changed life more than anything...'[28]

They had been a tough bunch of boys that Crom Price took on, many of them rejects from other schools, when the USC opened four years' earlier with sixty pupils. That the school flourished for twenty years under his headship was entirely due to Price's personality and gifted leadership. But it reacted like most other boarding schools of its day would have done, I suspect, when confronted with this extraordinary specimen of boyhood called Kipling. He became the butt of jokes – and worse – from the school bullies. On 10th March Alice wrote again to the head.

'It is some weeks since you told me if Ruddy told me in confidence of anything disagreeable to him to tell it to you, in confidence, and much as I hate to seem to complain I feel I really must send you an extract from his last letter. "I passed a very uncomfortable time yesterday from 9 p.m. to 11 p.m. I got 190/50/20/10/ Total 270 cuts with a brush on my seat of Honour. It doesn't hurt much until the first 50 are over and then it is unbearable. My seat bled a little. Anyone in the dormitory can bring any accusation they like against me, however trivial and I am sure to get licked for it. I got 190 for not watching the house match between Campbell's house and Green's – as if it mattered to me a fig whether my house won or not. I forgot to brush my teeth one morning as it was rather late...so I got 50 for that...I felt awfully uncomfortable as I got into bed, my body was as ice from being out of my bed so long (for I had to come to the fellows' beds as they never got out, and my seat stinging like nettles." You must not let Ruddy know that I have told you this – I am convinced that the boys exercise tyranny in the bedroom which ought not to be allowed and of which the masters know nothing...Forgive this letter, and don't hate me for bothering you.'[29]

For Ruddy it must have felt like Southsea – and Harry – all over again.

It took him a year to settle and make friends. He then romped through the next three years with a pen rarely out of his hand. Crom Price was a much-loved head, neither a clergyman nor a militarist; two positive virtues in the eyes of boys who resented being preached at one day and punished the next and who would have collectively cringed at an address on Patriotism by a 'Jelly-bellied Flag-flapper' of an MP (*Stalky & Co*) – if that story was anywhere near the truth.

In the form-room young Kipling had an abrasive relationship with his irascible classics master and the form got its money's-worth when Crofts hurled invective and argument (and one memorable day, a copy of Browning's *Men and Women*) at his precocious pupil's head. Rudyard had struck a gold-mine. Here were riches of language to be stored in his memory and gloated over for future use – especially the Browning. Now he understood why the sarcastic Crofts referred to him as 'Gigadibs the literary man' ('Bishop Blougram's Apology'). Crofts too saw a return on his investment. He would let Gigadibs run on when construing Latin because he made such a fairy-tale of the translation.[30] And what could he say to a sixteen-year old who, given a Horace Ode (Donec gratus eram tibi) to prepare as a punishment for forgetting to do some set work, turned it into broad Devonshire rhyming verse?

Rudyard read everything he could lay his hands on, with the blessing of the head who had given him the freedom of his 'brown-bound, tobacco-scented'[31] library as soon as he saw where the boy's interests lay; but, wisely, without letting Ruddy know he thought his work anything out of the ordinary. There on the shelves among ancient dramatists and English poets from Chaucer to Swinburne, he found 'thick brown books of voyages told in language like the ringing of bells.'[32] (Hakluyt) According to his study-mates Ruddy was, first and last, a bookworm who cared for nothing but words, 'gaudy' words, who read his way through every book in the school, six lines at a time, the book held within inches of his eyes, his spectacles pushed up on his forehead. He was also fat, unathletic and unsociable. But not enough to miss out on the running battles that Study Five waged against any masters or boys who incurred their displeasure.

Our heads were rough and our hands were black
With the ink-stain's midnight hue;
We scouted all, both great and small—
We were a dusky crew;
And each boy's hand was against us raised—
'Gainst me and the Other Two.

We chased the hare from her secret lair,
We roamed the woodlands through;
In parks and grounds far out of bounds
Wandered our dusky crew;
And the keepers swore to see us pass—
Me and the Other Two.

'The Dusky Crew'[33]

Precociously mature, Kipling was smoking heavily at sixteen, but only when out of bounds and under cover. The USC was one of the few schools where the prefects, that is, the Army Class, were allowed to smoke (pipes). Naturally it was a privilege they guarded jealously and with a heavy hand, as the head had foreseen.

He may have associated with the fish girls of Appledore, as he claimed, but militarism and imperialism were not words in his vocabulary. As for taking an interest in things mechanical: according to Beresford 'Gigger's attitude to machines was that of an amused, superior observer...From what deep well in his being he pumped up all this affection for pistons and connecting-rods one knows not; how compound marine engines and railway bogies came to claim him for their own is a dark mystery.'[34]

During his last two years at the College Kipling edited the school magazine and wrote much of its contents. The Horace translation was one of his contributions. *The Chronicle* was never to reach such literary heights again. He was a persuasive member of the debating society, where he always seemed to be holding forth for the winning side – even when his headmaster was speaking for the opposition. (He actually spoke in favour of abstinence – shades of his Methodist ancestors? – in spite of Study Five's occasional illicit bottle of port. But that was one debate he did lose, so justice was served.) He joined the new Natural History Society which attracted 'every boy in the School who had the poaching instinct'.[35] He acted in school plays (Sir Anthony in *The Rivals* at his last Christmas Pastimes) and pantomimes (Widow Twanky in an unofficial *Aladdin*, or Allah-deen as he insisted it should be pronounced) to some effect, except when he was plagued with catarrh; and generally filled the 'unforgiving minute', several notebooks and letters home with verse and prose, while somehow managing to get away with the minimum of schoolwork.

Mathematics was another matter, a closed door, and when it came to trigonometry he was not above cribbing from Stalky. All would have been well if the maths master had not been unkind enough to ask him what 'co-sine' meant. Collapse of Gigger – and the shameful truth was revealed. His school reports were outstanding in one respect: his masters' universal agreement that Kipling could do so much better if only he would *work*.

Four years earlier John had come over to supervise the Indian Exhibit at the Paris Exposition, and had taken Rudyard to France with him. It was the first time in seven years that father and son had met: since the day the two children were left at Southsea. On the channel crossing the boy noted that the boat was made of two steamers attached to each other at the sides, possibly the *Calais Douvres*, so designed to prevent sea-sickness – 'which even the gods themselves cannot do',[36] he was to say years later. While his father was occupied with the setting up of the exhibits Ruddy had the freedom of the Exhibition and all Paris on two francs a day. Never was a happier twelve-year-old left to explore that fair city. He roamed at will from the magnificent Notre Dame to the leafy splendour of the Bois de Boulogne where he and two chance-met English schoolboys played at paperchase, to the utter bewilderment of the gendarmes. ('Ah! Les Anglais...') His first cross-Channel visit was the start of a lifetime's love affair with France and a facility with the language (not all of which he had picked up through cheeking Parisian cabdrivers) which was to serve him well in the years ahead.

'I find Ruddy a delightfully amiable and companionable little chap,' his father wrote to Price after the Paris trip, 'but the way in which he only half apprehends the common facts and necessities of daily life is surprising. Vagueness and inaccuracy I fear will always bother him and they take curious forms...If there is anything in him at all, the steady stress of daily work in which exactness is required should pull his mind together a little. But I should think he will always be inclined to shirk the collar and to interest himself in out of the way things...'[37]

Of school food, always uppermost in a boy's mind, Kipling wrote years later that it would have raised a mutiny in Dartmoor. So perhaps the one thing guaranteed to 'pull his mind together' at Westward Ho! was when vital supplies of biscuits, condensed milk and other such life-savers were running low in Study Five and he was prevailed upon by Dunsterville (Stalky) and Beresford (M'Turk) to write articles for the local 'rag' at ten shillings a time until they were in funds again. Whether his father would have accepted this forced labour as part of 'the steady stress of work' is, I feel, debatable. Nevertheless, under this agreeable arrangement it seems that Study Five was never without funds – or food – for long. '...money came into the Syndicate honestly, for a London paper that did not know with whom it was dealing, published and paid a whole guinea for some verses that one of the boys had written and sent up under a *nom de plume*, and the study caroused on chocolate and condensed milk and pilchards and Devonshire cream, and voted poetry a much sounder business than it looks.'[38] The poem was published in *The World* in November 1882 *after* he had left school, so he must have been paid in advance, and not, as is usual today, at – or even after – publication. (These 'verses' were in fact a sonnet called 'Two Lives': 'Two lives, one sweet and one most sad, I lead;/ Two lives – and one is joy, the other woe...' on which he was to comment a year later: 'Not bad – a direct Shakespeare crib which I thought vastly fine when I wrote it.'[39]) And when even his pen failed to deliver the goods the Syndicate would pawn items of each others' clothing on a communal basis. Which was how young Kipling came to 'lose' the watch his mother had bought him when the other two mislaid the pawn ticket.

One way and another, Study Five had a reputation for more variegated insanity than the rest of the school put together.

During the holidays he stayed with his relations by turns; sometimes with his Kipling grandmother in Yorkshire and sometimes with his Macdonald cousins. Never before had there been such larks, my aunt Florence said, or so much laughter ringing throughout the manse. She would tell the tale of how Ruddy came in from the railway station one day and stormed about the house in a great rage. When asked what was the matter, he replied that a porter at the station had boxed his ears. 'What had you done to him?' – 'Oh, I expect I cheeked him!' He went on stamping about for a bit and then made for the door. 'Where are you going, Ruddy?' – 'Back to the station to cheek that porter again!' For most of the holidays, however, he was in the care of 'three dear ladies', one of whom 'wrote novels on her knee, by the fireside', in a book-filled house in Kensington, where the atmosphere of kindliness and culture did much to curb, though it did not cure, the roughness in his manners that had so worried his mother. These stimulating changes of scene provided a satisfying backdrop to the waking hours (and the often wakeful nights) of an imaginative boy who was still thousands of miles from home.

One day when he was fourteen and a half Ruddy returned to Southsea to call for Trix who was still living with Mrs Holloway. (This does seem to bear out the fact that Alice and John knew nothing of their son's unhappiness there.) With what mixed feelings Ruddy entered that house again we can only imagine. What we do know is how he felt when he left it: head over heels in love. Florence Garrard was one of Mrs Holloway's boarders, a year or two older than he was, a dark-eyed girl with a beautiful ivory face, slender figure and long hair. She might have stepped out of a Burne-Jones painting – straight into the heart of his impressionable nephew.

Back at school again his pen was scarcely out of his hand and his mother was pelted with verses by every post. Before the end of the year John Kipling was writing to a friend of his increasing concern over his boy's future. While admiring Ruddy's obvious talents, he wished that his son would add to them, 'application and perseverance. I have written him a wigging for his last school report and I confess (to you only) I felt how every word was a two-edged knife and that I got the sharpest one straight into my side.'[40]

A year later John had come to the conclusion that the regular daily work of a newspaper might be the answer. 'Journalism seems to be specially invented for such desultory souls.' When Ruddy was sixteen his father had an offer of a place for him on the local newspaper in Lahore where the Kiplings were now living. His son's letters and poems alone would have been all the recommendation necessary, but Stephen Wheeler, the editor, had interviewed young Kipling and been greatly impressed with him when on home leave earlier that year. Moreover he was 'sorely plagued' by his present assistant, a solemn Scot from Edinburgh University who had 'no spring or vivacity and put his dullness into the print', Kipling Senior reported to Price. Rudyard's final school report did nothing to dispel his father's anxiety over any 'career which begins with exams' for his son; although 'Alice says I am unduly harsh in saying Ruddy must be a journalist because he won't fit himself for anything else.'[41]

More to the point, perhaps, money was running out for the boy's continuing education. Alice and John were finding it ever more difficult to keep the Kipling family in three different establishments, and now that there was no chance of his gaining a scholarship there was no question of his going up to Oxford. The offer of a post on the *Civil & Military Gazette* was accepted on Ruddy's behalf and he was told to join his parents in India a year earlier than had been originally intended; by which time his affections were engaged elsewhere, his eyes on a different horizon. So it was a somewhat disgruntled youth who sailed from Tilbury in drizzling rain on the 20th September 1882. He was leaving behind the girl he considered himself engaged to for he knew not what, nor for how long.

The P & O *Brindisi* was a slower boat than her contemporaries, which may have suited the lovelorn Ruddy's mood as he settled down to write his 'Amour de Voyage'.

And I was a man who could write you rhyme...
And you were the woman I loved for a time...
We shall go our ways when the voyage is o'er...
With a dim remembrance rising at times...
Of a lovely face and some worthless rhymes.[42]

It was not the first, and by no means the last love poem he wrote for Flo, and he would remain faithful to her for many years.

Rudyard was not yet seventeen when he returned to the land of his birth, but in his newly-acquired side-whiskers, which his horrified mother ordered him to remove at once, he looked much older. On arrival in Bombay after an absence of eleven years he found his own way through the enlarged and rebuilt city to the place where he was born. It was a strange experience, he said long afterwards. With the sights and especially the smells all about him, his old life returned so that he found himself uttering words and phrases whose meaning he had long since forgotten. By the time he reached Lahore, after a four days' rail journey beneath India's immense skies, his English years had receded into the background. As if they had never been. In Lahore where his father was now Principal of the Art School and Curator of the Museum Rudyard was about to become one half of the editorial staff of the Punjab's daily paper. He was home at last; his 'seven years' hard' as a journalist about to begin.

---

1 *Something of Myself,* 1937.
2 *ibid.*
3 FWM to Harry Macdonald.
4 *The Macdonald Sisters.*
5 *ibid.*
6 *ibid.*
7 'Baa Baa Black Sheep', *Wee Willie Winkie,* 1888.
8 *SoM.*
9 JLK of himself, *The Macdonald Sisters.*
10 Mrs Holloway and her son Harry.
11 *SoM.*
12 RK to Gosse, 1907, *The Letters of Rudyard Kipling,* Vol 3, ed Thomas Pinney.
13 Lord Birkenhead, *Rudyard Kipling,* Weidenfeld & Nicolson, 1978.
14 RK to Chevrillon, 1919, The Kipling Papers.
15 RK to Herbert Baker n/d, KP.
16 Trix Fleming to Stanley Baldwin, 1945, KP.
17 Hannah Macdonald's Diary, 14th October, 1872, KP.
18 *SoM.*
19 Speech on Literature, 1906, *A Book of Words,* 1928.
20 CK Diary, 25th February 1920, KP.

21 Andrew Rutherford, *Early Verse by Rudyard Kipling*, Oxford, 1986.

22 *SoM.*

23 *ibid.*

24 Price Papers (Personal information).

25 *ibid.*

26 Beresford, *Schooldays with Kipling*, Victor Gollancz, 1936.

27 'A School Song', *Stalky & Co*, 1899.

28 AK to Cormell Price, PP.

29 *ibid.*

30 J H Griffith, KJ.

31 *Stalky & Co.*

32 'An English School', *Land & Sea, Tales for Scouts & Guides*, 1923.

33 Rutherford.

34 Beresford.

35 'An English School'.

36 *Souvenirs of France*, 1933.

37 JLK to CP 15th June, 1878, PP.

38 'An English School'.

39 Rutherford, Note in Notebook 1.

40 JLK to E Plowden, KP.

41 JLK to CP, PP.

42 Rutherford.

COMPRESSION 1882-1892

CHAPTER TWO

'Subversive pamphleteer' to Special Correspondent

Thus, the artless songs I sing
Do not deal with anything
New or never said before.
As it was in the beginning
Is to-day official sinning,
And shall be for evermore.

'General Summary', *Departmental Ditties*

Stephen Wheeler was a humourless man and a hard taskmaster, and according to John Kipling, a very tetchy and irritable one as well. In fact, Kipling Senior reckoned his son was 'training for Heaven as well as Editorship'[1] by reason of the patience and forbearance he had to exercise in front of his chief.

But Wheeler had reason to be tetchy with his precocious young assistant on the *Civil and Military Gazette*. Ruddy needed licking into shape after getting away with so little in the way of legitimate work at school for so long. He was quick to master the details of his new job but he was inclined to forget the boring local assignments and the proofs lying on his desk waiting to be corrected before they could go to press. Wheeler would rage at the youngster, rightly determined not to let him off any of his duties just because the paper's proprietors were friends of the boy's parents. As Kipling admitted later: 'A sub-editor is not hired to write verses. He is paid to sub-edit. At the time this discovery shocked me greatly.'[2]

His duties included dealing with agency reports, translations, telegraphic news from round the world, market quotations, sporting news and local notes of the dullest kind. Necessary matters, no doubt, but hardly original and therefore unlikely to catch the interest of this eccentric, bookish boy. Only when his editor was ill or on leave, and the responsibility for the paper's entire production fell upon his shoulders, could he stretch himself creatively and revel in the task.

This happened unexpectedly soon when shortly before his first Christmas in Lahore and his seventeenth birthday, Wheeler fell off his horse and was unfit to work for several days.

Afterwards one of the newspaper's proprietors complimented young Kipling on the way he had thrown himself into the breach, adding that he now had the 'fullest confidence' in him. 'I have grown at least six inches since then,'[3] he wrote to his old headmaster. A year later, in a letter to Crofts, his classics master, he remarked: 'Your theory about "giving a boy more work than he can do and he'll do it," works beautifully out here, though I didn't believe it in the Latin set. I have nearly always a little more than I can do on my hands and consequently it gets done.'[4] Kipling's handwriting is noticeably more legible and his English more formal than usual in this letter as if in belated deference to his former sparring partner. But the (almost) eighteen-year-old cannot resist mentioning his rise in pay to £300 a year. It must have made a senior master's salary look meagre by comparison.

As time went by the reins were slackened little by little as it began to be recognised – even by his editor – that he had a turn for the pen beyond all cure. He was sent on special assignments up and down country covering Durbars and state visits and the like; and as the paper's special correspondent was for once asked to write as much as he could – a rare treat after months of compression. There followed lengthy and intricate accounts of, for instance, how the armoured train went about its manoeuvres, or the bridge-builders went about theirs; each piece an object lesson in how to make technical minutiae leap off the page and grab the layman's interest until the last full stop. But where did Kipling, the least technical of men, pick up all this intricate knowledge? The simple answer was at the club. Under its roof could be found experts in every subject known to man, and a few more beside. (He was later to find this applied to London clubs too.) And with his extraordinary facility for extracting and remembering the core of each man's knowledge, Kipling could file it away in his head until required. (Much the same question was posed after the publication of *Plain Tales*: those story lines, where had he got them from? Kipling's reply was unequivocal. '...since the days of my first tail-coat men of all kinds have shot rubbish into my patient ear...and I have turned that rubbish into the shekels of the money-changer time and again...for it is wrong that a man should waste time and attention and pure priceless sympathy over a *man* for nothing.'[5])

The little *Civil and Military Gazette* began to sparkle as it had never sparkled before with vivid descriptive pieces, both serious and comic; sometimes even a story or poem. At first they were unsigned or pseudonymous, in line with their author's natural reticence, while at the same time providing a convenient smokescreen for the occasional broadside. Either way, having experienced his editor's wrath in the past, he was careful to point out that all such 'skits' and 'rhymed rubbish' were written out of office hours and for his own amusement. And if the *CMG* did not want a particular story then he was free to offer it elsewhere. This he did to other and larger papers throughout the sub-continent, gradually building up a widespread readership that came to identify and look out for his work. (There was always the "Disgusted from Dalhousie" type of reader to brighten his day: like the one who wrote to him complaining of the flagrant immorality of one of his *Plain Tales*. Where did the author think he would go when he died? Kipling was tempted to reply that he had made his own arrangements, thank you; but on reflection decided to leave "Disgusted" to his glory over a Lost Soul.)

He was a persistent pen-biter, reducing the ends to faggots and his father would dip them in quassia to discourage the habit. Ruddy was writing with both hands and a pen in his mouth, reported his mother, with all the satisfaction of an ambitious parent. (The same ambition which had prompted her to have *Schoolboy Lyrics* privately printed – a volume of her son's poems written while he was at school – without his permission and against John's better judgement? According to Trix, who was still in England at this time, when Ruddy found out on his return to India, he sulked for three days.)

That apart, he was as happy as any home-coming son could be who had rediscovered his parents after an absence of eleven years and found them to be everything he had dared to hope; and more. It could so easily have been otherwise after the traumas of Southsea. John and Alice were an unusual couple for that time and era: they were in demand socially *for themselves* rather than for John's indefinable position in the hierarchical pecking-order; and even more unusually, they entertained Indians in their home. John had been one of the pioneers of art education under government auspices in India and from the first had never attempted to foist western ideas on his students. He encouraged the native arts, weaving, carving, pottery and the like which were in danger of dying out. He had an encyclopaedic knowledge which was at the disposal of all who knew him, prompting one of his irreverent nieces to call him the 'Enquire Within'. Kay Robinson, who succeeded Wheeler as editor of the *CMG*, described John Kipling as 'a rare, genial soul with happy artistic instincts, polished literary style, and generous, cynical sense of humour – without exception, the most delightful companion I'd ever met. Mrs Kipling preserved all the graces of youth, with sprightly (occasionally caustic) wit, which made her society always desirable.'[6] Even unto the Viceroy. Lord Dufferin would often drop in at the

Kiplings' lodgings in Simla, where the government was in residence throughout the summer, to talk art and literature with John and enjoy Alice's sparkling conversation over a cup of tea. In his opinion dullness and Mrs Kipling could not exist in the same room.

When the fifteen-year old Trix joined them in 1884 the family square and their happiness in each other's company was complete. Even the infatuation of the viceroy's son with the incomparable Trix was only a temporary inconvenience. 'Don't you think, Mrs Kipling, that your daughter should be taken to another hill-station?" said Lord Dufferin. 'Don't you think, Your Excellency, that your son should be sent home?'[7] was Mrs Kipling's swift response. And the son it was who went. All the Kiplings wrote things, poetry, parodies and stories, and in '84 and '85 two small volumes of their work were printed. (*Echoes* and *Quartette*) But this time it was Rudyard who arranged their publication. The authorship of some of the unassigned pieces has been puzzling experts ever since, for even the authors themselves could not always agree who wrote what after a period of years.

Rudyard's work began to be quoted in other Indian newspapers. That it was not always his best work worried John who was concerned about his son's occasional lapses into 'vulgar smartness, over emphasis and other vices.' He wished someone would 'rap his knuckles for the unwholesomeness of *the phantom 'rickshaw* (sic)...and for some other reasons...But the Indian Press has given him only praise and his knuckles await a rapping.'[8] John himself felt too little of a judge and too involved in his son's eager, vivid life to do much about it. But in a letter to his niece Margaret, known to Ruddy as the Wop (she was the Wop of Europe, he the Wop of Asia) and a regular correspondent of his son's, John hints that any criticism from her or her mother (Aunt Georgie) would sink deep, with no fear of wounding him. 'He has the sweetest nature possible so far as criticism is concerned...the truest kindness is to speak and spare not.'[9]

Rudyard had inherited his mother's sunny nature as well as her Celtic colouring and was excellent company, bubbling over with laughter and good humour – at home and at work. But there were black days too when he could be difficult, mooning about the house or throwing things in temper in the office. And once again he did not conform to his surroundings, did not fit the accepted pattern of the British in India. His speech was unconventionally free and vigorous and his appearance as unprepossessing as his manners.[10] Beneath a mushroom-shaped hat his short, rumpled figure, bushy eyebrows, moustache and thick glasses were strangely at odds with his immature features. The more conventional Anglo-Indians such as Sir Francis Younghusband thought him 'bumptious and above his station',[11] like a member of the lower ranks who showed initiative. But that outwardly brash manner covered an unsuspected sensitivity and as he once confessed, 'a hide which is not so thick as it ought to be'.[12] He would rather dine alone at home than go to the club if he thought certain members would be 'taking him on' over the meal. It goes without saying, then, that he was not popular in some quarters because of his preference for studying the Tommy and the native rather than the brass hat and polite society. In his *British Social Life in India* Dennis Kincaid tells us that his memsahib grandmother always spoke of Kipling as 'a subversive pamphleteer given to criticising his betters'[13]; a telling phrase that the pamphleteer himself would have been the first to appreciate – and deserve.

His speech was often jerky and his movements uncoordinated so that teaching him to dance, a feat that Trix undertook when Rudyard's chief ordered him to polish up his social graces in preparation for Simla society, was only achieved with difficulty – and more laughter. For the same reason he was not a good horseman, he and his mount parting company more frequently than was customary; about once a week was a fair estimate. (In spite of this lack of cohesion, he did sometimes play polo, but only when his mother was away. It was the only secret he kept from her – 'a deep and Wopsome secret,' he told Margaret, 'and I trust to your sisterly honour not to divulge it. The Mummy thinks polo is dangerous...'[14]) And he was untidy. At the end of a long hot day in the office he resembled a Dalmatian, his white vest and trousers liberally spattered with ink from his dip pen as it jerked to and from the inkpot. 'Stand off!' his editor would shout each time his assistant darted towards him, a fully-charged pen stabbing the narrowing gap between them.

Whenever sleep eluded him – which was often – he would wander through Lahore's streets and gullies, his City of Dreadful Night, where few white men would care to go without an escort, entering the world of opium dens and liquor shops, native dances and puppet shows. At first he would be challenged by the police, until they came to recognise the short rumpled figure for his father's son. In the stifling night's heat corpse-like figures turn restlessly on rooftops and in courtyards, seeking the oblivion of sleep under the moonlit sky. At midnight the cry of the Muezzin is heard: 'Allah ho Akbar!' and the corpses rise to their feet in response. At dawn a wind comes up, briefly, and is gone. 'As one man, The City of Dreadful Night rises from its bed and turns its face towards the dawning day.' In the square 'something borne on men's shoulders comes by in the half-light...A woman's corpse going down to the burning-ghat, and a bystander says, "She died from the heat."'[15] He would return home, heavy-eyed through lack of sleep, in a hired carriage 'which stank of hookah fumes, jasmine flowers and sandalwood; and if the driver were moved to talk, he told one a good deal.'[16]

This was the India Kipling came to know and understand as few white men had done before him: its sensuous beauty but insupportable heat that hit you like a blow; the sudden fever, death and burial of a colleague in the space of twenty-four hours. A land of appalling poverty amid profligate luxury where the smells of spices and wood-smoke mingled with those of disease and death and where the dead, animal and human, lay in the road where they fell. A land of haunted ruins under huge skies, of stars so bright you could read by them, but a sun so blazing that it blinded without illuminating. A land that you either loved or hated – but trifled with at your peril – where Kipling's innate puritanism was continually at war with his sensuality. (His cousin Stanley Baldwin once said they both had 'common puritan blood' in them: a Wesley legacy.[17]) It was hardly surprising then that he suffered sudden swings of mood from despair to hilarity and back again.

For the young journalist fresh from England's chilly shores it was all a gift from Allah. But he hated the hot weather and being deprived of the company of his womenfolk for six months each year. Everyone else who could get away to the hills did so; even his busy father usually managed a few weeks away from the heat. The Wop of Asia liked it less each year, he told his cousin, and he felt it most on Sundays when the work 'won't be spread thin enough to cover the whole day'. Then it was that he wrote letters, nine or ten-pages long, to his relations in England and his mother in Simla. And early in 1885 he started to write *Mother Maturin*, a novel about Indian low-life that was an 'unfailing delight' to him, even though it never seemed to get finished.

That was the year he was sent on his first assignment as correspondent for the *CMG*. 'Ruddy goes to Pindi as special,' wrote his father to a friend. 'He has started his pony and tum-tum thither, and although a little nervous about his first big thing, I think he will do well.'[18] His job was to report on the Durbar and the politically important meeting between the Viceroy and the Amir of Afghanistan. For days little happened except rain and more rain. Conditions in the huge assembled encampment were miserable, while day after day the Amir kept putting off his arrival. In a single dripping afternoon he sent four contradictory telegrams from Jumrood. 'First he would and then he wouldn't: then he said he really couldn't.'[19] But come what may, or more likely may not, the newspaper required its daily injection of two or three columns, 'From our Special Correspondent on the northwestern frontier'. And that is what it received: thirteen articles (about 30,000 words in all) were written in the field and published over a period of three weeks. His own diary entries were brief.

3rd April: 'Wrote another Special. Certainly I haven't been to sleep for a week or so – wonder how much longer this is going to last. Camp in an awful condition. I myself not much better.

4th April: A blessed interval. Got a little sleep at midday. Feeling oh so tired.

Monday 6th April. (Bank Holiday). No bank holiday for me. Special of three columns on review. Fine weather at last but I *must* shut up with a click before long. Too little sleep and too much seen.

7th April Two column special today. Review and phantasm of hundreds and thousands of legs all moving together have stopped my sleep altogether. Top of head hot and eyes are beginning to trouble me.

8th April Two and a half columns about the big Durbar. Luckily got a good sleep last night and am fit for anything...Nothing but cannon all the day and half the night.[20]

Then it was back to Lahore and, oh blessed relief, up to Simla with its smell of wood-smoke and pine cones and its vista of snow-covered mountains; a world away from the palpitating heat of the plains. And this year instead of the usual one month's leave he was to represent his paper for the entire season. Simla was the summer capital not only for the government of the Punjab, but also for the supreme government of India, and where everyone who was anyone went to on leave. His advancement was celebrated with a bout of dysentery followed by an enforced 'rest cure': a walking tour in the Himalayas, for which, not surprisingly, he found he was out of condition. Back in Simla ten days later he was reduced to loafing and a little dalliance while waiting, Micawber-like, for something to turn up. When all four Kiplings were in their lodgings together working space was limited, so for a month he stayed with friends where space limitations produced a different sort of hazard. 'Wish they wouldn't put married couple next door to me with one ½ plank between,' he grumbled to his diary. 'Saps ones morality. (sic)' The next day: 'Same complaint. This is really ghastly.'[21]

Three and a half months in Simla among the great, the good, and the intriguing rest of the Anglo-Indians on leave taught him much. But not yet enough about the opposite sex, it would seem, as he was to find out when he returned on his own to Lahore and the office. In a long letter to Wop a few weeks later, he tells her not only about his fall from grace regarding polo, but confesses to having been 'taken in, made an ass of, bamboozled...by a "Daughter of Heth in Silk Attire." And it served me jolly well right for I was attempting to work the D of H to my own and the Old Rag's ends.'[22] But the D of H had guessed what he was up to and had written to tell him so, pointing out exactly where he had failed without bothering to spare his feelings. Now, in sackcloth and ashes, he had sworn never to pit his poor wits against a woman again. Further, he had got no sympathy from his mother when he told her about it. *She* would have done just the same had she been the woman.

His recent journalistic endeavours earned him a pay rise and another bout of fever. His note to the doctor miscarried, delaying his arrival by thirty hours, by which time the patient was delirious, cursed him fluently and offered to race him for a large bet. But it was the getting better alone that he hated most, when 'the whole house was full of noises and whispers and sighs and groans and chuckles from headachy dawn to delirious dusk. A return of this would drive me into instant matrimony...I began to understand then why so many good men perpetrate (it). It's temporary insanity superinduced by intermittent fever.'[23]

Once during a cholera epidemic when he was suddenly taken ill his servant gave him opium. Afterwards he described how the cramps left his legs and tummy, and he felt as though he was falling through the floor. But he was well enough the next day to go to the office, though 'with every sign of advanced intoxication'. He had discovered early in his apprenticeship that it was possible to work with a temperature of 104 'even though next day he has to ask the office who wrote the article'.[24] (In later years he was to speak of opium as the friend, and in some ways, the mainstay of millions of Indians, who unlike the whites, rarely took it to excess or succumbed to the endemic fever, but were strengthened by its consumption.[25]) On another occasion he cured himself of the after-effects, the suicidal post-fever depression, by a man he disliked telling him he was going to die. He revived on a two-point plan: to disappoint his enemy and win a bet with him into the bargain. His doctor provided the more orthodox cures, morphia and the application of leeches, although Kipling found that even those single-minded creatures could be 'coquettish' and refuse to stick on his temples where they should.[26] As always the doctor's advice to him was: 'Go slow and don't worry!' An easy prescription, his patient would reply, but, 'it ain't so easy to follow.' And downright impossible if your name was Rudyard Kipling and you had inherited your ancestors' work – and worry – ethic.

He regaled his Aunt Edith with the story of how an old Afghan who had fought against the British in the last Afghan War, had invited him to his house and then tried to bribe him. The old man was being kept under house arrest in Lahore, while his wives and women were at Cabul. The Sahib had influence, he had the ear of the Lat-Sahib (Lieutenant Governor). He must write something in his newspaper recommending that he (the Afghan) should be released. It was the sort of piece that under normal circumstances, that is, without bribes, Kipling would have done anyway in the course of a day's work. (According to Robinson "The Rag" was distinctly militant in those days.) But not now. First he was offered a large sum of money (an insult), then a beautiful Kashmiri girl ('but I didn't quite see how she was to be introduced into an English household like ours.'); and finally the choice of three of a string of the most beautiful horses he had ever seen. Regretfully he mounts his old waler – only to find a bag of uncut sapphires and big greasy emeralds pushed up under the saddle. It was enough to irritate the horse and infuriate its rider. He hurls the bag into an upper story window where it would be 'a good find for somebody...' And concludes, 'Wasn't it a rummy adventure for a Sunday morning.'[27]

In one of his many screeds to the liberal-minded Margaret, and presumably in reply to some searching questions on her part, he tells her something of India's complex problems: that its population 'dies from purely preventible causes; that in native states they are hideously misgoverned from their rulers' own folly...whereas a system of bunds, dams, channels...would at least store water and stave off drought for a year.' Similarly with the drains (a constant problem) and the prevention of fever...As to the 'natives'... 'A queer people indeed. Touchy as children; obstinate as men; patient as the High Gods themselves; vicious as Devils but always loveable if you know how to take 'em. And as far as I know, the proper way to handle 'em is not by looking on 'em as "excitable masses of barbarism" (I speak for the Punjab only) or the "down trodden millions of Ind groaning under the heel of an alien and unsympathetic despotism", but as men with a language of their own which it is your business to understand; [he was taking lessons and exams in Urdu with a native teacher] and proverbs which it is your business to quote (this is a land of proverbs) and byewords and allusions which it is your business to master; and feelings which it is your business to enter into and sympathize with. Then they'll believe in you and do things for you, and let you do things for them. But (and here you will think me wrong perhaps) never lose sight of the fact that so long as you are in this country you will be looked to by the natives round you as their guide and leader if anything happens. Therefore comport yourself as such.'[28]

He told her about Lady Dufferin's fund for 'the Medical education of native women who are dying from sheer want of medical attendance, English doctors not being allowed to see a zenana woman in her last agonies.' He touches on widow remarriage, which together with infant marriage and Drains were three of his pet investigative subjects. 'Thank Goodness you haven't any notion of the horrors of enforced widowhood out here.' These and 'whole hosts of abuses oppressions and unthinking wrongs' may one day be set right 'if you hammer long enough'. In other words, write columns about them in the newspapers. 'Keep on hammering. Get good men to write you leaders about it…get statistics and drive ahead.' And maybe…'write some verses with a lilting refrain that will take and catch the public ear…'[29]

This he was about to do on his own and the *Gazette's* account, writing verses that were born to fill a space, '"One-third column just proper,"' Rukn-Din, the foreman, would tell him; while 'Mahmoud, who set them up, had an unpleasant way of referring to a new lyric as "Ek aur chiz" – "one more thing" – which I never liked.' Soon 'Men in the Army and the Civil Service and the Railway wrote to me saying that the rhymes might be made into a book. Some of them had been sung to the banjoes round camp-fires, and some had run as far down coast as Rangoon…and up to Mandalay.'[30]

He hired the office-plant out of hours and devised a method of publication that would ensure his first book of verse landing on the desks (and getting under the skin) of some of the Anglo-Indians it satirised. Taking the form of a government docket in a brown paper wrapper imitating an envelope, it was tied up with red tape and addressed to all heads of departments and government officials. It sufficiently deceived the eye so as to be opened and studied before revealing its true provenance. By which time the bemused official was digesting the 'General Summary' from its first stanza (quoted below) to its last (heading this chapter).

> We are very slightly changed
> From the semi-apes who ranged
> India's prehistoric clay;
> Whoso drew the longest bow
> Ran his brother down, you know,
> As we run men down today.

There were twenty-six poems in the first edition of *Departmental Ditties and Other Verses*, the majority of them in keeping with the memsahib's image of him as a 'subversive pamphleteer'. It was so popular that a second edition came out before the end of the year, but under a publisher's imprint this time. Other editions followed, each a little fatter than the last as more poems were added. But it was the first edition – *My First Book* – that was the author's favourite: '...I loved it best when it was a little brown baby, with a pink string round its stomach; a child's child...'

A new editor took over the *CMG*. Kay Robinson was a very different character from Wheeler and he and Kipling got on famously together. Between them they restyled the paper's layout during the hot weather of '87.

'This took up for a week or so all hours of the twenty-four and cost me a breakdown due to lack of sleep. But we two were proud of the results,' wrote Kipling in his autobiography. It also introduced turnovers for the first time – a regular column and a quarter of 1200 words maximum designed to take contributions such as the assistant editor's apparently endless flow of stories, sketches and poems that the astute Robinson had noted. (Indeed, ten of his soon-to-be-famous *Plain Tales* appeared in this format in the first six months of the new editorship.) So Kipling had to 'write short' once more. His first turnover appeared on 4th August, hot on the heels of the exhausting change-over that had cost him so dear. It is not clear what he meant by a breakdown in this context, as it did not prevent his working, and continuing to work until towards the end of August when he went off to Simla for a month's holiday. But that first story reveals something about his mental state at the time. It was called 'The House of Shadows By its Occupant'. The said Occupant describes the unseen tenants that follow him about the house, watching him from behind his chair or screen, always just out of sight however quickly he turns round. One in particular worries him: the Man in the Next Room... 'I would endure the people who hide in the corners of the lamproom and rush out when my back is turned...or even the person in the garden who slides in and out of the ferash trees when I walk there, if I could get rid of the Man in the Next Room...One of these days, perhaps, if I enter my own house very, very silently, with bare feet, crawling through a window, I may be able to catch him and wring from him some sort of explanation; for it is manifestly absurd that a man paying seventy-five rupees a month should be compelled to live with so unsatisfactory a chum as the man in the next room.

'On second thoughts, and after a plain statement of facts to the doctor, I think it would be better to go to the Hills for a while and leave him to maunder about the empty house till he is tired. The doctor says he will be gone when I return; taking all the other persons with him.'[31]

This piece of writing seems to be a manifestation of Kipling's 'breakdown', a kind of hypnotic state where the conscious mind observes and takes notes of the subconscious. In a letter to The Wop a year earlier, he had described a rather similar experience when sent to report on a tragic accident at Lahore High School. The roof had fallen in killing three boys asleep underneath. He had known one of the boys. He saw the bodies laid out, smelt the smell of death, and already tired and used up with the heat, was violently sick on reporting back to the office. He had a fair notion of what would be in store for him that night. 'You know my peculiarity about eyes,' he wrote. 'It recurs whenever my tummy's out of order or I'm overworked or unstrung and it came back in full force that night. If I'd been a convicted murderer I couldn't have been more persistently followed by those things on the beds.'[32] This is the first reference to the disembodied eyes he had encountered at the Grange when staying with Aunt and Uncle Burne-Jones. 'At bedtime one hastened along the passages, where unfinished cartoons lay against the walls. The Uncle often painted in their eyes first, leaving the rest in charcoal – a most effective presentation. Hence our speed to our own top-landing...'[33] This horror of eyes following him was the innocent beginning of his night terrors as a child, which in later years led him to wander the streets of Lahore and London for hours on end 'when the night got into his head' and he could not sleep.

A week later he is describing his hemicrania, or migraine. 'It is a lovely thing. One mathematical half of head throbs and hammers and sizzles and bangs and swears while the other half – calm and collected – takes note of the agonies next door. Doctor says it's overwork again.'[34] And he overworked in order to cure 'the blue devils' – a vicious circle.

This was the other side of the coin from doing the work he loved: not only the inevitable eyestrain for someone with permanently weakened sight but the physical discomfort and mental turmoil of working throughout the hot season, apart from a month's oasis in the hills. That still left five red-hot months to be endured when the daytime temperature averaged 116 degrees F in the shade, when dust storms – and tempers – blew up in an instant, and the risk of cholera or typhoid was added to the endemic fever as an almost daily hazard; when men he had been yarning with in the club one evening were struck down by cholera the next. The nights were reckoned cool if the temperature fell to eighty-four degrees, and were often spent lying on the flat roof having water thrown over his parched body as he tried to sleep. It saved heat-stroke but brought on fever. 'I assure you, Auntie, that for one weary week my fear in the daytime was that I was going to die, and at night my only fear was that I might live to the morning.'[35]

Domestic life at Lahore was not without its distractions, if Rudyard's list of family pets and their hatred of one another is to be taken seriously.

Trix owned a Persian cat and a fox terrier pup, their father a raven and Rudyard a bull terrier called Buz. Later came Vixen (Vic), his beloved fox terrier, bought at the sale of a dead man's kit. She it was who shared his life from (and including) breakfast to bedtime. She could judge by the tone of his voice at the end of the day when it was more expedient to sleep under his chair than on his lap. And it was Vic's ecstatic welcome back after an absence of seven months in Allahabad during which time Rudyard confessed to having forgotten her, that prompted his 'egotistical' remark: 'I shall think better of myself henceforward.' – 'Hear him!' said his mother. 'Anyone but a man would have said he would think better of the dog.'[36]

In later years Robinson was to say that his young assistant had been a staff in himself, so hard did he work. But Kipling distrusted his own powers to the extent that to demand a leading article from him filled him with anguish – he would say it was 'above him'; and he scarcely wrote five in as many years. More to their mutual satisfaction were the 'sumptuous' rat hunts that the two men and their dogs revelled in after hours at the office.

He indulged in a few mild flirtations to the relief, and often to the amusement, of his family who were worried about his long-term attachment to Flo Garrard. One in particular about which Ruddy himself was 'vastly amusing', according to his father, was when he fell for the attractive daughter of an army chaplain. He would drive five miles to Mian Mir on a chilly Sunday morning to sit in a cold church and listen to the father's 'impossible' sermon to a company of soldiers and a handful of civilians, solely so that he might gaze upon the object of his affections. The Kiplings were not churchgoers, although in this case Trix would have gone with him if the weather had been better, purely to satisfy her sisterly curiosity. As it was, Rudyard, who admitted it was the first time in four years he had attended church, covered himself with glory by 'producing a card case instead of a prayer book and dropping a whist voucher into the collection bag.'[37] He was eventually introduced to the chaplain's daughter at a dance, only to fall foul of her halitosis. End of romance. For all that, he could not forget Flo, even though she had given him his *jawab* two years after he had arrived in India. (It had been an on/off relationship from the start; while still at boarding school he had written to a family friend that 'everything that has ever existed between myself and the fair F.G. *is entirely at an end.*[88]) But in spite of Flo's repeated wish to break with him he could not disentangle himself so easily, and eighteen months later was writing anxiously to Margaret begging her for news of his erstwhile sweetheart who was then studying art at the Slade. His 'miserably self-torturing nature' was also a loyal one, and time and distance seemed to make no difference to his feelings for Flo. He clung to her memory as if he needed to know that she (or *someone?*) was there in the background, the object of his hopes and dreams; his *amulet*, as it were, because without her – with 'Heart unfilled' – he was too emotionally insecure for his own good. Increasingly he was receiving pressing invitations from eager mothers of eligible, if plain, daughters (otherwise known as the 'fishing fleet') requesting the pleasure of his company. And who knew to what – and with whom – he might not commit himself in a moment of black despair?

When he had been in India for five years ('five years of perfect felicity at Lahore – in a damnable climate…but a home-life beyond compare')[39] and his name was beginning to be known in the land, the *CMG*'s proprietors sent him 800 miles south to Allahabad. He went reluctantly, even though he would be the star reporter on the *Pioneer*, the *Gazette's* big sister paper. Not only was it promotion but an opportunity to write more tales: about India, about soldiers and about a subject on which he appeared to be uncommonly *knowing*, at least in print: the opposite sex. It was, however, concerning one of the latter stories that the twenty-two-year old author felt unsure of his ground. So he sent the draft to his mother for her comments as he had often done before. He must have touched a nerve – or an eternal truth – for back came her reply: 'Never you do that again!' But of course he did.

At the beginning of 1888 *Plain Tales from the Hills* was published in India, forty slight, but acutely-observed tales that Kipling himself described as 'horrid bad'. Over half of them were set among Anglo-Indian society in Simla and were sufficiently scandalous for those days to ensure the book's immediate sell-out. Avid readers casting about among their acquaintances for the originals of some of the more questionable characters, were introduced to Mrs Hauksbee, a woman separated from her husband, who had 'big, rolling, violet-blue eyes', was 'clever, witty…and sparkling beyond most of her kind' – and who manipulated people, mostly for their own good, as if they were puppets. 'She could be nice, though, even to her own sex.'[40] This was the book that bore the famous, but unwise, dedication: To the wittiest woman in India. The young author had not foreseen, perhaps, that his chosen dedicatee, a certain Mrs Burton, would decline to accept the honour. Perhaps she guessed that she was supposed to be the original of Mrs Hauksbee. Or partly so, for there is something of Alice Kipling in the character too. Later he tactfully dedicated a copy of the third edition to his mother: 'The Most Excellent Lady of the Dedication from her unworthy son.' He was lucky to get away with that – if indeed he did.

In Allahabad Kipling worked at a furious pace, both editing and writing three or more pieces each week for the *Pioneer's* new supplement in addition to his everyday work on the paper, which entailed travelling widely and reporting on mines, factories and such like. No sooner had he settled in at the Allahabad Club than he was sent off for a month touring throughout Rajputana by rail and road – like a globe-trotter. The kind of man, he reported back, who '"does" kingdoms in days and writes books upon them in weeks...and is "much pleased" with everything.' (His book, or rather series of articles on the tour, would be called *Letters of Marque*.[41])

Leaning out of the carriage window in the early morning light he saw the Taj Mahal for the first time. In the low-lying mist its splendour seemed to be floating free of the earth. When the mists shifted and the sun shone it took on a hundred new shapes, each one perfect and beyond description – but full of sorrow. 'The sorrow of the man who built it for the woman he loved, and the sorrow of the workmen who died in the building – used up like cattle. And in the face of this sorrow the Taj flushed in the sunlight and was beautiful, after the beauty of a woman who has done no wrong.'

He visited the dead, desolate city of Amber, exploring the palace with its scores of venomous and suggestive little rooms; and found its death as nothing to that of Chitor whose ruins, from palace to tower to stinking water tank, emanated an evil he could not describe and from which he fled. And yet he returned there by moonlight, to the ruins and the tombs, as if a stronger force was pulling him. Among the shifting shadows where jackals lurked he heard again the malevolent chuckle of water – and believed that the soberest mind will 'credit every legend and lie that rises as naturally as the red flush of sunset, to gild the dead glories of Rajasthan'. Then at Boondi where he was shown round the outer rooms of a third and very much alive palace, he heard 'deep down in [its] bowels...a woman's voice singing, and the voice rang as do voices in caves. All palaces in India excepting dead ones...are full of eyes. In some...the idea of being watched is stronger than in others. In Boondi Palace it was overpowering...'

At Jeypore he noted the limitless luxury of the Maharaja's Museum where the South Kensington-type revolving cases and labels made him feel homesick – and savage when he considered certain 'starved' government museums of his acquaintance. And very far from the nearest railway line he came across a stretch of steel-blue water by yet another palace. Since returning to India he had been an exile from the sea, 'barred from anything better than the yearly swell and shrinkage of one of the Five Rivers.' He had seen enough of marble palaces. A soft-cushioned boat was found and...'the mutter of water under a boat's nose was a pleasant thing to hear once more.' And here providence favoured his artist's eye, his thirst for colour, for 'the bathing-ledge at the foot of the City wall was lighted with women clad in raw vermilion, dull red, indigo and sky-blue, saffron and pink and turquoise; the water faithfully doubling everything.' Further along the lake huge turtles lay on the shore, a stork had built her nest in a withered tree and water-fowl abounded.

Another year, a different direction and it was the turn of the railway workshops at Jamalpur, the Crewe of Eastern India, to come under his eye. There he made a profound discovery that was to reverberate throughout his life: 'An engine is a she – as distinctly feminine as a ship or a mine.' Naturally, then, they were also 'the "livest" things that man ever made. They glare through their spectacle-plates, they tilt their noses contemptuously, and when their insides are gone they adorn themselves with red lead, and leer like decayed beauties...' And he noted 'the soft sigh of a far-away steam-valve' and the language of the engineers that is 'beautifully unintelligible'.[42]

During his first few months in Allahabad leading a solitary life at the club, he met a Professor and Mrs Hill; and later in the year he moved into their bungalow, sharing expenses on a per capita basis: what the Anglo-Indians called "chumming". (He had first asked his mother's advice on the matter, acknowledging his 'ruffian' ways in the bosom of his family. The outspoken Alice had not minced her words: while it would be good for him having to be 'moderately genial' and civil she did not think the Hills – or anyone – would tolerate his moods and 'blue-devils'.) Mrs Hill's impressions of Kipling at this time are illuminating. He was already beginning to go bald, and at twenty-two he looked nearer forty. 'He was animation itself, telling his stories admirably, so that those about him were kept in gales of laughter. He fairly scintillated, but when more sober topics were discussed he was posted along all lines.'[43] He was all things to all people, talking equally well to a scientist or a high court judge; moreover she had heard that he could make 'first-class love to the latest belle in Simla.'[44]

It was at the Hills' bungalow that he wrote 'Baa Baa Black Sheep', stamping about the place in a tearing rage while doing so, according to his hostess. Yes, he could be a difficult house guest and was 'impossible' at times. But Mrs Hill came to understand his moods, perhaps because she was only a few years older than he, and soon became his confidante and friend. Kipling had never met a woman quite like 'Ted' Hill before: she was an American, the daughter of the president of an American college for women, and as unconventional and boyish as her nickname. When he was summoned back to Lahore to relieve the sick Kay Robinson, he wrote her long, gossiping letters almost daily. And now it was her advice, instead of his mother's (who was away in Simla, anyway), that he sought. In particular regarding 'girl talk' for 'The Story of the Gadsbys' (one of the many tales he wrote for the *Week's News* and which later 'took off' in the Indian Railway Library series); and over a certain nameless Maiden, 'the Incomparable She', with whom he professed to be in love. Was she real, this maiden he agonised over to Mrs Hill for a few weeks, and then never referred to again? Or was she a piece of pure fiction on his part, enabling him to ask advice of a married woman as to how she would react or respond to such-and-such a situation, in the interests of literary research? Mrs Hill's own comment on the maiden, years later, was that the girl in question was not worthy of him – 'she wouldn't marry such an "ineligible."' And that Kipling got 'bravely over' the affair.

Another possibility has been suggested: that he was in love with Mrs Hill herself but being unable to express his feelings except in the third person, invented his 'Maiden'. In which case he either fooled the intelligent Mrs Hill, or she was covering up for him. He was certainly devoted to her and depended on her support and advice *and* the prompt answering of his letters. But that is not the same thing as being in love. He was devoted to, and dependent upon, many women who filled the space in his life that no amount of work could fill: from his mother and sister to his aunts, honorary aunts and cousins. His frequent correspondence with Mrs Hill does not in itself imply anything more than that letter-writing was an essential part of his life, a pleasurable exercise, both physically and emotionally. The act of making marks on paper with a pen dipped in his own specially made Indian ink (never a pencil) was second nature to him, and in itself a sensuous delight. And when he was alone it was his only means of unburdening himself of the stresses of daily life, of getting something that troubled him 'out of the system'. For someone who lived on a knife-edge of nerves, as he did, letter-writing was a vital escape valve.

It was while he was in Allahabad that he received news of his cousin Margaret's engagement to an Oxford don with liberal views. 'My Wop, I envy you very bitterly, and I am pleased for your sake. Take my Wopsome love and – don't turn up your nose in scorn – if ever the time comes when you want help of any sort I, if I be above ground, am your servant and brother.'[45] He signed himself 'The Wop of Asia' for perhaps the last time. He felt he could no longer write to her with the same brotherly freedom after her engagement to 'a scholar of Balliol', nor would it be seemly for him to address her as 'Wop' after she was married. But he did, from time to time.

Acting as editor of the *CMG* through the heat of Lahore made Kipling ill again. His mother crisply told him it was time for him to go home. 'You are blue-moulded with India, fagged, dull and self-centred.'[46] She had also noticed a deterioration in his manners, never his strong point.

'You'll have to be civil, Ruddy.' Alice Kipling possessed a turn of phrase that would not have disgraced Jane Austen, one of her son's favourite authors. When Ruddy told her he was going up to Simla to 'make love to Miss E', she replied: – 'I shan't hinder you but she's yellowish green just at present and like a daguerreotype only shows in certain lights. It doesn't say much for your taste!'[47]

One way and another time was running out for Rudyard in India. 'The doctors say that unless I wish to leave my bones in the country – that is their elegant way of putting it – I had better quit.'[48] That would be reason enough for leaving India, but it was not the one uppermost in his mind.

Back in Allahabad Mrs Hill too had been very ill and temporarily insane with raving delirium, according to her lodger who had been keeping her amused during her convalescence by writing her lengthy letters after his day's work: from his rooms to hers. And readers of the *Pioneer* continued to appreciate his genius with words; never mind the fact that its star reporter had been showing a regrettable flippancy in prose and verse towards certain persons of state. It is quite possible that Kipling did this deliberately, due to an increasing restlessness of spirit, not entirely unconnected with the success of his *Plain Tales.* Its publication early in 1888 had crystallised his desire for a change of horizon; his need to move on. Four years' earlier he had written:

I am sick of endless sunshine, sick of blossom-burdened bough.
Give me back the leafless woodlands where the winds of Springtime
     range—
Give me back one day in England, for it's Spring in England now![49]

Now he wanted to 'see more of cities and men and write about them. The end of me when I have done my short studies for practice, will be a novelist; but in the meantime I've learned my trade and have a fair knowledge of special correspondents' duties…I've tried to get to know folk from the barrack-room and the brothel, to the Ballroom and the Viceroy's Council and I have in a little measure succeeded.'[50] More than anything else he wanted to be back in the centre of things, to put a face to the name – his name – that was beginning to be known in London's literary world.

He took stock of his assets. He had £1000 saved, the royalties from *Plain Tales from the Hills* were bringing in £300 a year, the handful of paper-backed railway bookstall volumes of his short stories were 'selling like smoke', and he had a commission to write *Letters of Travel* for the *Pioneer.* But first he must go to Lahore once more to say goodbye to his people. (And surely, to open his heart to them at last about his Southsea years. 'Baa Baa Black Sheep' had been published in the Christmas Supplement of the *Week's News*, and in the Indian Railway Library series, No 6, Price One Rupee.) His mother was very anxious to see him again and he confessed he would like to feel her arms around him once more before he left. 'I can get as much praise as I want in these parts but love is a scarce commodity and I hold the best is a Mother's...'[51]

So it was back to a welcoming 'fambly' where 'The Mother eyed me over and said: "Well, for a sick man you are looking uncommonly well cared for." We don't set to work on the packing till tomorrow – and the first days will, if I know my mother, be given up to the: – "Good Heavens, Ruddy, what is this disgusting rag?" business.' He knew his mother to a T.[52]

There was much for Alice to do in the short time her son was at home. But as she wrote to her sister Georgie: '...with maternal egotism I fancied no-one could do things as well as I. Indeed, it was good to be busy, for when the heart is full and the hands are empty it is hard to get through the last days of anything.'[53]

February in Lahore is when the Punjabi's passion for kite-flying is at its peak in celebration of the coming of spring. It is believed that a kite forms a bridge between heaven and earth, and earth and heaven. Had Rudyard ever flown a kite? Never! 'Then we'll get half a dozen and begin,' said his father. And off they went to the bazaar where kites of every hue and description were being sold as fast as they could be made.

'You never saw anything so funny in your life,' Rudyard wrote to Mrs Hill. 'There were not more than five hundred people watching me and my awkwardness. My kite went up with a rush and the line cut my hands and the population of Mozang (a local village) rocked and roared in rows – in battalions...Then without warning another kite swooped over mine, ducked and dragged its line across my kite line. There was a twang and my masterless kite pitched head over heels far to leeward while a shouting mob of little boys ran to catch it; the law of kite flying being that whoso first touches a fallen kite is its owner. Then the science of the game became apparent and I went baldheaded into the fun of cutting kite strings. I invested in a ball of glass powdered line (by the same token that cuts the hand) but mean little kites flown with greater skill swept my ventures away and I lost four in the afternoon. 'Tis a most fascinating game...You do not see and cannot tell who your antagonist is. He may be a quarter of a mile away and the spoils of battle fall to a third person equally unknown to you both. Very much like life isn't it...'[54]

In between the kite-flying (kite-*fighting* would be a more accurate description) he kicked his heels around his parents' house in unaccustomed idleness, teased the dog, wrote a turn-over for the *CMG*, drove his sister wild with rude remarks about her cooking, twisted the museum's turnstile until it registered more people than ever came in one day and generally made himself a 'surpassing nuisance'.

On 9th March 1889, in the company of Professor and Mrs Hill who were returning to America on a long leave, he sailed from Calcutta on the ss *Madura* with one small trunk and one large bag; eastward for England – and some spectacular kite-flying of his own under London's leaden skies.

1 JLK to EP, 1883, KP.
2 'My First Book', *CMG*, 1892, *Uncollected Prose 2*, Sussex Edition, 1938.
3 RK to CP, 1882, Pinney, *Letters*, Vol 1.
4 RK to Crofts, 1883, *Letters*, Vol 1.
5 RK to Mrs Hill, 1888, *Letters*, Vol 1.
6 Kay Robinson, *McClures Magazine*, 1896.
7 Charles Carrington, *Rudyard Kipling, His Life and Work*, Macmillan, 1955.
8 JLK to MB-J, 1885, KP.
9 *ibid.*
10 KJ
11 George Seaver, *Francis Younghusband*, John Murray, 1952.
12 RK to Mrs Hill, 1888, *Letters*, Vol 1.
13 Angus Wilson, *The Strange Ride of Rudyard Kipling*, Secker & Warburg 1977.
14 RK to MB-J, 1885, *Letters*, Vol 1.
15 'The City of Dreadful Night', *CMG*, 1885, *Life's Handicap*, 1891.
16 *SoM*.
17 Speech by the Earl Baldwin, 1967, KJ.
18 JLK to EP, 1885, KP.
19 *CMG*, 29th March, 1885, Pinney, *Kipling's India Uncollected Sketches*, 1986.
20 Pinney, *Rudyard Kipling, SoM & other Autobiographical Writings*, Cambridge, 1990.
21 *ibid.*
22 RK to MB-J, 1885, *Letters*, Vol 1.
23 *ibid.*
24 RK to EM, 1884, *Letters*, Vol 1.
25 RK in interview with American surgeon, KP.
26 RK to MB-J, 1886, *Letters*, Vol 1.
27 RK to EM, 1884, *Letters*, Vol 1.
28 RK to MB-J, 1885-6, *Letters*, Vol 1.
29 *ibid.*
30 'My First Book'.
31 'The House of Shadows', *CMG*, 1887.
32 RK to MB-J, 1886, *Letters*, Vol 1.
33 *SoM*.
34 RK to MB-J, 1886, Carrington, *RK, His Life and Work*, Macmillan, 1955.
35 RK to EM, 1884, *Letters*, Vol 1.
36 RK to Mrs Hill, 1888, Carrington.
37 RK to Crofts, 1886, *Letters*, Vol 1.

38 RK to Mrs Perry, 1882, *Letters,* Vol 1.
39 RK to Chevrillon 1919, KP.
40 'Three and – an Extra', *Plain Tales from the Hills,* 1888.
41 *From Sea to Sea,* Vol 1, 1900.
42 *ibid.*
43 Edmonia Hill, article in *Atlantic Monthly,* 1936.
44 *Reminiscences of RK,* KP.
45 RK to MB-J, 1888, *Letters,* Vol 1.
46 RK to Mrs Hill, 1888, *Letters,* Vol 1.
47 *ibid.*
48 RK to MB-J, 1889, *Letters,* Vol 1.
49 'In Springtime', *CMG,* 1885.
50 RK to MB-J, 1889, *Letters,* Vol 1.
51 *ibid.*
52 RK to Mrs Hill, 1889, *Letters,* Vol 1.
53 AK to GB-J, 1889, KJ.
54 RK to Mrs Hill, 1889, *Letters,* Vol 1.

CHAPTER THREE

From Sea to Sea: *a Globe-trotter returns*

I cannot write, I cannot think
I only eat and sleep and drink.—
They say I was an author once
I know I am a happy dunce
Who snores along the deck and waits
To catch the rattle of the plates,
Who drowns ambition in a sea
Of Lager or of Tivoli
I cannot write, I cannot sing—
I long to hear the meal-bell ring—
I cannot sing – I cannot write
I am a Walking Appetite.[1]

Kipling and the professor lazed on the *Madura's* deck in unaccustomed idleness. They were toying with matters of the utmost importance, such as whether Angostura bitters went well with whisky; and matters of no importance at all, such as the letter that one of them was supposed to be writing for his old paper. 'There is no such place as India; there never was a daily paper called the *Pioneer*. It was all a weary dream. The only real things in the world are crystal seas, clean-swept decks, soft rugs, warm sunshine, the smell of salt in the air, and fathomless, futile indolence.'[2] So ended the first of many despatches to a mythical newspaper in an unreal land. And so began Kipling's love affair with the sea. Here was the ocean in all its moods – and the despised globe-trotters in theirs. And always in the background was the insistent rhythm of unseen engines, the thresh of racing screws.

It was the shipping lines' belt-and-braces period when their vessels, although screw-driven, still retained masts and sails for auxiliary speed and stability. But it was the swan song of the romantic age of sail.

She was a three-masted schooner of the British India line, familiarly called the Mutton-Mail because of the nature of her regular cargoes between Calcutta and Rangoon. According to one of her passengers the day started something like this: 'It was pyjama-time on the *Madura*...and the incense of the very early morning cigar went up to the stainless skies. Everyone knows pyjama-time – the long hour that follows the removal of the beds from the saloon skylight and the consumption of chota hazri...The Captain, tastefully attired in pale pink, sat up on the signal-gun and tossed the husk of a banana overboard.'[3]

It was aboard the pot-bellied *Africa* bound for Singapore that Kipling started to hum a rhythmical tune as he leant over the ship's rail. 'Rum-ti-tum. Rum-ti-tum-tra-la.' The Hills recognised the signs, even before Rudyard announced his intention of writing some verses about 'Tommy Atkins'. But not yet. It was to be in a very different setting that *Barrack-room Ballads* would take off one at a time – like rockets – to startle an unprepared world with their brilliance.

They made an unscheduled stop at Moulmein where elephants, pagodas, tinkling bells – and a beautiful Burmese girl left a deep impression on Kipling. One of the pagodas had been built in honour of a priest from Mandalay...

By the old Moulmein Pagoda, lookin' eastward to the sea,
There's a Burma girl a-settin', and I know she thinks of me;
For the wind is in the palm-trees, and the temple-bells they say:
'Come you back, you British soldier; come you back to Mandalay!'

The haunting words of 'Mandalay', one of the original *Barrack-room Ballads*, would be set to music and become as much-travelled as their author. And surely only the pedantic would quarrel with the improbable siting of the dawn as it '...comes up like thunder outer China 'crost the Bay!' in the last line.

There is another change of ships at Singapore, for Hong Kong. This time it is the *Nawab* of the P & O line. It is overcrowded when it should have been half empty and does not find favour with Kipling. '...give me the freedom and cockroaches of the British India, where we dined on deck, altered the hours of the meals by plebiscite, and were lords of all we saw.' And later, on the *Ancona*: 'We do not laugh any more...because there is a cross-sea beneath us and a wet sail above. The sail is to steady the ship who refuses to be steadied. She is full of Globe-trotters who also refuse to be steadied. A Globe-trotter is extreme cosmopolitan. He will be sick anywhere.'[4]

There was little more to be said on the subject – except for 'It!', a delicately suggestive little tale in which the dread phrase is never once mentioned, but which all on board know will be the outcome as...'Suddenly and without warning our ship curtsied. It was neither a bob nor a duck, nor a lurch, but a long, sweeping, stately old-fashioned curtsey.'[5] He could not have found a more appropriate word to describe that sinking feeling as the deck gives way under your feet, closely followed by the pit of your stomach.

The voyage is further enlivened by the presence on board of a much-travelled American child whose precocity and atrocious manners leave an indelible impression on Kipling.

> I cannot call it a boy though officially it is only eight...When it has nothing else to do it will answer to the name of Albert...and it lives in the smoking-room financing the arrangements of the daily lottery...I was afraid of it, but it followed me, and in a level expressionless voice began to tell me how lotteries were constructed. When I protested that I knew, it continued without regarding the interruption, and finally, as a reward for my patience, volunteered to give me the names and idiosyncrasies of all on board...Some day a schoolmaster will get hold of it and try to educate it, and I should dearly like to see at which end he will begin.[6]

One day Albert would get his come-uppance from Kipling's pen. In the meantime he would settle for the more immediate limerick:

> There was a small boy who was proud
> And smoked where he wasn't allowed
> Till a java cigar
> Lit the bestest so far
> And he quit – in a Pillar of Cloud.[7]

They spend some days in Hong Kong where he is taken by a young man in a bar to see 'what they call Life, with a capital Hell', among the 'ladies of the Ancient Profession'. After living in India for so long he is shocked to 'meet again Englishwomen in the same sisterhood'. At the end of the evening he has seen all that he wishes to see of their wretched, drink-sodden lives. 'And mine was the greater sin. I was driven by no gust of passion, but went in cold blood to make my account of this Inferno, and to measure the measureless miseries of life.' We shall hear more about this episode in six months' time during his tour of America.

In his letter to the *Pioneer*, which despite his protestations to the contrary he is despatching regularly throughout the voyage, Kipling describes a steamer trip in the *Honam* from Hong-Kong to Canton, 'a big blue sink of a city full of tunnels, all dark and inhabited by yellow devils.' It is obvious that Kipling has taken an unaccountable dislike to the Chinese people. He senses that they despise the white man and he feels threatened by their myriads. 'There was of course no incivility from the people, but the mere mob was terrifying.' The professor, a man of science, chides him for being intemperate in his attitude towards the Chinese, which is fair comment, but...'He did not see Canton as I saw it – through the medium of a fevered imagination.' The professor persuades Rudyard to visit the Temple of Horrors with him. This is a sort of Chinese Madame Tussauds showing lifelike models of men enduring every manner of torture; not the kind of place to take someone of Kipling's sensitivity. The visit makes him feel sick and unhappy. By the end of the day's sightseeing he is 'wearied and scared and sullen'. Nothing more is revealed in the despatch, and it is only later that we learn he was suffering from fever at the time. (When he was living alone in London and on the verge of a breakdown, he would write to Mrs Hill: 'My head has given out and I am forbidden work and I am to go away somewhere. This is the third time it has happened – the last was on the *Ho-nam* in the Canton river...'[8])

But according to Mrs Hill later, Kipling did not see Canton: 'R.K. had a bad attack of Indian fever when we reached Canton and had to stay in his berth.' She and the professor had told him all about it afterwards.[9]

In his next despatch Kipling is writing from Japan, where their stay coincides with the Japanese 'prodigality of Spring': three weeks of sensuous peach and cherry blossom and its attendant festivals. By contrast with his instinctive reaction to China, he is enchanted with Japan and its people who are always laughing; and especially is he enchanted with the small children. 'Can the people help laughing? I think not. You see they have such thousands of children in their streets that the elders must perforce be young lest the babes should grieve. Nagasaki is inhabited entirely by children. The grown-ups exist on sufferance. A four-foot child walks with a three-foot child, who is holding the hand of a two-foot child, who carries on her back a one-foot child, who – but you will not believe me if I say that the scale runs down to six-inch little Jap dolls such as they used to sell in the Burlington Arcade. These dolls wriggle and laugh. They are tied up in a blue bed-gown which is tied by a sash, which again ties up the bed-gown of the carrier. Thus if you untie that sash, baby and but little bigger brother are at once perfectly naked. I saw a mother do this, and it was for all the world like the peeling of hard-boiled eggs.'

He was less than enchanted with the bathing habits of the adults. 'They bathe often with nothing on and together.' He goes to the hotel bath-house, where there are no bolts on the door, and, when he is dressed only in his virtue and a pair of spectacles, is joined by a pretty girl. The latter senses that the blushing white man is not happy about bathing *à deux* and retires, giggling. All Japan giggles.

But in praise of the food and its service in certain hotels he would have no hesitation in writing a leading article – 'if the *Pioneer* were a medium for puffs...No, it should be a poem – a ballad of good living.' He was also enjoying the other comforts of a civilised life: spring mattresses, gas, electric bells and hot and cold water taps. 'We in India are cheated out of our birthright in all these things.'

They visit a curio shop in Kobe where an old man shows them his treasures and Kipling discovers that the joy of possession lives in the eye. 'The Professor raves about the cabinets in old gold and ivory studded with jade, lazuli, agate, mother-o'-pearl and cornelian, but to me more desirable than any wonder of five-stoned design are the buttons and netsuke that lie on cotton wool and can be taken out and played with.' They behold a procession of fifty-three priests, 'each one clad in at least four garments of brocade, crepe, and silk' that even to a mere male were 'marvellous beyond description', so that he 'broke the tenth commandment in fifty-three places...(with) wicked thoughts of looting and a rush by the next train to the sea...Mercifully the last priest and the last little acolyte went by ere crime had overcome me...' Even the usually calm professor was 'dancing mad with suppressed photography' – but without his camera.[10]

A writer's emotions are legitimate and necessary aids to his pen, but sometimes when a sensitive nerve is touched without warning, they can get out of control – or *are allowed to do so,* as part of the creative process. When Kipling came across American 'pirated' copies of one of his books in Yokohama he stormed out of the bookshop in a rage worthy of the five-year-old Ruddy – without buying what he had gone in for: reading material for himself and the Hills for the 'infinite monotony' of the voyage to San Francisco. His omission must have aggravated and inconvenienced his friends. *He* always had his pen to fall back on and the mix of passengers aboard the American boat to observe for copy. ('For all practical purposes she is the United States.') Had he allowed himself to be driven by his emotions? As always when he had the bit between his teeth, discretion lost out and nothing short of catalepsy could have stopped him from 'bolting' into print on the subject of American piracy. But not merely on his own account. He listed the names of a dozen well-known authors whose works had suffered a similar fate to his, including Haggard, Stevenson and Thackeray. The shop, he fumed, 'which unhappily is not yet burned down...sold every novel of any pretensions that has been published within the last five and twenty years at a uniform price of twenty cents, or something between six and nine pence...by a nest of filchers called the "Seaside Publishing Company".' (This company was to pirate eleven of his books in as many years.) And being an American company it had naturally 'improved' the spelling. 'When Thackeray is made to talk about "travelers" and "theaters" it is time for England to declare war.'[11] Kipling already had. Well into his stride now, he roundly and rudely cursed the Seaside Library and the United States that bred it in some 350 inflammatory words. One gets the impression that, beneath all the surface anger, he was rather enjoying himself. And relieving the monotony of the voyage at the same time. After all, the letter was destined only for an Anglo-Indian readership. (It was published in the *Pioneer* that November and would be heavily edited before appearing in *From Sea to Sea.*) Unfortunately for Kipling, however, it suffered a similar fate to the pirated books. It too was 'lifted' along with many others from the *CMG's* and the *Pioneer's* files by unscrupulous agents and published, warts and all, in the USA early in 1891 under the title *American Notes.* Oddly enough Dickens had used the same title almost fifty years earlier after his visit to the States; and his 'Notes' too had caused offence.

The voyage took seventeen days instead of the scheduled fifteen in the under-engined four-masted *City of Peking.* According to the captain they will do better when they get a wind. They get a beam sea instead. '"She's a daisy at rolling," murmured the chief steward, flung starfish-wise on a table among his glassware...We dined to a dashing accompaniment of crockery, the bounds of emancipated beer-bottles livelier than their own corks, and the clamour of the ship's gong broken loose and calling to meals on its own account...No one slept very heavily that night. Both arms were needed to grip the berth...Twice I know I shot out of my berth to join the adventurous trunks on the floor...'[12]

Arrived at San Francisco, Kipling parted company with his friends for the time being, but not before he had been pointedly rude about American west-coast fortifications observed as they had entered the harbour. (This 'Letter' too was to suffer the same fate as the previous one.)

On his own again, he felt 'very lonesome...in this big raging tearing city' – until he received a letter from Aunt Georgie inviting him to stay with them until he had found somewhere to live in London.'...and then the sky brightened'. He called on a resident who had also sent him an invitation, on the grounds that she knew his Uncle Ned and Aunt Georgie. '...and there was Uncle Ned's portrait and photoes of his paintings in the room. So we fell into each other's arms...She lives in a funny little house all of painted wood, (which is the custom in Frisco – and has refined – that is to say, unAmerican – daintiness about her).'

He was, he told his aunt, now writing for three newspapers, making money almost as fast as he was spending it and 'running a lady typewriter' to keep pace with the work. One reporter had described him as a 'handsome but bashful Englishman' – how he must have changed since the old days. But he could not love the Americans en masse. 'They spit even as in the time of Dickens, and their speech is not sweet to listen to – 'specially the women's'.[13]

For nearly four months he quartered North America by rail, almost as industriously, but by no means to the same divine purpose, as his maternal great-grandfather had quartered the north of Ireland on foot or horseback a hundred years earlier at the same age. But where James Macdonald had studied the scriptures and preached to the people, Kipling studied the people and – preached gospels of praise and insult by turns, in interviews and in print. He was acting like a small boy who has been released from the confines of a strict environment and is determined to indulge himself to the limit. Once again his inflammatory words took off round the world and boomeranged back at him. By which time he had revised many of his ideas about the country, with particular reference to its intelligent and attractive girls. It was the beginning of a love/hate relationship with America and the Americans that was to have life-and-death consequences in the years ahead.

But travelling on his own again after the companionship of the Hills he found the loneliness overwhelming: 'it seemed so strange unnatural and wrong to be seeing all this loveliness alone.'[14] He continued to write regularly to Mrs Hill in Pennsylvania while he was touring and writing up his travels. On a more practical note, the packing of his bags each time he moved on utterly defeated him. The result was a 'most horrible mess'. Not quite as bad as it had been in India when there had been his bedding to wrestle with as well. It would 'swell up like whipped cream' each time he tried to strap it down. But now there was another cross to bear. He had split his dress trousers and buttons were beginning to 'rot off' his shirts. 'I try to cobble things together but it's very hard work,' he complained. 'I'd sooner write a leading article on the Silver question.'

He was happy to hear that Mrs Hill was safely home again with her mother, but '...in the midst of your happiness don't forget to send an occasional line to me...just now a letter means so much – so much.' He was suffering from raging toothache and a swollen face at the time. Once again his dependence on letters in lieu of companionship is noticeable. 'I'm like a Ruddyless ship without you...' But there were good days too. He met 'three jolly Parsees' from India and 'spake in the sweetest of vernaculars' to them to their mutual joy. And there was the day in Boston when he came across two English reviews of his Railway

Library stories that made him 'foolishly happy.' But 'the more I wander about the world and realise the utter insignificance of literary aims and aspirations...the more assured I am that there is only one thing in the world worth having. And that is not Fame.'

He decided to call on Mark Twain, the man he had loved and admired from fourteen thousand miles away. It was not, however, until he was standing on Twain's doorstep, unannounced and uninvited, that it occurred to him that the great man 'might possibly have other engagements than the entertainment of escaped lunatics from India, be they never so full of admiration...How was I to explain that I only wanted to shake hands with him?' And to ask him some questions. Were his readers ever going to hear of Tom Sawyer as a man? And to protest at any thought of the author killing Tom off because '"...he isn't your property any more. He belongs to us."'[15] It was all rather impertinent, an invasion of privacy that the older Kipling would never have tolerated from any newspaperman. Fortunately for the younger man, Mark Twain did not take it amiss. On the contrary one gets the impression that he enjoyed the occasion, and not least the conversation, quite as much as his unexpected guest. In later years he would say of Kipling, whom he met again at an Oxford degree-giving ceremony: 'Between us we cover all knowledge. He knows all that can be known, and I know the rest.'[16]

While in New York Rudyard called on Uncle Harry, his mother's elder brother, at his Wall Street office. Harry had not seen Alice for thirty years and the thought made her son feel suddenly old. Time had not dealt kindly with his uncle although he seemed to be comfortably off. He called Rudyard 'my boy' and yarned away to him about literature. But first he handed his nephew some mail that was awaiting him: an envelope containing an 'enclosure'. Describing the matter in a letter to Mrs Hill, Rudyard said he was horrified to discover that his 'damphool' editor had sprung his letter about the Hong Kong brothel on an 'innocent Anglo-Indian public' that June. So presumably the envelope contained the relevant tear-sheets from the *Pioneer*. Kipling does not mention showing the article to his uncle, but I would be surprised if he had not done so, there in his office with no women present.

Over dinner that evening with his aunt and uncle (they had no children) Rudyard had to tell them all about himself and his life in India – and apparently did nothing to dispel their notion that he was some sort of 'wandering scapegoat'. Was there a link here, in their minds, with his brothel story? In return he was regaled with 'much' family history. (It was Harry, we must remember, who at nineteen had earnestly hoped that his brother Fred's behaviour was in keeping with a Macdonald cadet, etcetera. So Harry knew what he was talking about in this regard.) And what was Rudyard's reaction to the family history? It was 'doubtless very interesting,' he wrote to Mrs Hill, '—if I had only listened to it.' What? Kipling, the journalist who was interested in all things, not listening to what his uncle had to say about his ancestors? It is more likely that it was his way of saying, politely, to his pal that he did not want to discuss it – implying, perhaps, that it was not sufficiently interesting anyway. It would seem that he decided there and then to keep the family history to himself for the reasons already suggested.

The last leg of the journey to England was in the *City of Berlin,* designed on the one hand to capture the Blue Riband and on the other to dazzle her passengers with her spaciousness and luxury. Not only did she have a 500 ft long promenade deck but she still clung to a bowsprit and figurehead, one of the last passenger liners to do so. The three miles of lead piping throughout the ship ensured running water in the cabins and ample bathing facilities in the white marble bathtubs. By arrangement with the steward the passenger's name was put on a slate outside the bathroom door, and at the allotted time the passenger claimed his place on the rota and in the bath. (No risk of Rudyard being embarrassed by extra-ablutionary companions here.) The public rooms, Ladies', Smoking, Officers' and so on, opened on to the deck on either side, and the dining saloon was furnished in Spanish mahogany and purple velvet. None of which luxury prevented the age-old hazard of seasickness – or for that matter, one of the ship's more poetic passengers relaxing into rhyme on the subject, on the back of a convenient dinner menu.

> There were passengers thirty and three
> And they sailed along o' we
> On the North Atlantic Sea
> In the *City of Berlin.*
> And they none of 'em laughed or spoke—
> (They were far too queasy to smoke)
> And they couldn't stomach a joke
> In the *City of Berlin...*
> But we (who are Never Ill)
> We watched 'em load and unfill
> And laughed – we are laughing still—
> On the *City of Berlin...*[17]

Rudyard was happy and at ease once again. For company on the voyage he had Mrs Hill, her sister Caroline Taylor and four other

members of their family, the professor having gone on ahead to visit
his people in Ireland.

In October 1889, seven years after he had left it as a precocious
schoolboy, Rudyard Kipling returned to England. On the train journey
from Liverpool to London he would have had plenty of time to catch
up with all the latest news, from a rail crash to royalty, from a pit disaster
to a police raid. In London's theatreland Beerbohm Tree was appearing
at the Haymarket, the D'Oyley Carte Company was performing *The
Yeoman of the Guard* at the Savoy and at the Lyceum Ellen Terry and
Henry Irving were in a play about the French Revolution.[18] (Irving was
to become a favourite actor of Kipling's, and eight years later – after
putting a box at the author's disposal and meeting him backstage after
the performance – appeared 'rather keen' on Rudyard writing a play
for him. Kipling rather liked the idea too but, for whatever reason, it
never came to anything. Actors were rummy folk, Kipling confided to
a friend.[19] In the meantime, until fame overtook him, he preferred to
queue for the pit rather than have a seat for the asking: it was better for
studying people.) The weather forecast was unsettled and there were
letters to the editor complaining about the unpunctuality of the train
service. *Plus ça change...*

Young in years though he was his experience of the world – two
worlds, East and West – gave him a certain advantage over his peers;
although it is unlikely he saw that as compensation for his self-conscious
lack of a university education. It was suggested that he should do a
course of English Literature at Oxford and live with the dons for six
months. His reply that a bull in a china shop would be easier than he
up at Oxford was probably no exaggeration, even if it was tinged with
regret for what might have been but now could never be so. But what if
this galvanising relationship had come to pass? One thing is certain:
the experience would have left its mark – and not just on Kipling.
Something of his raw genius would have been lost to the world. Apart
from isolated sneers at his being no intellectual – a condition he would
be the last to claim, or want, for himself – few biographers have deplored
his lack of higher education. It would not have been in their interests
to do so. Nevertheless it was largely the intellectuals of a liberal
persuasion who decried him and his works. A few continue to do so to
this day with a fine head of derogatory steam, although even they are
running out of puff as the literary world re-evaluates the man and his
work.

But oh how good it was to be in his aunt and uncle's company once
more! After seven years' absence he found The Grange was still on the

edge of the countryside at Fulham, but its staff had increased and now included a butler, parlour maids and studio assistants. Rudyard relaxed in the comfort of his aunt's loving concern, set the world to rights with his uncle among the familiar studio smells, and felt at home again after six months of living out of suitcases. (Ned Burne-Jones made a wonderful uncle with his delight in the so-called vulgarities of life. His comic letters and drawings – the one of 'A Prominent lady on her honeymoon at Rottingdean' immediately comes to mind – and his boisterous enthusiasm for jokes, both practical and verbal, endeared him to children of all ages. They were his way of letting off steam, an escape from the high-minded idealism of his 'piccys'.) Rudyard rediscovered his cousins, played trains with the seven-year-old Hugh (Poynter), whom he persisted in regarding as a nephew, acted as father-confessor to Hugh's older brother, Ambrose, and to Philip (Burne-Jones), who separately brought him their troubles and their tragedies (Ambo's was in blank verse and ran to five acts) for his expert opinion. To Ambo he gave 'a sight of good advice – I'd be sorry to follow it all myself',[20] and he helped to get Phil out of the clutches of shady publishers to whom that young man had foolishly entrusted his autobiography.

But more than anything Rudyard wanted a place of his own. He found it, off the Strand; that lively, noisy thoroughfare which seemed to consist entirely of restaurants, jingling horse-drawn vehicles – and mud. His rooms high above a narrow street that ran down to the river were far removed, in every sense, from the Burne-Jones and Poynter households. And there, three – or was it five? – floors up, he was alone throughout a working day that often extended into the small hours, unless one of his cousins happened to drop in for a smoke and more good advice. In those days Villiers Street was a place 'primitive and passionate in its habits and population',[21] where a man could cut his own throat without disturbing its inhabitants any longer than it took for the body to be carted off and a bucket of water thrown over the bloodstains. The area had not entirely thrown off its Dickensian atmosphere, although the old Hungerford Market had long since disappeared under the railway lines that crossed the new Hungerford Bridge.

Did Kipling know that the twelve-year-old Charles Dickens had worked at a blacking factory by Hungerford Stairs, little more than a stone's throw from his own lodgings? He would have if he had read John Forster's biography of Dickens published some years earlier, the first of many to be written about the famous novelist, in which the young Charles's experiences in the factory were revealed for the first time. But if Kipling, the eternal journalist, had read it would he not have commented on its proximity to Villiers Street, either when he was living there, or later in his autobiography? Not necessarily. For someone of Kipling's sensibilities it would have been unthinkable to draw attention to a period in Dickens' childhood which had in some respects paralleled his own: the parents' apparent rejection of their son in alien surroundings, following a happy early childhood. (Charles' father had been a clerk in the Navy Pay Office at Chatham until he went bankrupt and was sent to the Marshalsea debtors' prison in London where the family was then living in poor circumstances. Charles was sent out to work labelling bottles in the ramshackle, rat-infested factory that was almost tumbling into the Thames. He earned six shillings a week for a twelve-hour day and then walked the four miles home to fend for himself in his lonely room, while his mother and younger siblings shared their father's room at the prison.)

Like the younger Ruddy at Southsea, Charles had confided his feelings of misery and rejection to no-one. And although he was in the factory less than six months, compared with Ruddy's almost six years at Lorne Lodge, those months were to haunt Dickens for the rest of his life and profoundly influence his writing. While he was working on *Oliver Twist* and the largely-autobiographical *David Copperfield* in particular, he suffered recurrences of a painful boyhood illness. But, unlike Kipling, he had an additional cross to bear that he never got over: the shamefulness of his employment and the discredit it brought upon his parents. In particular on his mother who had not wanted her son to leave the factory when his father was in a position to take him away. Charles was then earning eight shillings a week and Mrs Dickens was reluctant to lose the extra money. The real grinding tragedy of Dickens' life – which would have been immediately recognisable to Kipling, whose love for his own parents was the bedrock of his – was that Charles could never forgive his mother for that. The blacking factory episode was never afterwards referred to in the Dickens family and when Charles married he did not even confide in his wife.

Both Dickens and Kipling fictionalised their early traumas; but only Dickens, in his portrayal of society's victims, their deprivations and insecurity, allowed them to dominate his writing. We can only speculate whether this would have been the case had he been able to unburden himself of those 'shameful' childhood memories by talking them over with his family.

What we do know, however, is that within a year of Kipling's arrival in England, during which time his meteoric rise to fame was being compared to that of the young Dickens who had also worked as a journalist, he had written his first – and only – story set in the East End: 'The Record of Badalia Herodsfoot'. Why did he write it? I suggest there were two reasons: firstly, as a tribute to the great novelist one of whose manuscripts in a 'big bluish book' he had gazed upon with wonder as an eleven-year-old in the old South Kensington Museum. ('That man seemed to me to have written very carelessly; leaving out lots which he had to squeeze in between the lines afterwards.'[22]) Secondly, it was written as a testament to the East End woman (a new breed to Kipling) who despite deprivation and brutality remained true to her faithless man.

Badalia is a 'godless' costermonger's girl and…'there is a legend in Gunnison Street that on her wedding-day she, a flare-lamp in either hand, danced dances on a discarded lover's winkle-barrow, till a policeman interfered, and then Badalia danced with the Law amid shoutings.'

Two years later her husband leaves her – 'over her senseless body' – for another woman. And the baby he has left her with, dies. But Badalia refuses all proposals from other men because: "'My man…'ll come back one of these days, and then, like as not, 'e'd take an kill me if I was livin' 'long o' you…'"

The local clergy recruit her for her special knowledge of the sick and needy in the street who have the right to relief. "'The men they'll shif' for themselves…The women they can't shif' for themselves – 'specially bein' always confined…women is cruel put upon in Gunnison Street.'"

'To her unbounded pride Badalia [is] appointed the dispenser of a grant – a weekly trust…for the benefit of the street.' She faithfully keeps a record of every penny she spends, on whom and why. And when the money runs out she 'begged clothes…for the scrofulous babes that multiplied like the green scum on the untopped water-cisterns'.

And then after two years Badalia's husband returns to Gunnison Street, drunk and demanding the money he has been told the curate gives her every week. Badalia is glad to have her man back. But: "'Anythin' else but that, Tom, I'll give willin' and true. That money's my trust.'"

Badalia refuses, just as she refuses to give her man away when later that night the priest and the curate are called to what is left of Badalia after her husband had finished with her.

"'Who was it?' said the curate.

"'Man from outside. Never sees 'im no more'n Adam. Drunk, I s'pose. S'elp me Gawd that's truth!…an' it's all right…I never guv up a copper o' the trust money – not a copper. You look under the chist o' drawers – all wot isn't spent this week is there…'"

'It was a seven pound fifteen shilling funeral, and all Gunnison Street turned out to do it honour.'[23]

The story, which was taken almost directly from life, tends towards the sentimental, but together with the later poem, 'Mary, Pity Women!'

expressed Kipling's compassion for the unloved or deserted woman; as he had in 'Lisbeth', the first of his *Plain Tales.*

It aren't no false alarm,
The finish to your fun;
You – you 'ave brung the 'arm,
An' I'm the ruined one!
An' now you'll off an' run
With some new fool in tow.
Your 'eart? You 'aven't none...
Ah, Gawd, I love you so!...

When a man is tired there is naught will bind 'im;
All 'e solemn promised 'e will shove be'ind 'im.
What's the good 'o prayin' for The Wrath to strike 'im
(Mary, pity women!), when the rest are like 'im?[24]

Kipling's rooms were above Harris the Sausage King at No 19 (later 43) Villiers Street. It was easy to find, he would explain to first-time callers, because sausages were always frying in the window. The proximity of a ready meal suited him well, apart from ensuring a reasonable rent, for he would have been quite helpless in the matter of feeding himself. (Even his daily shave required the services of a barber, another instance of how India, where his servant used to shave him while he slept, had spoilt him for 'normal' life.) He could subsist, he said, on twopennyworth of sausage and mash from breakfast to dinner 'when one dined with nice people who did not eat sausage for a living'.[25]

'The chambers stood much higher than the other houses, commanding a hundred chimneys – crooked cowls that looked like sitting cats as they swung round, and other uncouth brick and zinc mysteries supported by iron stanchions and clamped by S-pieces. Northwards the lights of Piccadilly Circus and Leicester Square threw a copper-coloured glare above the black roofs, and southward lay all the orderly lights of the Thames.'[26] From the back he could see the Victoria Embankment and the river while from the front he could look through the fanlight of Gatti's Music Hall under the arches across the street, almost on to its stage.

Before they sailed for India Mrs Hill and Caroline saw him settled in his rooms, helping him arrange the few treasures he had picked up during his travels. (Visitors described Persian rugs and prayer-mats, pictures of military subjects and shelves-full of magazines, while the furniture was of the most basic bed, table and two chairs variety.) Once again he had a fiancée across the sea to bombard with earnest love-letters, for he had become engaged to Caroline within a few days of arriving in England. He continued to write regularly to Mrs Hill, from time to time describing his feelings of loneliness that it seemed he would always be prey to, and never more so than when gazing across water. From his window high above the street he would watch the departure of the continental night mail across Charing Cross Bridge almost with tears in his eyes – for him it was a link with the India he had left behind.

———

Kipling erupted onto the London literary scene like an oil-well in a conservation area; and to much the same effect. It was the *fin-de-siècle* and the afternoon of the Beardsley period. With all the great Victorian writers either dead or dying, there was more than a whiff of decadence about late nineteenth century literature in spite of the robust presence of such as Thomas Hardy, Rider Haggard and Conan Doyle. The Aesthetic Movement was palely in love with its own image of 'art for art's sake'; melancholy hung in the air like early morning mist on the river, and to slightly paraphrase the words of one of its proponents: 'They are not long, the days of wine and roses,' so 'I cried for madder music and for stronger wine.'[27] Not surprisingly, the world-weary Aesthetes regarded Kipling's work with horror. A horror which was returned with interest:

> But I consort with long-haired things
> In velvet collar-rolls,
> Who talk about the Aims of Art,
> And 'theories' and 'goals',
> And moo and coo with women-folk
> About their blessed souls.
>
> But that they call 'psychology'
> Is lack of liver-pill,
> And all that blights their tender souls
> Is eating till they're ill,
> And their chief way of winning goals
> Consists of sitting still.
>
> It's Oh to meet an Army man,
> Set up, and trimmed and taut,
> Who does not spout hashed libraries
> Or think the next man's thought,
> And walks as though he owned himself,
> And hogs his bristles short.[28]

On the voyage to England he had been appalled to see white stewardesses waiting on the passengers and the way some of them were treated. Now he was shocked all over again to see how the English treated their female servants while asserting, the more radical among them, that 'the British in India spent violent lives "oppressing" the Native. This in a land where white girls of sixteen, at twelve or fourteen pounds per annum, hauled thirty and forty pounds weight of bath-water at a time up four flights of stairs!'[29] He came to the conclusion there was a 'fine-crusted, slave-holding instinct in the hearts of a good many deep-bosomed matrons – a "throw back" to the times when we trafficked in black ivory.'[30]

The literary world had been given an early warning of what was in store for them with *Departmental Ditties* and *Plain Tales*, and a foretaste of those 'deplorable' privates, Mulvaney, Ortheris and Learoyd, in *Soldiers Three*. Suddenly the word went round that their author was actually living in the capital. Who was he, this writer with the odd-sounding name, who discoursed so knowingly on life in India – and so intimately on the natives and er – 'Tommies'? 'He is so clever, so fresh, and so cynical that he must be young,' said Andrew Lang[31] shrewdly, before anyone had set eyes on him. How old was he? Not yet twenty-four? Good God.

There was no precedent for Kipling's vigorous writing in which the army was represented by the common soldier with all his human frailties in good working order, and never more so than when he was 'drunk and resisting the Guard!/ Mad drunk and resisting the Guard.'[32] The more Tommy dropped his aitches (or 'aspirates' if your name was Oscar Wilde) the more flurries of apostrophes assaulted the eye of the bewildered reader, while editors and publishers fell over themselves to engage his attention. Some wanted to sign him up exclusively, but after seven years in harness he was not to be bought by any man, even though he was almost penniless after his extended holiday. All his life he was mistrustful of praise. Only when the abuse began, as it had after the publication of *Departmental Ditties*, did he feel that he was getting somewhere, that his work was not so bad.

In the next few years he was pronounced to be, by turns: 'a new star out of the East'[33] about whom 'one feels as if one were seated under a palm-tree reading life by superb flashes of vulgarity...He is our first authority on the second-rate, and has seen marvellous things through key-holes'.[34] (Wilde again) Kipling's was 'the voice of the hooligan';[35] he was 'the most complete man of genius'[36] whose 'fairy godmothers were all tipsy at his christening.'[37] And so on.

The writer and critic Edmund Gosse described him as: 'Not a commonplace young gentleman...nor do I suppose that anyone has a sweeter and more deferential smile and a more awful use of language, both at the same time on tap.' His conversation and company fascinated Gosse 'horribly', while admitting that their effects were like 'long potations of green chartreuse. They make one's hand tremble and one's eyes see visions.'[38] It was Gosse who would encourage him to go and see Ibsen's *Hedda Gabler* while Kipling was praising the superiority of the music hall over the 'new theatre'. ('This is why my style is curt and severe, at present date of writing,'[39] Kipling confided to an editor after seeing the play.)

But critics there were by the close of the century; in particular those who allowed political prejudice to get in the way of criticism. There was much sharpening of quills and uncorking of vitriol, as everyone who thought himself anyone in the world of letters raised his voice in praise or protest, lining up in opposite camps of opinion. And with many a Kipling broadside to follow in the years ahead, the critical fires were never in danger of dying out. Succeeding generations and their opinions have changed sides many times, and even today, more than sixty years after his death, his name still arouses controversy; seldom indifference.

Kipling had a horror of patronage and when the 'Hupper Sukkles' took him up he made it a point of honour when introduced to the great and the good not to be impressed by them; but then it came over as arrogance or, at the least, offhandedness. His manners still lacked polish, in spite of his mother's warning to 'be civil, Ruddy'. He was known to forget or altogether ignore some of the more important invitations that were starting to arrive at his modest lodgings, while others of less importance received a reply that would be treasured always.

A certain literary group wrote to ask Kipling if he would speak at their forthcoming dinner. He replied:

To Certain Odd Volumes/Folios, Quartos, octavos and all others innominate – from a small Pamphlet Salutation:

For the kindness of that invitation all thanks to your Bound and Beautiful Selves. For myself Sorrow Sincere upon that day I am out upon Loan for such hours as you mention: yet seeing that odd volumes so notoriously circulate beyond the use of Complete Sets it is my hope that I may later meet you, Individual or Collect on the shelves of that great Library which, lacking all catalogues, men are content to call the world. R.K.[40]

Now, back at the hub of things, his head was filled with tales and more tales queuing up to be told, but he was too proud to ask for any money in advance. He set to and worked the sort of hours that would give a Trades Unionist a coronary to contemplate, and when thus engaged would pin a 'DEAD!' notice on his door. Typically, his first poems were published under pseudonyms, but not for long. 'The Ballad of East and West', for instance, could not have been written by anyone else, and even the aged Tennyson admitted that the young author from India was 'the only one of them with the divine fire'. (For those readers still worried about that controversial first line, taken out of context: 'Oh, East is East, and West is West, and never the twain shall meet,' it is essential to read the entire first verse – better still, the whole ballad – to appreciate Kipling's meaning.)

For fourpence, which included a pint of beer, he could gain admission to Gatti's opposite – and a whole new world of the music hall, the off-duty play-ground of Cockney barmaids and red-coated Guardsmen. It was here, under the arches of Charing Cross that he learned about London's street life at first-hand, from the comic ('Brugglesmith') to the tragic ('Badalia Herodsfoot'). Surely, he thought, the millions of Londoners whose only amusement this was needed a poet of the Music-Halls? Then *he* would be that poet, and defend their so-called 'vulgar' songs as a popular art form. There had been a campaign against the 'immorality' of the music-halls, but he had found that many a West End theatre had 'nudities and lewdities' at least as offensive, and nobody complained about *them*.

He wrote a ballad with the immortal refrain: 'And that's what the girl told the Soldier'.

> At the back o' the Knightsbridge Barricks,
> When the fog's a-gatherin' dim.
> The Life-Guard waits for the Under-Cook,
> But she don't wait for 'im.
> She's married a man in the poultry line
> That lives at 'Ighgate 'Ill.
> An' the Life Guard walks with the 'ousemaid now,
> An'...she can't foot the bill!
> Oh, think o' my song when you're goin' it strong,
> And your boots are too little to 'old yer,
> And don't try for things that are out of your reach,
> And that's what the girl told the soldier,
> Soldier! Soldier!

The horns and fiddles accompanied, the gallery – and the stalls – rocked with delight as the red-coats lustily joined in the refrain that had been tailor-made for them. And if they substituted a few of their own words as they beat out the rhythm with their tankards, who cared?

'Providence has sent me many joys,' said its author, 'and I have helped myself to others, but that night, as I looked across the sea of tossing billycocks and rocking bonnets – my work – as I heard them give tongue, not once, but four times – their eyes sparkling, their mouths twisted with the taste of pleasure – I felt that I had secured Perfect Felicity...and afterwards the dark street was vocal with various versions of what the girl had really told the soldier, and I went to bed murmuring: "I have found my Destiny."'[41] A slight exaggeration, but it made a colourful tale to send to his old newspaper in Lahore; and it triggered off his work on *Barrack-Room Ballads*, first thought of aboard the schooner *Africa*. As always it was a tune or a rhythmic beat that he had to get into his head first. The words followed by themselves, falling neatly into place like soldiers on parade. 'Danny Deever', the first of the ballads to be published, in the *Scots Observer*, was a sensation. 'Here's Literature at last!' cried a grave English professor waving the journal at his students.

> 'What makes you look so white, so white?' said Files-on-Parade.
> 'I'm dreadin' what I've got to watch,' the Colour-Sergeant said.
> 'For they're hangin' Danny Deever, you can hear the Dead March play,
> The Regiment's in 'ollow square – they're hangin' him to-day;
> They've taken of his buttons off an' cut his stripes away,
> An' they're hangin' Danny Deever in the mornin'.

Kipling, through the ballads, was paying homage to Thomas Atkins, warts and all. 'And, Thomas, here's my best respects to you!' But he also had something to say about a society that treated the common soldier with: '"We serve no red-coats here."' A society 'makin' mock o' uniforms that guard you while you sleep...' Until, that is, 'The drums begin to roll, my boys, the drums begin to roll,' and then it's '"Thin red line of 'eroes" when the drums begin to roll.'[42]

As the all-enveloping winter fogs descended on London he was shut away from the world for days on end in his eyrie high above Charing Cross. In a gesture of defiance he had put a notice on his door: 'To Publishers. A classic while you wait!' He had not experienced such isolation since the nightmare Southsea days when he had been banished to the dank, unheated basement as a punishment for his misdeeds. Suddenly London was a vile place. Not so very long ago he had been heartily sick of India's sunshine. Now he longed for it again; the more so now that he could no longer glimpse the East-bound boats making their way down London's murky river.

1 Inscription in Mrs Hill's copy of *Wee Willie Winkie*, 1889.
2 *From Sea to Sea*, Vol 1.
3 'A Menagerie Aboard', *Abaft the Funnel*, Authorised ed, Doubleday, Page & Co 1909.
4 *From Sea to Sea*, Vol 1.
5 'It', *CMG*, 1889.
6 *From Sea to Sea*, Vol 1.
7 Rutherford.
8 RK to Mrs Hill, 1890, *Letters*, Vol 2.
9 W M Carpenter, 'RK's Allahabad Home', *Letters*, Vol 3.
10 Hugh Cortazzi & George Webb, *Kipling's Japan*, Athlone 1988.
11 *ibid*.
12 *From Sea to Sea*, Vol 1.
13 RK to GB-J, 1889, *Letters*, Vol 1.
14 RK to Mrs Hill, *Letters*, Vol 1.
15 *From Sea to Sea*, Vol 2.
16 Mark Twain, KJ.
17 Rutherford.
18 Morton Cohen, *Rudyard Kipling to Rider Haggard*, Hutchinson, 1965.
19 RK to Conland, 1897.
20 RK to Mrs Hill, *Letters*, Vol 1.
21 *SoM*.
22 *ibid*.
23 'The Record of Badalia Herodsfoot', 1890, *Many Inventions*, 1893.
24 'Mary, Pity Women!', 1896.
25 *SoM*.
26 *The Light That Failed*, 1890.
27 Ernest Dowson, 1867-1900, 'Cynara'.
28 'In Partibus', *CMG*, 1889.
29 *SoM*.
30 'The New Dispensation'—1, *Abaft the Funnel.*
31 Andrew Lang, literary critic, Lancelyn Green, *The Critical Heritage*, R&KP 1971.
32 'Cells', *Barrack-room Ballads*, 1892.
33 Edmund Gosse.
34 Oscar Wilde.
35 Robert Buchanan.
36 Henry James.
37 RL Stevenson.
38 Ann Thwaite, *Edmund Gosse, A Literary Landscape*, Secker & Warburg, 1984.
39 RK to WE Henley, Editor of the *Scots*, later the *National, Observer, Letters*, Vol 2.
40 c 1890 from Embankment Chambers.
41 'My Great and Only', *CMG* Turnover, 1890 & *Abaft the Funnel.*
42 'Tommy', *B-r B.*

CHAPTER FOUR

London: fame – and fever

Yes, I have sighed for London Town
And I have got it now:
And half of it is fog and filth,
And half is fog and row...
I cannot tell when dawn is near,
Or when the day is done,
Because I always see the gas
And never see the sun,
And now, methinks, I do not care
A cuss for either one.

'In Partibus'

It was the 'wail of a fog-bound exile'[1] crying out for the sunlight of his motherland, '...so ignorant, I never guessed...that trains could take me to light and sunshine a few miles outside London.' But it was not only the weather that was depressing his spirits. While editors and critics on the one hand were pointing out the wisdom of identifying himself with a literary 'set', one of those sets – 'the long-haired literati' of the Savile Club – was putting it about that he had invented his soldier-talk in *Soldiers Three*. That made him angry. He knew that not one of those gentlemen would venture within earshot of a barracks if he could avoid it. 'But this is only the beginning of the lark. You'll see some savage criticisms of my work before spring. That's what I'm playing for.'[2]

Brave words. But the other side of that coin, as writers have discovered down the centuries, is the isolation that clamps the spirit like a vice when the day's work is done and there is no loved one to turn to – in Kipling's case to provide the emotional ballast that he needed, at times, desperately. His first Christmas Day in London was spent alone until the evening when he went out to dinner with Uncle Ned and Phil, who were also on their own. (The Burne-Jones cottage had been virtually doubled in size that year by the acquisition of the

next-door property. Aunt Georgie had gone down for Christmas with
the now-pregnant Margaret and her husband, but Ned could not face
Rottingdean's icy draughts and stayed at The Grange with Phil.) The
proprietor of the Italian restaurant where the three men presented
themselves at the usual hour was not expecting any diners that night,
but he invited them to join in his family celebrations, and gave them a
bottle of wine because he thought they looked lonely. He was not far
wrong. At midnight Kipling wrote to Mrs Hill: 'Christmas is a beastly
season...There are five million people in London this night and saving
those who starve I don't think there is one more heartsick or thoroughly
wretched than that "rising young author" known to you as Ruddy.'

The new year started badly for Kipling and then progressed in a
series of peaks and troughs, like an over-worked melodrama, parts of
which he was to use in his first full-length work of fiction before the
year was out. At the end of January he was ill again with influenza topped
up with a recurrence of his old Indian fever and some sort of mental
collapse. 'My head has given out and I am forbidden work and I am to
go away somewhere...I must go on alone now till the end of my time. I
can do nothing to save myself from breaking up now and again...I am
physically in perfect health but I can neither work nor think nor
read...You (Mrs Hill) and the doctors always laughed but I knew that
the smash would come some day. It's nobody's fault but my own.'[3]
According to Mrs Hill he was always fearful of losing his mind, although
on this particular occasion he blamed the drugs prescribed by his doctor.
And it is possible that they were stronger than those currently available
in India. But Mrs Hill, drawing on her own experience, thought it more
likely that he was suffering from an acute attack of post-fever depression
brought on by six weeks alone in his rooms, 'too weak to commit suicide'
and prey to an over-active imagination. He once told an editor who
had called on him at Embankment Chambers that when he was working
late 'a phantom of himself had formed the disquieting habit of sitting
opposite him at his desk'; this he took as a sign to 'knock off.'[4] About
this time he wrote 'At the End of the Passage', a macabre tale in which
a similar phenomenon occurs, and like 'The House of Shadows' written
three years earlier, it gives a clue to his mental state.

Hummil, an assistant engineer of a state railway line under
construction in a remote area of India, lived alone and 'understood
the dread meaning of loneliness'. He was under thirty 'which is too
soon for any man to possess that knowledge'. He becomes unwell during
the hot weather but will not go sick because his relief, a young married
man, would only bring his wife and baby with him. '"If she came, – and
[he's] one of those selfish little beasts who are always talking about a
wife's place being with her husband, – she'd die."...Every door and

window was shut, for the outside air was that of an oven. The atmosphere within was only 104…and heavy with the foul smell of badly-trimmed kerosene lamps; and this stench, combined with that of native tobacco, baked brick, and dried earth, sends the heart of many a strong man down to his boots, for it is the smell of the Great Indian Empire when she turns herself for six months into a house of torment.'

After nights of sleeplessness interspersed with horrific nightmares in which 'A blind face that cries and can't wipe its eyes…chases him down corridors', the doctor gives Hummil a morphia injection. Hummil sleeps and the next morning the doctor departs. 'Hummil turned on his heel to face the echoing desolation of his bungalow, and the first thing he saw standing in the verandah was the figure of himself. He had met a similar apparition once before, when he was suffering from overwork and the strain of the hot weather.'

When the doctor (with Lowndes and Mottram who made up their weekly whist foursome) calls a week later Hummil is dead in his bed. 'In the staring eyes was written terror beyond the expression of any pen.' The doctor photographs the dead eyes, develops the film – and destroys it immediately. '"It was impossible of course. There was nothing there…"

'"That," said Lowndes, very distinctly, watching the shaking hand striving to relight the pipe, "is a damned lie."'[5]

(Scientists would agree with the doctor that it is not possible to photograph 'things in a dead man's eye'.)

In February he spent an evening with his cousin Margaret and her husband in their little Kensington house situated next to the Greyhound Inn mentioned in Thackeray's *Esmond*. In a letter to Caroline Taylor describing the occasion and the young couple's conjugal happiness there is a note of longing for a home of his own, and all that that would mean. In the meantime, Aunt Georgie was going to give him a cat when it was old enough to take up residence with him. (Next to the indispensable galley, the companionable cat deserves a place on the Macdonald crest.) And then one day in the street he met Flo Garrard again – whether by chance or design is uncertain – and knew in an instant that his feelings for his childhood sweetheart were as strong as ever.

It must have been shortly after this meeting that Trix called on him in his rooms. (She had married the army man to whom she had been twice engaged, soon after Rudyard left India, and now with her new husband was home on leave.) She was shocked to find her brother looking so ill and despondent, so apparently indifferent to his longed-for literary success. Brother and sister had always had a close relationship, sharing their joys and sorrows equally, and it was with visible emotion that he told her of his meeting with Flo and the terrible mistake he had made in getting engaged to Caroline.

1 *Above left* – James Macdonald (1761-1833), born Ballinamallard, Enniskillen. The first of three generations of Methodist ministers, he was Rudyard's maternal great-grandfather.

2 *Above right* – George Browne Macdonald (1805-1868), his surviving son, was in harness to the ministry at twenty.

3 *Below* – Hannah Macdonald (1809-1875), George's wife and mother of Alice; inclined to melancholy but 'a paragon of mothers'.

4 *Above left* – Frederic W Macdonald (1842-1928), Rudyard's uncle and the third generation of Methodist ministers.

5 *Above right* – Alice Kipling (1837-1910), Rudyard's mother, eldest of the 'garden of girls'.

6 *Below left* – Ruddy, not yet six when he was left at the 'House of Desolation'.

7 *Above* – 'Twelve bleak houses by the shore'. The United Services College at Westward Ho!

8 *Below* – Young Kipling, complete with moustache, in the centre of a group of USC boys.

9 *Top left* – India. The young journalist in Simla.

10 *Top right* – The incomparable 'Trix' Kipling (1868-1948) had many admirers in India, including the Viceroy's son.

11 *Below* – The last leg of Rudyard's journey Home in 1889 was in the *City of Berlin* out of New York.

"The ploughman stilts the share
More deep in the sodging clod,
'The corn and the cattle are all my care
And the rest is the will of God.'
— Rudyard Kipling

J. Lockwood Kipling
19 September 1890.

12 *Above left* –John
ockwood Kipling (1837-
911). His genial wisdom
rompted a niece to call
m the 'Enquire Within'.

13 *Above right* – Father
nd son trying out ideas
for JLK's *Beast and Man
in India*.

14 *Below right* – The
eloved Josephine in the
nursery at Naulakha.

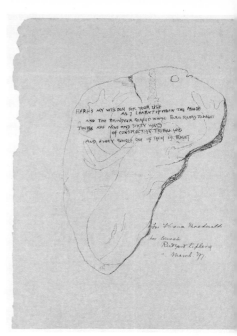

15 *Left* – Josephine and her nurse at Naulakha.

16 *Above right* – 'In the Neolithic Age' depicted for cousin Florence at Rock House.

17 *Below* – Carrie with Nip and Tuck and the cockney coachman at Naulakha.

8 *Above* – Arundell House, 'the hired girls' school' in Tisbury where they spent the summer of 1894.

9 *Below* – Rock House, near Torquay; enviable outlook but a brooding atmosphere. After seven months they moved to Rottingdean.

20 *Above* – North End House, Rottingdean. Uncle Ned's seaside home, where John Kipling was born and Rudyard wrote 'Recessional'.

21 *Below* – Rudyard & Carrie rented The Elms, across the green from the Burne-Jones', for five years (1897-1902).

Earlier in the year, longing to see his parents again and in the knowledge that he had a thousand pounds saved and could afford to pay for their passages – which he was not allowed to do – he had sent them a cryptic telegram: Genesis XLV 9 ('Haste ye, and go up to my father, and say unto him, Thus saith thy son Joseph, God hath made me lord of all Egypt: come down unto me, tarry not.') How gratified 'Aunty' would have been, had she been privy to this evidence of her religious fervour bearing fruit, even unto chapter and verse. To Rudyard's great joy (and I have no doubt, his salvation) they came for an extended leave that May. By which time *The Times* had devoted a leading article to the young author of the *Barrack-room Ballads* that had been astounding the literary world since the end of February.

For the next few months the Family Square was reformed while his prodigious output continued. Now he no longer felt isolated and alone. Sometimes his father would come over to Embankment Chambers and work with him there. More often he stayed under his parents' roof in Earl's Court Road until he finally gave up his rooms and moved in with them altogether. John Kipling was working on a book of his own, *Beast and Man in India*, which would be published the following year (1891), and to which Rudyard contributed some verses. 'As always, they seemed to suggest nothing and interfere nowhere. But they were there – my Father with his sage Yorkshire outlook; my Mother, all Celt and three-parts fire...'[6]

But still the bouts of illness continued. He had broken off his engagement to Caroline and knew he had to see Flo again, to plead his case once more. At the end of May he went over to Paris where she was studying art, and there in that romantic city Flo made it abundantly plain to him that men had no part in her life; she was not interested in anything but her work. It was Rudyard's final, bitter rejection.

During June and July he was working more furiously than ever; poems, ballads, a book of short stories and his first novel flowed from a pen that seemed in perpetual motion. He chose the sea as the background for his farewell to India, 'The Galley-Slave'. He could not have hit upon a more appropriate metaphor for a journalist than that of the slave chained to his oar; nor, in 'galley', have chosen a word with more significance for a newspaperman.

> Oh, gallant was our galley from her carven steering-wheel
> To her figurehead of silver and her beak of hammered steel.
> The leg-bar chafed the ankle and we gasped for cooler air,
> But no galley on the waters with our galley could compare!...
> But today I leave the galley. Shall I curse her service then?
> God be thanked! Whate'er comes after, I have lived and toiled
>   with Men![7]

By August, while confessing he was feeling anything but well, he was working night and day to finish the book for *Lippincotts Magazine* by the fifteenth of the month, the printer's deadline.[8] *The Light that Failed* is the story of Maisie, a girl who thought more of her painting (she was an indifferent artist who lived in expectations of painting a masterpiece) than of the devoted Dick who wanted to marry her.

'Maisie, darling, come with me and see what the world is really like...you're half a gipsy...and I – even the smell of open water makes me restless. Come across the sea and be happy!'[9] (Again and again Kipling would visualise happiness as being over the water – beyond the horizon. Perhaps beyond reach?) But Maisie, like Flo on whom she was undeniably based, had her own self-centred plans. *The Light that Failed* was all the more demanding and flawed for being written at speed – and for being semi-autobiographical. (Chapter One is Southsea all over again.) And he wrote it too soon after that final rejection when ten years of his emotional life had been excised as if by a surgeon's knife.

Now there was no woman in his life – excepting always one. The one to whom he dedicated the book's English publication with its original sad ending – which he knew his mother did not like.

> If I were hanged on the highest hill,
> *Mother o' mine, O mother o' mine!*
> I know whose love would follow me still,
> *Mother o' mine, O mother o' mine!*

But why was Kipling juggling with alternative endings at this stage of his writing career? The previous summer he had started on a collaborative work with a young American literary agent and writer. Wolcott Balestier had come over to England to 'collect' British writers for the American market. He charmed his way into London literary circles with his engaging personality rather than his ability as a writer. And he 'collected' Kipling, not only by looking after his always-tricky American interests, but by actually persuading him to collaborate over a novel. This was an event in itself and one that was never repeated: Rudyard Kipling, the author who valued his independence above rubies, acting entirely out of character. Was Wolcott as charismatic as all that? By comparison with Rudyard who, we are told, had an uncanny power of irritating people he disliked[10] and whose manner could be awkward, even brusque in polite society, the answer is, yes he was. The young American attracted all who met him. But there was more to it than that. Wolcott happened to be in the right place at the right time – and with an intriguing proposition. Rudyard had known Wolcott for several months during which time the two had become friends and colleagues, but it was not until after his Paris trip that *The Naulahka* collaboration really took off. It is not difficult to see why. For the first time in a decade, with Flo and Caroline out of his life, Rudyard's personal horizon was empty, his focal point vanished. And if a hook were needed to catch the Anglo-Indian author, the book's sub-title: *A Story of West and East* (the west being the American West and the East, India) would have been that hook. He was able to draw upon many of his journalistic pieces for the Indian chapters which formed the major part of the story and these he would dictate to Wolcott while pacing up and down the room. Compared with the frenetic pressure of working to deadlines it was a relaxing and leisurely pursuit slotted into their respective work schedules.

The Naulahka, the name of a fabulous jewel, was a good adventure story, but it would never be the jewel in Kipling's crown. He had still to prove himself in a full-length work as he had in the short story. And he knew it. He confessed to being mystified how anyone could make a beginning, middle and end to a 'really truly' long story. He could think up plots by the score but '…I have not the hand to work out the full frieze. It's just the difference between the deep-sea steamer with twelve hundred people aboard…and the coastwise boat with a mixed cargo of notions.'[11]

In August he took a much-needed break and left London in search of the English sun. 'Then it rained and hailed, and rained again, and I ran up and down this tiny country in trains trying to find a dry place. After ten days I came back to town, having been stopped by the sea four times. I was rather like a kitten at the bottom of a bucket chasing its own tail.'

A little later in the month he tried again and was rewarded with three perfect days at the seaside. 'A milk-white sea, as smooth as glass, with blue-white heat haze hanging over it, one little wave talking to itself on the sand…and half the babies in Christendom paddling and yelling…There was a baby…with whom I fell madly in love. She lived down at the bottom of a great white sun-bonnet; talked French and English in a clear, bell-like voice, and of such I fervently hope will the Kingdom of Heaven be. When she found that my French wasn't equal to hers she condescendingly talked English and bade me build her houses of stones and draw cats for her through half the day. After I had done everything that she ordered she went off to talk to some one else. The beach belonged to that baby, and every soul on it was her servant, for I know that we rose with shouts when she paddled into three inches of water and sat down, gasping: "Mon Dieu! Je suis mort!"'[12]

In September his health broke down again and he took ship for Italy where he had been invited to stay at Lord Dufferin's villa. (His host, the former Viceroy of India, was the subject of 'One Viceroy Resigns', a clever pastiche of Browning's 'Bishop Blougram's Apology', which had appeared in the *Pioneer* and *CMG* shortly before Kipling left India.) On his return to London a month later Kipling was immediately plunged into more controversy. Wolcott, as his American agent, had despatched the alternative, happy-ending version of *The Light that Failed* to America for publication. And its author was not pleased. (It is likely that it was Wolcott who persuaded Kipling to write the other ending in the first place, which he then sent across the Atlantic while Rudyard was out of the country.) But worse by far was the almighty storm that had blown up over copyrights – a new version of the old story – with American publishers. And this time three much respected authors on this side of the Atlantic, whom Kipling had met at the Savile Club, appeared to be appeasing those same publishers in print. This was too much to swallow. Kipling's wrath exploded in a long satirical ballad, which he later said he wished he had made shorter by at least twenty lines.[13] In 'The Rhyme of the Three Captains' three English sea captains refused to acknowledge a Yankee pirate for what he was, because they themselves had not suffered at his hands. In a single line he worked in the names of the three 'appeasing' authors – Besant, Hardy and Black: 'We are paid in the coin of the white man's trade – the bezant is hard, ay, and black.' The sea was a favourite allegory in many of Kipling's ballads, and the sustained rhythm of a beam-sea roll is used here to some effect. Its delivery relieved his outraged feelings, and in as much as he had written it, 'in part, [in] pure revenge',[14] on a matter touching his honour, he would not accept payment for the ballad. But publishers as a breed went down another notch in his estimation. (He had learned something about that gentlemanly profession when he had published *Departmental Ditties* in India. 'Every copy sold in a few weeks, and the ratio of expenses to profits, as I remember it, has since prevented my injuring my health by sympathising with publishers who talk of their risks and advertisements.'[15])

That November he met Wolcott's sister, Caroline, who had come over from America with her mother and sister on a long visit; and early in December he called on Mrs Hill and her sister at their London hotel to pay his respects and bid them farewell. The two women were on their way back to the United States after the sudden death of Alex Hill in India. Kipling was never to meet either of them again. Another chapter of his life had ended, although in the years ahead he would keep up an occasional correspondence with Mrs Hill.

With the Family Square still intact, his second Christmas in England followed by his twenty-fifth birthday, was as joyous as the first had been miserable. His father's genial wisdom and his mother's intuitive grasp of mood and atmosphere provided a soothing background. They understood each other so well that words were often unnecessary between them – unless words were what he needed, when 'the Mother' would throw in the occasional suggestion. That resounding line: 'And what should they know of England who only England know?' ('The English Flag', April 1891) was his mother's, as he proudly acknowledged. (Tennyson liked the poem, and his son, Hallam, wrote to Kipling to tell him so.) But there is another side to a mother's intuition where sons are concerned. After meeting Caroline Balestier Alice said: 'That woman is going to marry our Ruddy.' And there was little enthusiasm in her voice.

News from America that Uncle Harry was sick sent Fred Macdonald hastening across the Atlantic to his brother. None of the family, except Rudyard who had met his uncle two years earlier, had seen Harry since 1870 when he and his wife had spent sixteen months in England. Rudyard, feeling restless and unwell, decided to join his uncle on the voyage for another brief holiday. To avoid recognition he travelled under the name of J Macdonald, but his moustache, eyebrows and glasses, to say nothing of his conversation, were too distinctive to disguise. And when Uncle Fred, a man of the cloth, was challenged by reporters as to the true identity of his companion he could not tell a lie. By now Kipling was as celebrated in America as he was on this side of the Atlantic; more so in some respects due to the pirating of his work and the consequent rash of unauthorised publications – including those written for the Indian papers in which he had impartially insulted America and the Americans, as we have seen. By the time the ship reached New York the world's press was waiting for him; but Uncle Harry had died.

Kipling returned home immediately, unwilling to be a target for reporters while his uncle was seeing to his brother's affairs; and in any case, he had *The Naulahka* to finish. He returned feeling no better for the out-and-back-again voyage, while the boiled pig's feet and sauerkraut served up as the ship wallowed in choppy seas, did nothing for his equilibrium. He vowed he would never go on a German liner again. But he did.

Work of any kind was now forbidden him by his doctor. He complained to a friend that he did not know what to do with himself, or how to do it.[16] And this time it was more serious; there was stiffness in his left arm and side which could indicate the reason for his doctor's concern: that the right side of his brain, the intuitive, artistic side, was not functioning as it should. He went to the New Forest for a short holiday and to the Isle of Wight with the Balestiers; and in between gorging himself on raspberries and cream, 'three helps a day', and trying to 'educate' his 'pesky' arm by playing golf, he and Caroline came to an understanding.

It was while he was on the island that the idea came to him for another weird tale, again typical of his mental state. 'The Disturber of Traffic' is about a lighthouse keeper whose head 'began to feel streaky from looking at the tides so long'. He eventually goes mad but recovers after six months in a survey ship, 'cured of his streaks by working hard and not looking over the side more than he could help...and now he's a wherryman from Portsmouth to Gosport, where the tides run crossways and you can't row straight for ten strokes together.'

That month saw the publication (in *Contemporary Review*) of an even stranger tale in which once again the sea plays an important role. 'The Finest Story in the World' hinges on the extraordinary visions of a very ordinary clerk who aspired to write great poetry but could never achieve more than 'wondrous bad' verse.

Charlie Mears is a twenty-five-shillings-a-week London bank clerk who has 'never been out of sight of a made road'. He is befriended by the narrator (Kipling), to whom he unburdens himself of his dreams which, by agreement, the narrator writes down for his own use. Charlie describes the life of a Greek galley-slave down to the smallest horrific detail: the banks of oars to which the rowers are chained, the overseer with a whip walking up and down 'to make the men work', the men on the lower deck, whose only sunlight squeezes through the oar-holes as they sit up to their knees in water. And so on. Charlie continues to have these 'dreams', which he thinks nothing of compared with his own writing efforts. He jots down words that are meaningless to him, and which an expert declares to be a particularly corrupt Greek such as an illiterate person might attempt. In translation: 'I have been – many times – overcome with weariness in this particular employment.' (Longfellow's version which Kipling had hacked out of his desk at Embankment Chambers with a razor-edged kukri, goes: 'Oft was I weary when I toiled at thee.')

The narrator tells us that this is a form of metempsychosis, in which 'the Fates that are so careful to shut the doors of each successive life behind us had...(in Charlie's case) been neglectful'. He too must have died scores of times, but because he could have made use of such knowledge as Charlie had been shown, for him the doors remained shut. Then Charlie describes a sea-fight with another galley whose leader, a red-haired man with a red beard, came from the north. The narrator realises that Charlie is now describing a later incarnation when he was captured by Vikings and forced to sail with them.

Kipling's work schedule suggests that he wrote this story on the heels of Flo's final dismissal and, with his nerves at breaking point, the rapid completion of *The Light that Failed*. If the novel was meant as a cathartic exercise in revoking past unhappiness, (as in the writing of 'Baa Baa Black Sheep' in Allahabad when he had stamped about the house in a retrospective rage after an interval of many years) it failed. Indeed in the short term it probably had the opposite effect – of lacerating an open wound and bringing him a step nearer complete collapse.

What should we make of 'The Finest Story in the World' in which re-incarnation is the pivot on which the story turns? Bearing in mind Kipling's ancestry and the mental pressure he was working under at the time, I suggest that he was describing his own visions or memories glimpsed through the door the Fates had left ajar. But not quite in the same way as Charlie had done.

The answer, for Charlie, was simple. He fell in love – and his mind was emptied of all visions, except that of his beloved. The doors of his past lives had shut for good. And Kipling could see why. 'It is that we may not remember our first and most beautiful wooings. Were this not so, our world would be without inhabitants in a hundred years...Charlie had tasted the love of woman that kills remembrance, and the finest story in the world would never be written.' End of story.

But what of Kipling's remembrance? Whether its origins lay in a provident imagination or in his subconscious, this story is arguably one of his finest. But if we say it can only be a work of his imagination then we should also bear in mind that he once described imagination as a form of imperfect memory – which brings us back to his subconscious and his ancestral memory. Even if he had not been aware of his ancestry before he met his uncle in New York, Harry Macdonald, the eldest grandson of James, scion of the Macdonalds of Ostaig, would surely have regaled him with the details when he told his nephew 'much' family history.

It seems logical to assume that if we can, as we do, inherit certain physical and mental characteristics from our ancestors, that we could also inherit their memories. Most of us, no doubt, will be relieved to know that the ability to tune in to the right wavelength – to be a receiver, to use Kipling's own expression – is not given to many. But bearing in mind his ancient Scottish and Viking ancestry (clan historians state that every Macdonald who can trace his line back to Somerled has the blood of the Norse Kings of the Isles in his veins) it does shed fresh light on the subject that has been puzzling scholars for decades: why Kipling wrote with such feeling about the sea, and with such insight into the Vikings and their galleys.

But if we dismiss the whole idea as preposterous, inconceivable, what about the house martins? Year after year succeeding generations of house-martins return to their nests under the eaves of our houses after over-wintering in Africa. And year after year in the autumn they and their young fly unerringly south again – *with the young leaving before their parents.* Scientists tell us that migratory birds navigate thousands of miles by some sort of inherited map (and seasonal clock) which enables them to fly by the stars or the sun or by electro-magnetic waves to their destination. It is a miracle that never fails, although scientists themselves are still unable to tell us precisely how it works.

The two short breaks had not been enough to restore Kipling's health and at last medical and parental pressure prevailed. At the end of August he set off again, before the first chapters of *The Naulahka* appeared in print (in the American *Century* magazine), even before the last chapters were written – on an extended, leisurely voyage half round the world. Others too had urged him to go, but for very different reasons. Some critics, like Gosse in the *Century*, were afraid he was publishing too much and would write himself out. 'Go back to the East, Mr Kipling! Come back in ten years' time…Go and learn about life at a deeper level…' And he went alone on the long trail, despite Dick's declaration (*The Light that Failed*) that the yearned-for Southern Cross was not worth looking at unless someone was with you to share it. But at least there was an understanding between himself and Carrie to hold on to; as there had been barely two years since with Caroline Taylor, and seven years before that with Flo. On each occasion the understanding or engagement preceded a lengthy separation overseas. For Rudyard, but possibly not for the first Caroline and certainly not for Flo, the commitment was like a continuous silken thread reinforcing the complex pattern of his life while they were apart.

Aboard the ss *Mexican* and in time to the rhythmic thump of her triple expansion engines beneath his feet, Kipling put the finishing touches to 'The Long Trail'.

You have heard the beat of the off-shore wind,
And the thresh of the deep-sea rain;
You have heard the song – how long? how long?
Pull out on the trail again!
Ha' done with the Tents of Shem, dear lass,
We've seen the seasons through,
And it's time to turn on the old trail, our own trail, the out trail,
Pull out, pull out, on the Long Trail – the trail that is always new!

There is an early draft of this poem in an American library which must have been written before he became engaged to Caroline; probably on one of his two previous sea voyages, in which the fifth line of the verse runs: 'Ha' done with the Tents of Shem, dear lad.' It has been speculated that the 'dear lad' was Wolcott, the Tents of Shem the business world of Europe in which the American had been overworking, and that the poem was originally a plea to Wolcott from its author to join him on the long trail.[17] Kipling was devoted to his friend – as he had been to Mrs Hill in India – and as we have already seen, there were never any half measures about his feelings, innocent though I believe they were in each case. And now just to confuse matters, a third version has recently been discovered in manuscript draft form, also in the USA. Entitled 'L'Envoi', it was dedicated to CK and uses the phrase 'dear heart' throughout: 'Ha' done with the tents of Shem, dear heart'.[18] The only constant would seem to be the 'stamp and ring' of the engines as the 'Southern Cross rides high'. And the demands of his Daemon.

He spent two weeks in sleepy, dusty little Cape Town, where teams of oxen ambled down the main street, and the British and the Boers lived amicably together. He visited the naval base at Simon's Town where he was able to study the blue-jackets for the first time and absorb the atmosphere of the Senior Service. There he met a Captain Bayly who was to invite him to cruise with the Royal Navy in the years ahead. Another outcome of the visit, although not immediately, would be his first naval story, 'Judson and the Empire', the precursor of many more such tales. It concerns 'Bai-Jove' Judson, more properly known as Lieutenant Judson, RN, and his first command, an impossibly-shallow-draught gun-boat that resembles a flat-iron with a matchstick mast. She draws five feet or less, her single gun forward sends her compasses into convulsions – and altogether she is Judson's pride and joy, lacking only (in his opinion) a line of gold-leaf to relieve all that dreary grey paint. With the grace of God and a fair wind, she was just about capable of defending a river – and that was exactly where Judson's Admiral sent him and her: on a mission up an African river where a small foreign power was throwing its small weight about – plus the odd pot-shot at inquisitive little gunboats. After some inspired naval and diplomatic manoeuvring on the part of Judson the situation is happily resolved with a party aboard the 'enemy' boat, which the admiral joins (unofficially, of course). As reparations the little gunboat acquires the one thing she had always lacked in Judson's eyes: an (unofficial) line of gold-leaf to relieve all that dreary grey paint. The story was said to be founded on fact, and is bizarre enough to be so. (A certain admiral[19] has since claimed that the story was based on his first command at Simon's Town of just such a small gun-boat, *Gryper* by name, which he took very seriously although no-one else did. In real life, the small foreign power had taken alarm at the show of strength preparing to leave Simon's Bay – his and one other gun-boat – and had capitulated. Which was just as well, in the admiral's opinion, as they progressed almost as fast broadside as they did ahead.)

When Kipling left South Africa on the *Doric* he could not have guessed how much that beautiful country would mean to him in the future, how often he would return to its welcoming climate and the longed-for sight of the Southern Cross.

Of more immediate importance to him on that September day was the long lonely run to New Zealand in an almost empty ship that spent the entire three weeks trying to 'fill her boats at one roll and empty them down the saloon skylight the next'.[20] With no companions to distract him during the voyage he had plenty of time to consider the racing screws as the hull alternately lifted and wallowed; to ponder on the hidden power that threshed the dark water into angry white foam; and to seek out the 'dour Scots engineer, the man they never knew'. He found the huge 'slam-banging' engines beating out their satisfying rhythm with the regularity of a metronome. And he found the engineer tending them as lovingly as a mother tends her children, and like any proud parent, only too willing to show them off, to explain their mysterious workings and even more mysterious jargon to an unusually sympathetic ear. This was indeed a new angle on sea travel to add to Kipling's journalistic repertoire. But it was to be much more than that: it was the beginning of a love affair with motive power and all things mechanical that was to last for the rest of his life, and provide him with all the metaphor – and rhythm – he could desire. 'M'Andrew's Hymn', a powerful soliloquy by an old Scots engineer was the outcome of that voyage although again, not at once. Like a slow-maturing wine it lay quietly working at the back of his mind for two or three years. By which time he could recite all 188 lines off by heart before committing any of them to paper. Now that is the sort of memory I should like to have inherited.

While he was in the southern hemisphere Kipling planned to visit Robert Louis Stevenson, an author he had admired since his youth, who was then living in Samoa with his American wife. Stevenson, in his turn, had written to express his admiration for the creator of Terence Mulvaney of *Soldiers Three*. But the irregularity of the sailings to the island made the visit impossible. Instead he made lightning tours of New Zealand, from Auckland ('a most beautiful city...') to Invercargill ('the Last Lamp-post in the World'), complete with his unique brand of commentary: instant and often tactless. And this time, as a world-famous author, journalists were falling over themselves to catch his every word. Wellington, 'the windy town', reminded him of Portland, Oregon; but the girls – and in particular, the ten maidens who rowed him round the harbour for a moonlit picnic – were 'wonderful'. Even if he did catch a chill afterwards. He wanted to see all the sights, he said, and he did; the Maoris, the hot springs, the geysers and the wild horses. In return, and quite unconsciously, he provided one of the sights himself at the local bath-house, bathing with his spectacles on. After six hours in Christchurch where he was shown round by a journalist before briefly meeting F W Haslam, one of his old classics masters, he reported that Christchurch was more like an American town than an English city, as he had been told. And he knew of only one other country where the trains were slower than they were in New Zealand.

One of the lasting memories he took away with him on the stormy crossing of the Tasman Sea from Bluff to Melbourne, was of the face and voice of a woman in an Auckland bar who sold him beer. It would lie at the back of his mind for several years before coming away 'in a rush' in South Africa in 1904: the unfathomable 'Mrs Bathurst'.

Now it was Australia's turn to lionise the author of *Plain Tales* and *The Light that Failed.* He took tea with the ladies at their salon, dined at the club with the men, and gave an interview to *The Age.* Melbourne, he said, was very 'second hand American'; but he liked their trams whose bells were 'like music'. They reminded him of San Francisco. He admitted that when he was in America he would be 'railing' at that country, but away from it he wanted to go back. He thought there was too much politics in Australia for a country 'with its character still to make'.[21] And he referred to New Zealand's public funds being wasted on the unemployed, instead of setting them to work clearing scrubland for farming; and that the inhabitants didn't know what work was. A twenty-four hour visit to Sydney produced the remark in *Something of Myself* over forty years later that Sydney was populated by 'leisured multitudes all in their shirt-sleeves and all picnicking all the day'. Two years earlier in a despatch from Japan he had written: 'Man isn't made to picnic.'[22]

Later, in the four-line verses of 'The Song of the Cities' he again managed to ruffle a few feathers, but without lasting damage. And in 1901, from the safe haven of Rottingdean, he told a visiting Australian poet: 'You people in Australia haven't grown up yet. You think the Melbourne Cup is the most important thing in the world.'[23] (From the personal experience of one who arrived for her first visit down under on Cup Day, they still do.)

Nevertheless, in 1933, when Melbourne's Shrine of Remembrance was being built as part of the city's centenary celebrations, it was to

Rudyard Kipling that the Premier of Victoria turned for the dedicatory verses on the occasion of the shrine's dedication. The poet responded with an ode of thirty-five lines which may be seen today inscribed on a hand-beaten metal panel in the shrine.[24] He had actually been asked by Australia's High Commissioner early in 1934 if he would open the Melbourne Centenary, but after some consideration declined, probably because of his poor health at the time.[25]

Kipling left Adelaide for Colombo on 25th November. As they approached Ceylon's coastline he smelt 'the smell of damp earth, cocoanut oil, ginger, and mankind' telling him he was nearing home and 'the dearest places in all the world; even the first sniff of London had not caused so big a choke in the throat...'[26] Travelling by rail northwards through the unfamiliar territory of Central India, (this was the nearest he ever got to Mowgli's neck of the jungle) he was in Lahore about a week before Christmas. The first morning home found him sitting in his old office chair correcting proofs on the same yellow paper, with an excited foreman printer telling everyone that 'Kuppuleen Sahib' had returned; and with the opportunist editor asking if Kipling could 'give us something' while he was there.

But Rudyard was destined not to spend Christmas with his parents. A telegram from Carrie Balestier brought the news that her brother Wolcott had died of typhoid fever in Germany. (According to Gosse the wire read: WOLCOTT DEAD. COME BACK TO ME.[27]) As if pulled by an invisible cord, he immediately packed his bags, took leave of his parents and left India for the last time. He paused in Bombay only long enough to visit his old ayah, before taking ship for home. Two weeks later he arrived in London, to be met at Victoria Station by Carrie, her mother and her sister. The capital was in the grip of a killer influenza epidemic. He put up at the Langham Hotel and just eight days after his return, on 18th January 1892, he and Carrie were married at All Souls' Church, Langham Place. Ambo Poynter was best man and Henry James gave the bride away. William Heinemann and Edmund Gosse and his family also attended but everyone else was in bed with flu. Even the bride had to leave her new husband at the church door, under the scandalised gaze of the minister, to tend to her mother while the bridegroom glowered at a precocious news placard announcing his marriage.

Why did he get married so impetuously – and so soon after Wolcott's death – without even waiting for the flu epidemic to subside? Both Rudyard and Carrie had been devoted to Wolcott and had been through 'troubled waters together', whatever that phrase may imply. And Kipling had been adrift in some pretty troubled waters on his own in London and had no desire to repeat the experience. And now that Wolcott was dead there would be nothing to detain the Balestier family in England. We have seen how he envied his cousin Margaret's domestic happiness and how it had underlined his yearning for what always seemed to be beyond his reach. More than ever he needed an anchor – and an anchorage; although whether he saw his needs in quite those terms is another matter. But surely the strong-minded Carrie did, now that the brother she had assisted so ably was beyond all earthly needs and sisterly concern. Surely she saw her life's work laid out ahead of her: to nurture this man whom half the world called a genius at the age of twenty-six, to make a home for him where he might continue his work undisturbed by the importunate or the idly curious, and to regulate his life so that never again would he suffer breakdowns in health through stress and overwork. Carrie was to take charge of every aspect of her husband's life, bar one: his imagination. To that even she did not have the key. Henry James described her as 'a hard, devoted, capable little person whom I don't in the least understand his marrying.'[28] Rudyard's father had remarked on her universal competence and that she was 'a good man spoiled', and we have already observed his mother's instinctive reaction. But perhaps Rudyard needed a strong-minded woman to look after him, as he had been used to all his life. Repeating patterns, like habits, are hard to break – even had he wanted to do so. Writing his autobiography almost half a century later is it not significant that he chose to call this chapter of his life, his two years alone in London, The Interregnum?

Whatever the reason for their precipitous marriage on that foggy January day he was, as he wrote to Aunt Louie on his wedding eve, 'riotously happy'.[29]

And that was really all that mattered.

---

1   RK to Mrs Hill, Nov 1889, *Letters*, Vol 1.
2   *ibid.*
3   *ibid.*
4   Robert Barr of 'The Idler', Thurston Hopkins, *Rudyard Kipling, The Story of a Genius*, Cecil Palmer 1930.
5   'At the End of the Passage', 1890.
6   *SoM.*
7   'The Galley-Slave', 1890.
8   RK to Margaret Clifford, August 1890, *Letters*, Vol 2.
9   *The Light that Failed*, pub Nov, 1890 in USA (happy ending); March, 1891 in UK (sad ending).
10 Carrington, KJ.
11 RK to Mrs Humphrey Ward, *Letters*, Vol 2.
12 'Letters on Leave', 1890, *Abaft the Funnel.*
13 RK to Gosse, December 1890.

14 RK to MacColl, Editor, *Athenaeum*, 1891, *Letters*, Vol 2.
15 'My First Book'.
16 RK to Mrs de Forest, July 1891, *Letters*, Vol 2.
17 Wilson.
18 The Kipling Collections at Marlboro College, Vermont, KJ.
19 Admiral de Horsey, KJ.
20 *SoM*.
21 Orel, Vol 2, *Kipling Interviews & Recollections*, Macmillan, 1983.
22 *From Sea to Sea*, Vol 1.
23 RK to AB 'Banjo' Paterson, *Happy Dispatches*, Angus & Robertson Ltd, 1935.
24 Julian Moore, *Rudyard Kipling's Ode*, Kipling Society of Australia, 1999.
25 CK Diary.
26 'Home', *CMG*'s Christmas Supplement, 1891, Uncollected, KJ.
27 Ann Thwaite, *Edmund Gosse*, 1984.
28 Henry James to his brother William, February 1892, Carrington.
29 RK to Mrs Alfred Baldwin, *Letters*, Vol 2.

EXPLOSION 1892-1914

CHAPTER FIVE

Home-building, but '...gypsies by birth'.

Out of the dark of the gorgio camp,
Out of the grime and the gray
(Morning waits at the end of the world),
Gipsy, come away!...

Both to the road again, again!
Out on a clean sea-track—
Follow the cross of the gipsy trail
Over the world and back!...

Follow the Romany patteran
West to the sinking sun,
Till the junk-sails lift through the houseless drift,
And the east and the west are one.

'The Gipsy Trail'

Early in February Henry James, Gosse, Heinemann and Bram Stoker saw the newly-weds off at Liverpool; from the same dockside at which an obscure Anglo-Indian journalist had disembarked a little over two years earlier, intent upon making his name known in London. To what extent Rudyard Kipling had succeeded may be judged by that quartet of literary figures who had taken the trouble to journey north to wish the bridal pair God-speed.

In one respect at least the honeymoon trip was to be no novelty for the bridegroom. It would be another open-ended, world-wide voyage and with a second try at calling on Stevenson in Samoa. (The author of *Treasure Island* had preceded him on the long trail, also with an American wife but without the younger man's life expectancy.) This time, though, Kipling would be travelling with the longed-for companion. In fact, he had *three*. Carrie's mother and sister accompanied them on the first leg of their honeymoon journey across the Atlantic.

The *Teutonic*'s modern, uncluttered lines and lack of supporting sails had already earned her the Blue Riband for the fastest Atlantic crossing. 'Fate was kind on that voyage,' observed an American historian who made the bridegroom's acquaintance on board. 'Rudyard Kipling...dashed over the passenger his exuberant fountain of gaiety and wit – as though playing a garden hose on a thirsty and faded begonia. Kipling could hardly ever know what peace of mind he gave, for he could hardly ever need it himself so much; and yet, in the full delight of his endless fun and variety, one felt the old conundrum repeat itself. Somehow, somewhere, Kipling and the American were not one, but two, and could not be glued together...'[1] An unfair comment, perhaps, with the bridegroom's mother-in-law at large on the ship; but characteristic of its author.

The newly-weds spent a few days in New York – long enough for Kipling to despatch 'The Gipsy Trail', a pre-nuptial song that he had been working on during the voyage and for which he was paid $150 – before leaving for Brattleboro, Vermont to meet the rest of Carrie's family. '...to the lands where the snow lay...Thirty below freezing! It was inconceivable till one stepped out into it at midnight, and the first shock of that clear, still air took away the breath as does a plunge into sea-water.' And there Beatty Balestier, Carrie's happy-go-lucky younger brother, was awaiting them in his sleigh. They were wrapped up in hairy goatskin coats, caps that covered their ears, buffalo robes and blankets. 'The night was as keen as the edge of a newly-ground sword...and the eyes wept bitterly because the horses were in a hurry to get home...But for the jingle of the sleigh-bells the ride might have taken place in a dream for there was no sound of hoofs upon the snow...and all the sheeted hills round about were as dumb as death...In the morning the other side of the picture was revealed in the colours of the sunlight. There was never a cloud in the sky that rested on the snowline of the horizon as a sapphire on white velvet.'[2]

The crispness of the New England winter not only took Kipling's breath away in every sense, it also made him feel strangely at home. It was the view over to Mount Monadnock: it reminded him of his schooldays and a line of Emerson's about this very mountain. '"Happy," I said, "whose home is here!"' He too would be happy to make his home here.[3] Put down roots. (Did he also recall another line of Emerson's: 'Hitch your wagon to a star'?) To mark the occasion he built a swag-bellied Buddha in the crisp snow, to the amazement of some locals passing by on a sledge. From their outspoken comments he concluded that its 'imperial and reposeful waist' was out of fashion in Vermont. Before they left to continue their honeymoon trip Rudyard and Carrie negotiated a deal with Beatty for ten acres of Balestier land where they would build a house on that same hilltop facing Monadnock where he had made the snow-Buddha. The locals were in for some more shocks from its creator.

At Vancouver they embarked on one of the latest passenger ships of the CPR, the white-painted *Empress of India*. The old-fashioned crossed yards and flush decks of her predecessors were gone and she rejoiced in every refinement and comfort. But she still retained the graceful lines of a yacht, with overhung stern, clipper bows – and a figurehead of Queen Victoria breasting the Pacific waves. Very Kipling. A few days out and Rudyard has a touch of liver, slanders his wife's native home and is generally 'sweet to live with', according to Carrie. However he is fit enough to recite 'The Ballad of the *Bolivar*' at the ship's concert the following night. The *Bolivar* was one of the infamous 'coffin-ships' that were 'Overloaded, undermanned, meant to founder...' in order that their owners could claim the insurance money. Rudyard had written it out from memory in half an hour in the office of the *St James Gazette*, for fifteen guineas cash on the nail, a few days before sailing for America with his bride. Six months earlier he had given a broad hint of the ballad's form in a letter to Henley, and according to Carrie's diary had been working on it the day before. Carrie kept a diary from the week before their marriage until the day her husband died, for which unconscious service to literature Rudyard's biographers must be eternally grateful. (The diary survives today only in summary, the original having been destroyed when Rudyard and Carrie's daughter died, according to her wish.)

Three years almost to the April day after his first enchanted visit to Japan Kipling returned to 'The Edge of the East', as he refers to it in his *Letters of Travel*, to a welter of cherry blossom and azaleas 'aching to burst into bloom'.

'There are ways and ways of entering Japan. The best is to descend upon it from America and the Pacific – from the barbarians and the deep sea. Coming from the East, the blaze of India and the insolent tropical vegetation of Singapore dull the eye to half-colours and little tones.'[4]

He finishes a P & O ballad, 'The Exiles' Line', and is 'sociable' in Tokyo and Yokohama. (From which we must assume that in Carrie's opinion her new husband is not always so disposed.) The garden where they are staying overhangs the harbour and...

we look down upon a heavy-sterned fishing-boat, the straw-gold mats of the deckhouse pushed back to show the perfect order and propriety of the housekeeping that is going forward. The father-fisher, sitting frog-fashion, is poking at a tiny box full of charcoal, and the light, white ash is blown back into the face of a largish Japanese doll, price two shillings and threepence in Bayswater. The doll wakes, turns into a Japanese baby something more valuable than money could buy – a baby with a shaven head and aimless legs. It crawls to the thing in the polished brown box, is picked up just as it is ready to eat live coals, and is set down behind a thwart, where it drums upon a bucket, addressing the fire-box from afar. Half-a-dozen cherry blossoms slide off a bough, and waver down to the water close to the Japanese doll, who in another minute will be overside in pursuit of these miracles. The father-fisher has it by the pink hind-leg, and this time it is tucked away, all but the top-knot, out of sight among umber nets and sepia cordage. Being an Oriental it makes no protest, and the boat scuds out to join the little fleet in the offing.

Kipling takes note of the sailor ashore. 'The sailor in port is the only superior man. To him all matters rare and curious are either "them things" or "them other things." He does not hurry himself, he does not seek Adjectives other than those which custom puts into his mouth for all occasions; but the beauty of life penetrates his being insensibly till he gets drunk, falls foul of the local policeman, smites him into the nearest canal, and disposes of the question of treaty revision with a hiccup.'

At the time of Kipling's first visit the once-isolationist Japan was energetically pulling itself out of feudalism by its collective obi, before discarding the sash in favour of Western clothes – for the men. A new constitution had been drawn up, a two-tier parliament (*Diet*) of limited powers promulgated and a handful of treaty ports opened to Western merchants and visitors. Then he had found it 'sufficiently Europeanised in its shops to suit the worst and wickedest taste. To-day it is still worse…' The wealthy globe-trotters headed for the curio shops as soon as their feet touched Japanese soil, 'advised by their guide-books to do so, lest the land should be suddenly civilised between steamer-sailing and steamer-sailing.' And they were not far wrong: already those curio shops were filled with 'things which are prepared for them – mauve and magenta and blue-vitriol things.'[5] The Made-in-Japan industry was under way.

Kipling too had become something of an industry in the past three years. He was now a world-famous author, as Japan was quick to recognise and its prestigious Tokyo Club to honour. Based on the lines of a traditional London club, its members were prominent Japanese and foreigners: ambassadors, senior officials and expatriates. Kipling was entertained to dinner, welcomed by its foreign vice-president, an American legal adviser from Vermont – and then without apparently knowing that a speech was expected of him, had to reply. He too belonged to the 'outlying colonies of men whose life is severed from that of their fellows at home; the little isolated communities beyond the seas who are looked upon so curiously and sometimes so curiously misrepresented by wondering tourists...the men...who are the builders of trade, the makers of ways, and the teachers of all good influences...' The same type of men as those among whom he had been bred and trained. 'And it is as such that I salute you.'[6]

Seal-poaching in the Bering Sea was a sensitive issue between England, America and Russia about this time. A few years earlier three British sealing boats had been captured by the Americans with serious diplomatic consequences; and while Kipling was in Japan the local press, which he would almost certainly have read, extensively reported a court case involving the crews of another three sealers. He had already picked up enough knowledge of the industry from a passenger aboard the *Empress of India* to write the delightful story of 'The White Seal' (*Jungle Book*), after his return to the USA, and it is more than likely that he also met some of the seal poachers based in Yokohama: tough men who sailed under the colours of any nation that suited them and who would fight another ship's crew for their cargo of skins. In the long ballad 'The Rhyme of the Three Sealers' which he was working on in Yokohama, there is the crackle of skulduggery from the first lines:

Away by the lands of the Japanee
Where the paper lanterns glow
And the crews of all the shipping drink
In the house of Blood Street Joe,

to the last:

Ever they greet the hunted fleet – lone keels off headlands drear—
When the sealing-schooners flit that way at hazard year by year,
Ever in Yokohama port men tell the tale anew
Of a hidden sea and a hidden fight,
When the *Baltic* ran from the *Northern Light*
And the *Stralsund* fought the two.

Rudyard and Carrie pay a visit to Kamakura, twenty miles from Yokohama, where 'the great bronze Buddha sits facing the sea to hear the centuries go by. He has been described again and again – his majesty, his aloofness...the smoky little shrine within him, and the plumed hill that makes the background to his throne.' He ponders on the tourists who scrawl their 'ignoble' names over the inside of the bronze plates that form the giant figure…'Think for a moment of the indignity and the insult!' But then, 'Buddha said that a man must look on everything as illusion – even light and colour – the time-worn bronze of metal against blue-green of pine and pale emerald of bamboo – the lemon sash of the girl in the cinnamon dress, with coral pins in her hair, leaning against a block of weather-bleached stone – and, last, the spray of blood-red azalea that stands on the pale gold mats of the tea-house beneath the honey-coloured thatch. To overcome desire and covetousness of mere gold, that is conceivable; but why must a man give up the delight of the eye, colour that rejoices, light that cheers, and line that satisfies the innermost deeps of the heart?'[7]

And despite two very different kinds of shock in quick succession he saw no reason to give up those delights in a hurry. On 3rd June a violent earthquake was felt in Tokyo shortly after seven a.m. It lasted seven minutes and 'at least one bewildered sleeper suddenly awakened saw his empty boots where they "sat and played toccatas stately at the clavicord"'.(Browning again)…Then a clock fell and a wall cracked, and heavy hands caught the house by the roof-pole and shook it furiously.'[8] A few days later the Oriental Banking Company failed. The Kiplings were left with £10 in the local equivalent of 'mere gold', their return tickets and the loss of almost £2000. (About £60,000 today.) No wonder that, with hindsight, he called the earthquake 'prophetic' – but there had been no suggestion of his boots playing a quick march rather than a toccata on the bedroom floor. He was not disposed to leave Japan a moment sooner than need be. He had been despatching travel sketches to *The Times* and other journals throughout the voyage, had finished *The Naulahka* on the *Teutonic*, and was now working on short stories and verse; Thomas Cook's was pleased to refund him the money on his cancelled on-going reservations (including the trip to Samoa – he was fated never to meet his boyhood hero); and his credit was excellent world-wide. So for almost three more weeks he continued to rejoice in the delights of the eye, confident that any financial embarrassment would be only temporary. Perhaps, too, with that inner sense that was never far beneath the surface, he felt he should make the most of his stay in Japan as he would not pass that way again. One of the ways he did so was to store up half-a-dozen 'pictures' in his mind's eye of his visits to the Far East (typically, four of them were seascapes) and with more success than the artist he had met on his earlier visit who was '…swearing horribly. He had been trying to paint one of my pictures…Most naturally he failed, because there happened to be absolutely no perspective in the thing…'[9] No such problem besets the mind's eye. (The artist may have been Alfred East who was sent out in 1889 to paint Japanese landscapes for a Bond Street dealer whose "Art of Japan" exhibition the previous year had been such a success.)

Nevertheless he was returning to Vermont from a much-publicised honeymoon trip, virtually penniless and certainly homeless; and with Carrie now pregnant (even as his mother had been pregnant on her honeymoon voyage to Bombay twenty-seven years earlier). For any young husband faced with the prospect of living under his mother-in-law's roof and among a people with whom he had enjoyed less than harmonious dealings in the past, the immediate future must have looked daunting indeed.

Three days out from Yokohama aboard the *Empress of China* (figurehead a Chinese dragon) Rudyard 'recited' 'The Taking of Lungtungpen' at a ship's concert. He could have chosen an easier tale to tell. Mulvaney's rich Irish brogue requires skill and confidence to put over. But if he rendered it half as well as he would later render M'Andrew's Glaswegian accent, his shipboard audience was royally entertained. (Rudyard was a curiously good character actor – according to Trix; it was a talent he shared with other members of the Macdonald family. His uncle Fred's gift for mimicry and oratory as a young man had provoked Rossetti to declare him 'born to raise the fallen fortunes of the British stage',[10] and for a while my grandfather was torn between acting and preaching. He may even have narrowed the gap between the two callings when he became known as the 'silver-tongued orator of Methodism'.) It could be that Rudyard chose to tell a *Soldiers Three* story as his valediction to the Tommy now that the sailor and the sea were firmly entrenched in his affections and in his work.

Back in Vermont Carrie's mother offered them the use of the hired-man's house, Bliss Cottage, for $10 a month rent. (a little over £2.) They took it, furnished it simply and moved in on the 10th August. He wrote of painting floors and hunting for lost gimlets – but he did not think Heaven had made him for putting up bedsteads. His days were divided between '...stables and sewers and furniture and the settling down of a house'. It was all great fun and prevented him dwelling too much on words and their composition. 'We don't talk about Art here.'[11]

They bought a huge second-hand hot-air stove which they installed in the cellar. 'We cut generous holes in our thin floors for its eight-inch tin pipes (why we were not burned in our beds each week of the winter I never can understand) and we were extraordinarily and self-centredly content...When our lead pipe froze, we would slip on our coonskin coats and thaw it out with a lighted candle. There was no space in the attic bedroom for a cradle, so we decided that a trunk-tray would be just as good. We envied no one.'[12]

Money was beginning to flow in again from royalties on both sides of the Atlantic. Although, outwardly, he had not let the loss of all his money worry him as it would have done a year ago, there was no denying it was a 'poor return' for three years' hard work. (He did eventually get all his money back.) Carrie was now able to employ a maid at $18 dollars a month and Rudyard sent his mother 100 dollars for Christmas. And then: 'My first child and daughter was born in three foot of snow on the night of December 29th 1892. Her Mother's being the 31st and mine the 30th of the same month, we congratulated her on her sense of the fitness of things, and she throve in her trunk-tray in the sunshine on the little plank verandah.'[13]

On the last day of the year Rudyard wrote in his wife's diary: 'All well – and the Good God be thanked for the ending of the happiest year in my life.'

How he adored his little Josephine. His love of children had been noticeable ever since as a schoolboy he would sit beside a visiting baby's cradle at his Uncle Fred's, marvelling at the perfection of the tiny hand he was holding in his own grubby one. And he never outgrew that devotion. Like many shy men he was relaxed and at ease with children and throughout his life, given the choice, preferred their company to most adults; preferred nursery to drawing room – and did not care who knew it.

So now, seated in his seven foot by eight workroom in Bliss Cottage (which they had soon renamed The Blizzard), the snow level with the window-sill from December to April, he settled down to write – letters. By the score and largely on a single topic.

'The Baby flourishes mightily,' he informed his cousin Margaret. 'She has a chin, ear and nose which is a ridiculous plagiarism from her father – specially the chin, but I can't understand how the hair comes to be downy fluff...Tomorrow she'll be three weeks old and tonight she is having a musical evening to celebrate it. Yet it is true (don't laugh) that if I say:– "Joss, stop this nonsense," she is still for quite half a minute. She's wickedly and uncannily like me in profile but I wish I could understand her hair. It ought to be black or potato brown at least.' A few weeks later: 'She has smiled once or twice since she was a month old and I am sure it isn't wind – unless it be that from cherub's wings.' But then: 'Do you think it is all good for Angela (Margaret's three year old daughter) to learn ballads so soon? I have an extreme dread of Jo learning anything for the first six or eight years of her life.'

When he had finished rhapsodising about The Baby, it was the weather's turn. It 'only goes above freezing for half an hour at midday sometimes: and yet is dancing, clear, dry buoyant weather...Day after day the sun comes up in a cloudless sky burns across the snow and goes out, clear to the last glitter...The trees are Emperors with their crowns on and icicles five and six feet long hang from our eaves. It's all like life in a fairy tale – life when one sings and shouts for joy of being alive.'[14] In spite of the low temperatures he had never been cold as he had been in London, never had to wrap up his throat, nor had a cold or cough since living there.

When he wrote to cousin Stan two years later on the birth of his first child, it was as an old hand at the game of fatherhood. 'Were I near you I could overwhelm you with much unprofitable advice...Lord what a time you have in front of you – angina pectoris when baby is hoarse, paralysis when she coughs more than once, and the baser forms of heart disease when she comes out in a rash – likewise yells; likewise broken nights and such. But you'll find it well and well worth anything...Let us know how the wife does and (this is worth knowing) you must be more than gentle with her these next months to come. A woman isn't well before her child comes bodily but it's her spirits and mind that are all on edge afterwards.'[15]

The spring of 1893 saw work begin on the house that was to be called Naulakha (correctly spelt this time) in memory of Wolcott. By the end of the summer they moved in to the long narrow (ninety feet by twenty-five) frame house that lay on the hilltop like a ship riding a wave. John Kipling, when he came to stay, referred to it as that sage-green shanty because of its covering of dull green shingles. On the brick fireplace in Rudyard's study he affixed the words, modelled in clay: 'The Night Cometh when No Man can Work', neatly providing a title, *The Day's Work*, for his son's next volume of stories.

Rudyard's workroom, as he called it, was at the far end of the house with a door on to a verandah. From there he could step down into a terraced enclosure filled with sweet-smelling flowers and protected from view by a high wall. The room could only be entered through Carrie's boudoir where daily she sat at her desk, on guard. No one could disturb him without her permission and that was not readily given – and certainly not to importunate journalists who would turn up unannounced, in the confident expectation of an interview with the famous English author. (Within two months of their moving into Bliss Cottage two reporters from Boston were on his doorstep demanding interviews and, according to Carrie's diary, wrecking their day. When Kipling said he had nothing to say to them, they replied: '"If ye hevn't, guess we'll make ye say something."' Which they did, lying 'copiously' and at some length.[16] It is surprising that Kipling, with bitter experience of American publishers, was unaware of the habits of the American press in this regard; that they were, in fact, years ahead of every other country in this new 'art' form. The 'interview' had been born in the

USA out of a New York newspaper some thirty years earlier, giving the Americans a head start. Approval was not universal, however, and it was confined to that country for several years. One New York journal vowed that the interview made fools of great men, another that it made journalism an offence. But by the 1880s the 'New Journalism' as it was called, had crossed the Atlantic and was establishing itself in London. The rest is history.[17])

This was to be the pattern of their lives for the next forty years. In order that he could work in peace, the devoted Carrie protected him from a world that increasingly desired to beat a path to his door. It suited his Daemon, of course; but what of Rudyard Kipling, the man himself? In those early happy years it is safe to say that he neither wanted nor needed anything or anyone more than the loving companionship of his wife and growing family and their friends within the four walls of his own home. They were riches enough for any man. Without Carrie's immaculate organisation his life would become as unmanageable as the bulging suitcase of bachelorhood whose lid would refuse to shut for him. And so when a young friend asked him one day which hotel they would be staying at in New York during a forthcoming trip, he replied happily: 'Why bless you, I don't know. I'm no more than a cork on the water when Carrie is with me.'[18]

Friends and family – and especially children – were another matter and they were always made welcome at Naulakha. The Kiplings were genial and thoughtful hosts and gave parties for the local children at which Josephine's Daddy would tell them wonderful tales in his special story-telling voice. Best of all was when John Kipling came over to stay. He and Alice were now retired after almost thirty years' service in India and would soon be settling in Tisbury, Wiltshire for the rest of their lives. John was a confirmed globe-trotter even in his retirement but Alice preferred to stay on dry land after years of necessary but hateful travelling. That summer while John was in America she spent three months at Rottingdean with her sister Georgie, exhausting Ned's patience – and he was a patient man – so that he went up to London more often than usual.[19] Across the Atlantic father and son went off on a trip to Canada just when Carrie, with servants giving notice at the last moment, could have done with Rudyard's help over the move into the new house. It is doubtful, though, if he would have been of much practical use: he once admitted that when he was around 'pretending to help pack' he would make more mess than two women could clear up behind him.[20] Whether this was done deliberately to get him out of the whole business of packing is not clear, but as usual Carrie coped magnificently and all was in order by the time the recalcitrant pair returned.

John's comment on his son's apparent isolation 'upcountry' was that Ruddy seemed to find it 'most congenial...I fancy something of this is congenial as well...a country life of itself seems to be no great hindrance – and there is much to be said for that of towns and the contact of one's fellows. But I have always noticed that the influence of London Literary society which one would be inclined to consider stimulating and encouraging is in the long run irritating and depressing to his temper.'[21] His son greatly enjoyed the simple pleasures of life and extracted enormous satisfaction out of his hillside home, his ponies, the woods and the farmers around him. And when all was said and done, John was well content with Rudyard as he was. There was undoubtedly a freer outlook from America for a man who preferred to think for himself than there was from London.

But his son had not entirely settled down. When Charles Stoddard, an American writer friend, sent him a copy of his 'South Sea Idyls' it reminded Rudyard that twice he had missed taking a trip through that fairyland...'"Here you come with your old music," [Browning's 'Toccata' again] and give me as bad an attack of go-fever as I've had for a long time past...You have broken the peace of an ordered household and set two folks who are gypsies by birth or inheritance longing to take ship again and GET OUT. In return please to accept as an example my sober and continent verses [*Barrack-Room Ballads!*] which have nothing to do with roving and roystering or racketing on far-away beaches. Yours hungrily, admiringly and upsettedly...'[22] And when news reached him of Stevenson's death in Samoa at the end of 1894 he was so upset he could do no work for a week.

His go-fever did not, however, respond to an offer of a lecture tour in the States. He might have considered it, he said, if he had had two mortgages on his house, a bill of sale on the furniture, writer's cramp in both hands – and had not already wandered over most of the land. But there was not enough money in sight to face again some of the hotels and railway systems he had met with. He thought America a great country – but not for lecturing in.[23] As always with requests from strangers, however tiresome or time-consuming they might be, he would reply personally and with courtesy, if not always in the manner expected of him. There was, for instance, the reverend gentleman who wrote to him on behalf of the Board of Foreign Missions of the American Presbyterian Church who wanted to know Kipling's views on their work among the 'heathen'. But as Kipling pointed out in his plain-spoken reply, the views he expressed were unlikely to assist their cause or be accepted by any conference on foreign missions. He ended his letter by thanking his correspondent for giving him an opportunity to testify on a matter very near to his heart: the (to him) cruelty of white men who confounded 'their fellow creatures with a doctrine of salvation imperfectly understood by themselves and a code of ethics foreign to the climate and instincts of those races whose most cherished customs they outrage and whose gods they insult.'[24]

Two days earlier *The Times* had published one of his poems, the first of many to appear in that newspaper. 'The Native-Born' was the name given to those Anglo-Indians, like himself, who were born in India of British parents.

> We've drunk to the Queen – God bless her! –
> We've drunk to our mothers' land;
> We've drunk to our English brother,
> (But he does not understand);
> We've drunk to the wide creation,
> And the Cross swings low for the morn.
> Last toast, and of obligation,
> A health to the Native-born!

The Times' manager, Moberly Bell, wrote to thank Kipling for the 'really beautiful poem you have allowed us to publish...', explaining that it was the first time they had taken a poem not written in relation to any one particular event. This had caused them to hesitate – 'as a good old conservative institution' – but as they read and re-read it 'their scruples disappeared'.[25]

For his part, Kipling said afterwards that he would never have thought of trying the 'austere old *Times*' but for Charles Norton's advice. The Harvard professor had been one of the pre-Raphaelite circle in London when Rudyard was a boy and had become their good friend in New England.

The four years in Vermont were probably the happiest and certainly the most carefree of his life. On each New Year's Eve he would add his message of thanksgiving in his wife's diary for another perfect year ended. 'The Lord has been very good to us...well, content and most unspeakably happy. C and I and J.' (He had also earned $25,000 or £5000 that year, 1894) He had his own home, he had a wife and family who were the delight of his heart – Josephine had grown into an imaginative and enchanting little maiden with blue eyes and fair hair – and he had 'sunshine and a mind at ease...' Everything indicated that he would never need to look at both sides of the family shilling again – although with his background and upbringing he would find it a difficult habit to break – and in any case Carrie took care of all his business affairs quite splendidly. They lived in a climate where the long winters gave him not only 'time, light and quiet, three things hard to come by in London' to work in, but also sledging, skiing and snowshoeing for relaxation and fun.

It was all like a fairy-tale, he said, when one sings and shouts for joy of being alive. As to snowshoes, never the easiest of appendages to manage, it was 'as tho' you put a semi-detached villa on each hoof and then quarrelled with either landlord for rent.'[26] A couple of winters later when the snow lay five or six feet thick Carrie reported that Rud was now so clever on his snow-shoes that he went out on them most days, if only to Maplewood and back where Beatty and his family lived: Rudyard had been devoted to their little daughter Marjorie from the first day they met. Soon the Kiplings would be off to Washington – they usually planned their city visits in mud time – where they whirled 'social whirls of the whirliest...' But there was a snag to everything, for 'tho' the vittles is splendid and the people is glorious and fine and the houses is palaces a little of it goes a dam long way...this is a bad place to work in. People knock and ring all day long.'[27]

He had done his best to sell his 'unnecessary Pillywinkie' (a "Gem" windmill that pumped up the water) to Norton – cheap. It was a 'kind and affectionate windmill without any flaw' and it was painted a tender sage-green, presumably to match the house. But despite its owner's persuasive character reference there was no sale. Nor three weeks later was there a Pillywinkie even to give away. While it was being dismantled a fortuitous gale blew it down and saved them the trouble, luckily without any casualties. The windmill was replaced by an 8-inch Rider engine operating a deep-well pump which it was Kipling's 'disgustful duty to oil'. Farmers came from miles around to look at 'Eugene', as it had been christened, and were surprised to see no steam. "Where in Hell's the boiler?" they wanted to know and thought its owner was joking when he told them it worked on air.[28]

The locals never quite got the measure of this odd-looking Englishman who had married 'one o' them Balestiers' with their high-flown 'Frenchy' ways. (This was a reference to the family's Huguenot ancestors and affluent lifestyle that included dressing for dinner every evening and drinking wine instead of decent whisky.) 'This yere Kipling' would walk down Main Street in old clothes looking like a nobody-at-all; he'd coast downhill on his bicycle with his feet on the handlebars and coat tails flying. Folks said he'd made a heap o' money out of book writing, enough to buy his missus a carriage and pair and pay the wages of two maids, a nanny and an English coachman. Then, darnation if he didn't sink a well 300 foot when their water supply played up. Eccentric? Take that new-fangled game of golf: he'd practise it over two feet of snow. Lost all the balls, o' course – until he took to painting 'em red. Yip. 'That yere Kipling' – still this side o' thirty – sure was eccentric.

But there was at least one neighbour among the lonely hills who had reason to bless their arrival, as Rudyard and Carrie discovered when they called on her one day. She was a wild-eyed woman living in an isolated farmhouse across the valley who could see Naulakha 'riding on its hillside like a little boat on the flank of a far wave. Said the woman, fiercely: "Be you the new lights 'crost the valley yonder? Ye don't know what a comfort they've been to me this winter. Ye aren't ever goin' to shroud 'em up – or be ye?" So, as long as we lived there, that broad side of Naulakha which looked her-ward was always nakedly lit.'[29]

New friends were made, old friends came to stay. They went on a cruise to Bermuda and they made two consecutive summer visits to England and stayed near his parents at Tisbury, where Rudyard found himself homesick for Naulakha. As for the English summer: 'This climate is only fit for marine monsters,' he wrote to Henry James one typical July day in '94. 'We abandon room after room in this hired girls' school of ours and huddle over one fire like bears in a cave...Never was man so anxious to leave his all too native land behind him, as I am and I would I were a Byron that I might fitly curse it...Our house is dry and we burn a ton of coal every ten days. More shall be added when you come and the garden walks shall be relaid with piping hot water bottles. We will come down to breakfast with counterpanes and coverlets upon our shoulders and dine atop of a kitchen range. More we cannot do.'[30]

No indeed. Nor do we know if such drastic action was required when James joined them at Arundell House at the end of the month. In any case Rudyard had the infallible answer to raising Henry James' temperature, if not his blood pressure: he read him 'M'Andrew's Hymn'. James and all things mechanical were incompatible. Even the *Jungle Book* he found 'thrilling, but so bloody'. As he explained to a mutual friend: 'In his earliest time I thought he perhaps contained the seeds of an English Balzac; but I have given that up in proportion as he has come down steadily from the simple in subject to the more simple – from the Anglo-Indians to the natives, from the natives to the Tommies, from the Tommies to the quadrupeds, from the quadrupeds to the fish, and from the fish to the engines and screws.'[31] James never used one word where he could get away with half a dozen.

Rudyard and his father had been down to his old school at Westward Ho! a few days before James' visit. Crom Price was retiring after twenty years' headmastering and his world-famous old boy, after an undistinguished four years at the college, was to be the guest of honour. In his speech on behalf of the old boys, Rudyard spoke of the head 'advising them and chastising them for their souls' good' and congratulated him on having created 'the best school in the world'.[32] If an extremely proud old boy, his ears still ringing from his resounding welcome, exaggerated a little, it made excellent copy for the *College Chronicle* whose editor he used to be.

The college had, in fact, fallen on hard times and in the years to come would be losing its individuality in an amalgamation with Haileybury; thus coming full circle, for Price had left Haileybury, where he had been head of the modern side, in order to become the USC's first headmaster.

This was the year that Rudyard, Carrie and Josephine spent three months at Tisbury with Rudyard making frequent trips to London where he seemed for once to enjoy being lionised at regimental dinners, banquets and the like; while back in Wiltshire they were kept busy hobnobbing with their county neighbours. They talked of making a trip to India that year and when Ambo came to stay there was even talk of a cottage by the sea to be built for them by Rudyard's architect cousin. By the end of a week's fireside planning the cottage had assumed baronial proportions, if only in Ambo's imagination. Neither plan came to fruition; perhaps they were merely pipe dreams conjured up in idle moments in the 'infamous climate'.

But they did have one or two warm, even hot days in June and on one of them went on an excursion '...as wild as anything in a dream' to Lulworth Cove. Suddenly they found themselves in the middle of 'Macbeth's blasted heath' (Hardy's Egdon Heath, actually)...and there was an 'enchanted castle – Lulworth Castle – bobbing in and out of the haze'.[33] (Kipling was to return to Hardy country three years later and with the great man himself make a rather different sort of excursion into Dorset.)

Even when the weather did improve it only produced in Rudyard a 'lively' desire to be back in Main Street Brattleboro and have the 'iron-headed old farmers loaf up and jerk out: – "Bin in Yurope haint yer?" and then go home...through the deep white dust with the locust trees just stinking to heaven and the fire flies playing up and down the swamp road...' As for New York, 'won't [it] be hot just!' He could smell it 'with the naked eye'.[34]

He had survived four months of an English summer and now he understood why the English went forth and colonised the earth – because nothing could surprise them in the way of temperatures. But weather apart, Heaven had been kind to him in England, he told a friend on his return.[35] He had been safely delivered of several poems, four new jungle stories and a piece of broad farce, 'My Sunday at Home', that was 'even viler' than 'Brugglesmith', the tale that had brightened the dark days of '91 London for him.

One day, not long after they had moved into Naulakha, Rudyard told Carrie that he felt the return of the great strength that had come to him when he first arrived in London and met the men he was up against in the literary world.[36] And his output of poetry and prose during his Vermont years – *The Jungle Books, The Seven Seas, Captains Courageous*, most of *The Day's Work* and several of the tales in *Many Inventions* – seem to bear this out. The next day was spent 'playing about', humming over to himself all his half-completed verses. Kipling was not musical, could not even sing in tune, and once said that if he did try to sing the dog got up and left the room. But he had what was more important to a poet, a strong sense of rhythm. (Swimming at school off the North Devon coast, he would practise his side-stroke to Swinburne's *Atalanta in Calydon*. 'Who shall seek – who shall bring/ Who restore us the day [Half roll]/ When the dove dipped her wing/ And the oars won their way [Other half roll'].[37] But when Dunsterville decided that young Kipling should join the school choir, he had little success trying to teach him a tune. Losing patience with Kipling's lack of ear, he had resorted to kicking him, 'by the old parallel bars under the trees', as Kipling reminded his old friend many years later.[38])

For months, on and off, he wrestled with his 'Song of the Deep Sea Engines', in which he was trying to suggest how the soul of a ship was born: 'From the mine head – from the well-mouth – to the try-pit we rose/ Till a soul that was not man's soul was born of the blows.'[39] The poem itself was still-born; not so the soul. When 'M'Andrew's Hymn' was at last written out – Carrie knew something was brewing when Rudyard started marching round the house humming 'The Church's One Foundation' – it was seen that the doughty Scots engineer was of the same mind.

> Mill, forge and try-pit taught them that when roarin' they arose,
> An' whiles I wonder if a soul was gien them wi' the blows.

When Conan Doyle came to stay at Naulakha he too was treated to a reading of 'M'Andrew's Hymn' and was impressed by his host's dramatic power which enabled him to sustain the Glaswegian accent throughout the long poem, 'so that the angular Scottish greaser simply walked the room'.[40]

> Lord, Thou hast made this world below the shadow of a dream,
> An', taught by time, I tak' it so – exceptin' always Steam.
> From coupler-flange to spindle-guide I see Thy Hand, O God—
> Predestination in the stride o' yon connectin'-rod....

And then, after showing 'our Viscount loon' round the ship:

'Mister McAndrew, don't you think steam spoils romance at sea?'
Damned ijjit! I'd been doon that morn to see what ailed the throws,
Manholin', on my back – the cranks three inches off my nose.
Romance! Those first-class passengers they like it very well,
Printed an' bound in little books; but why don't poets tell?
I'm sick of all their quirks an' turns – the loves and doves they
    dream—
Lord, send a man like Robbie Burns to sing the Song o' Steam!

The Lord, it seemed, already had. But a year or so later the critics
who had taken M'Andrew on the chin, were rocked on their heels by a
series of 'filthy-technical' stories. There was the anthropomorphic 'Ship
that Found Herself', in which the different parts of a new cargo boat
talk together during her shake-down trip until by the end of the voyage
they find the unifying voice 'which is the soul of the ship'; there was
'The Devil and the Deep Sea', a story of another cargo-boat of many
disguises and little virtue whose engines were damaged – in considerable
technical detail – by a shell, followed by a blow-by-blow account of how
they were repaired; and there was '.007', a tale of more talking
machinery, only this time it was American locomotives doing the
talking…Whatever, the exasperated critics asked – though do not
trouble to tell us! – whatever is a coupler-flange, a brake-shoe, a
condenser-tube? When they had suggested, earlier, that Mr Kipling
should go away and learn about life, goings-on of a technical nature
were not what they had in mind.

The author himself had already posed the question: 'It's clever, but
is it art?' in 'The Conundrum of the Workshops'.

The tale is as old as the Eden Tree – and new as the new-cut tooth—
For each man knows ere his lip-thatch grows he is master of Art
    and Truth;
And each man hears as the twilight nears, to the beat of his dying
    heart,
The Devil drum on the darkened pane: 'You did it, but was it Art?'

And it was a conundrum for Kipling. How far was a man justified in
using onomatopoeic metres to reproduce the beat of engines? Where
does legitimate art end and sheer trick-work begin, he asked a fellow
writer.[41] But he was cheered by the American Navy's chief engineer
thanking him for 'at last seeing the romance of the engineer and
drawing attention to his good qualities'; and most of all for the chief's

103

comment that in his professional opinion the author had made no technical errors in 'M'Andrew's Hymn'. 'There's richness for you,' he wrote to Henry James. James' reply would have been worth hearing, but like the rest of the incoming mail in the Kipling household, it would have been recorded, acknowledged by the addressee, and finally destroyed by Carrie. Later Kipling was asked why he had used the term 'follower-bolts' in preference to 'junk-ring bolts', the former being an American term. Typically, he had gone into the matter thoroughly, seeking the comments of several engineers with differing views. In the end he stuck with 'follower-bolts' because of its open sound, whereas 'junk-ring bolts' produced the effect, to his ear, of a knock in the engine-room.[42] Did that make it legitimate art or sheer trick-work? No matter; he was soon writing a companion set of verses, 'The Mary Gloster', even finer than 'M'Andrew's Hymn'.

Despite this welter of technicalities Kipling was not yet ready to switch off from his Indian background. Mowgli and his brothers were born at Brattleboro, the two *Jungle Books* were published, and he was incubating what was to be his finest novel, set in India. Increasingly, however, his thoughts were turning towards things mechanical, and one gets the impression that had the great age of technology not dawned obligingly when it did, Kipling would have invented one: a copper-bottomed fairyland of his very own to play in. Not only because it provided excellent 'copy' and unrivalled imagery, but because to a cack-handed layman like himself it was all endlessly fascinating and romantic.

> 'Good-bye, Romance!' the Skipper said:
> 'He vanished with the coal we burn…'
> 'Romance!' the season-tickets mourn,
> '*He* never ran to catch His train,
> 'But passed with coach and guard and horn—
> 'And left the local – late again!
> 'Confound Romance!'…And all unseen
> Romance brought up the nine-fifteen.
>
> 'The King'

There was 'a perfectly splendid volume' of tales to be written about the machinery of the Victorian age, he told a London editor,[43] but as it would take him about five years to do he did not think the publishers would be pleased. Sorry though he was, they would have to count him out. Also counted out was any suggestion of writing to order. When Tennyson died after forty-two years as Poet Laureate, Kipling was 'sounded' about the laureateship. He was not interested, although he had several suggestions to make, not all of them serious, regarding the great poet's successor. But for himself he knew it would mean loss of power and ultimately, of self-respect. Indeed, there were times when he yearned to tell tales of 'extended impropriety – not sexual or within hailing distance of it – but hard-bottomed unseemly yarns.'[44] He wondered if people got a 'tithe of the fun' out of his tales that he got out of writing them. Laughter was good for the soul (and the digestion) and 'one can't be serious always'.

One of their new American friends who soon became an old friend, was James Conland, the doctor who brought Josephine into the world. Conland had served in the cod-fishing fleet off the Grand Banks as a young man and had a fund of 'fish-yarns' about life aboard a fishing-boat. The two men made several trips to the doctor's old haunts round Boston Harbour and Gloucester, where Rudyard was initiated into the mysteries of the fishing industry; on one occasion soon after the doctor had safely delivered their second daughter Elsie in February 1896.

'We assisted hospitable tug-masters to help haul three – and four-stick schooners of Pocahontas coal all round the harbour; we boarded every craft that looked as if she might be useful, and we delighted ourselves to the limit of delight...And Conland took large cod and the appropriate knives...and demonstrated anatomically and surgically so that I could make no mistake about treating them in print...And he sent me – may he be forgiven! – out on a pollock-fisher, which is ten times fouler than any cod-schooner, and I was immortally sick, even though they tried to revive me with a fragment of unfresh pollock.'[45] Thus, through painful travail was born *Captains Courageous, A Story of the Grand Banks*, and his third full-length work.

For the chapters in which a rail journey from San Francisco to New York had to be made in record time, Kipling had the help of a railroad magnate of his acquaintance who supplied him with a detailed time-table. The magnate was so impressed when he read the finished story that he ordered his own private car to be hitched up to a succession of locomotives to try and beat Kipling's time (in the book) over the same route. And with typical American thoroughness he did so.

The story concerns Harvey Cheyne, an objectionable, spoilt American boy and the son of a millionaire, who falls overboard from a luxury liner (while being sick) and is picked up by the seventy-ton fishing schooner, *We're Here*, on her way to the Grand Banks on a three months' fishing trip. The precocious boy demands to be taken back immediately to New York, where his father would 'pay anything any one chose to name..."I'm grateful enough for being saved...but I want you to understand that the sooner you take me back to New York the better it'll pay you."' Harvey's first lesson follows hard on the heels of referring to the *We're Here* as a 'dirty little fish-kettle' and accusing the crew of stealing his money: a punch on the nose from her skipper. For the first time in his pampered life he has to work for his bread and ten and a half dollars a month. But slowly and painfully he responds to the circumscribed, uncomfortable new world into which he has literally tumbled.

> The little schooner was gambolling all around her anchor among the silver-tipped waves. Backing with a start of affected surprise at the sight of the strained cable, she pounced on it like a kitten, while the spray of her descent burst through the hawse-holes with the report of a gun…
>
> Wop! She sat down in the moon-path on the water, curtseying with a flourish of pride impressive enough had not the wheel-gear sniggered mockingly in its box.
>
> Harvey laughed aloud. 'Why, it's just as if she was alive,' he said.

The tough life aboard the fishing boat, the hauling, gutting and salting of the catch, the gruesome sight of drowned men at sea, all have their effect, of which the unfamiliar roughness of his palms and the gurry-sores on his wrists are only the outward signs.

> Harvey began to comprehend and enjoy…the hurry of the wind working across open spaces and herding the purple-blue cloud shadows; the splendid upheaval of the red sunrise; the folding and packing away of the morning mists, wall after wall withdrawn across the white floors; the salty glare and blaze of noon; the kiss of rain falling over thousands of dead, flat square miles; the chilly blackening of everything at the day's end; and the million wrinkles of the sea under the moonlight, when the jib-boom solemnly poked at the low stars, and Harvey went down to get a doughnut from the cook.

Harvey is (of course) a changed boy by the time they return to port three months later.

> Over and above the darkness…Harvey could feel the land close round him once more, with all its thousands of people asleep, and the smell of earth after rain, and the familiar noise of a switching-engine coughing to herself in a freight-yard; and all those things made his heart beat and his throat dry up

as he stood by the foresheet…somebody waked with a grunt, threw them a rope, and they made fast to a silent wharf…and lay there without a sound.

Then Harvey sat down by the wheel, and sobbed and sobbed as though his heart would break…[46]

Soon he is reunited with his railroading parents who have hastened across two thousand-odd miles from seaboard to seaboard in their own gilded car in the record time already mentioned.

Harvey's prototype was that rampaging young American boy – once endured, never forgotten – that Kipling had noted on his homeward voyage seven years earlier. (Did that young man ever read *Captains Courageous* and recognise himself in print? Probably not; prototypes seldom do.) This was what Kipling meant when he wrote: '…it seems to me that every card in my working life has been dealt me in such a manner that I had but to play it as it came.' And he ascribed 'all good fortune to Allah the Dispenser of Events'.[47] Here he does himself less than justice; to say nothing of serious card players the world over – of which he was not one – who devote half their lives to learning how best to play the cards dealt them. But what of those unforgettable descriptions of the sea? If he claimed nothing else, they at least were inimitably his own. Not so, said their author, they were the work of his Daemon. All he had to do was to 'drift, wait and obey' – with a pen in his hand.

'You're dead wrong about my "sustained fiction,"' he told the Editor of the *Idler*. 'There ain't two cents' worth of plot in the blessed novel – it's all business – cod-fishing on the Banks; and no love at all. Wish I hadn't told you now in such enthusiastic terms but I was bung full of it when I wrote. It's in the nature of a sketch for better work: and I've crept out of possible holes by labelling it a boy's story.'[48]

At the end of 1895 Rudyard wrote in his wife's diary: 'So ends our fourth and best year.' And indeed his family was thriving and *The Second Jungle Book* was out with an initial print run of 35,000 copies on the strength of advance orders. But politically all was not well. Storm clouds were gathering between Britain and America over the Venezuela/British Guyana crisis, to the extent that he would have been relieved he had decided against taking out American citizenship. Early in the new year he wrote to Norton that he feared time was running out for them in 'a hostile country'. The situation put an end to his 'good wholesome life here: and to me that is the saddest part of it. We must begin again from the beginning elsewhere…'[49]

And then in May came a devastating row between Carrie and her hot-tempered brother after a year in which the two families had barely been on speaking terms. As usual it was over money and Beatty's increasing dependence on the Kiplings for paid work which, in Carrie's eyes (and it was she who paid him) was done in a slipshod manner. Beatty objected to being harangued by his bossy older sister while she doled him out trifling amounts of money and Rudyard objected to 'carrying' a good-for-nothing brother-in-law. But the latest row was more serious. Beatty, drinking too much and in debt had brought shame on them all by petitioning to be made a bankrupt. One day the brothers-in-law met by chance round a bend in the road, Beatty driving his horses furiously as usual and Rudyard riding his bicycle. Beatty pulled his team up with a jerk and Kipling fell off his bicycle. Beatty, a large man, brandished his whip at Rudyard and threatened him. Kipling, alarmed at his brother-in-law's wild appearance and even wilder words, took the threat seriously and to court. It was said afterwards that if it had not been for the wives refusing to allow their respective husbands to back down, the sorry affair would have been settled amicably enough with an apology from a repentant and sober Beatty. As it was, Carrie's entry in her diary for 9th May read: '...so far the most wretched and unhappy day of my life. Beatty arrested on a charge of threatening to kill Rud.'

They were in court for over five hours during which time the packed court room gave itself up to the spectacle of their celebrated neighbour being given the third degree in the witness box; almost as if he were the guilty party. Beatty enjoyed the publicity as much as his brother-in-law patently shrank from its relentless exposure. He was among his own people who turned a blind eye to his drunkenness and rowdy ways, he had a pack of reporters to play up to, and he was quite prepared to go to jail. In the event Beatty was remanded on bail. Immediately Kipling offered to pay the sum required, an extraordinary gesture under the circumstances. But this stealing of his thunder at the end of an otherwise satisfying day, did not suit Beatty and he put up the money himself. If the whole episode had not been so sad, so unnecessary, it would have been farcical. It had all the hallmarks of as vile a piece of farce as anything Kipling would ever write – except that he was very far from laughing. He was, in fact, a 'total wreck' for days afterwards, at the mercy of his high-strung nerves and unable to work. Three months later, shortly before Beatty's trial was due to be held before a Grand Jury, the *New York Times* of 2nd September reported that: 'Rudyard Kipling, the novelist, accompanied by his wife and children, sailed yesterday on the North German Lloyd Steamship *Lahn* for Southampton. Mr Kipling will be gone for several years. He goes direct to Torquay, a small fishing village situated in the south of England. Although he has removed all his furniture from his home in Naulakha, Vt., he did not take it with him, but stored it in Rutland, Vt.'[50]

But Kipling was never to return to Vermont nor see his beloved Naulakha again. For whatever reason, political or personal, it was no way to leave the country he had grown to love and the home where his two daughters were born – as if the hounds of Hell were behind him. Which in a sense they were, for that was how he had come to regard American newspaper reporters who had given him no quarter since the Beatty affair. As for his brother-in-law, over thirty years later Beatty was still talking about his old protagonist: 'He never has come back to Vermont. He never will, while I'm alive.'[51]

One of the last poems Kipling wrote at Naulakha, born of a morning's pacing up and down, was 'Sestina of the Tramp-Royal'. (A sestina is a particularly demanding verse form.)

Speakin' in general, I 'ave tried 'em all,
The 'appy roads that take you o'er the world.
Speakin' in general, I 'ave found them good
For such as cannot use one bed too long,
But must get 'ence, the same as I 'ave done,
An go observin' matters till they die....
Therefore, from job to job I've moved along.
Pay couldn't 'old me when my time was done,
For something in my 'ead upset it all,
Till I 'ad dropped whatever 'twas for good,
An', out at sea, be'eld the dock-lights die,
An' met my mate – the wind that tramps the world!

The words of a poet making capital of circumstance – in his own words, playing the cards that had been dealt him – or a man haunted by his need for the haven that still eluded him? On his last day at Naulakha friends found him pacing the terrace. 'There are only two places in the world where I want to live – Bombay and Brattleboro. And I can't live at either.'[52]

Aboard the *Lahn* Kipling wrote to Conland: 'We ran the Banks in brilliant sunshine, and passed within half a mile of the living image of the *We're Here*, slatting under riding sail and the dories bobbing on the swell round her. It made me think of old times with you...'[53] There would always be vivid reminders of the past in the midst of present sorrows. 'It is hard to go from where one has raised one's kids, and builded a wall and digged a well and planted a tree.'[54]

And, he might have added, where already there were two towns named after him: Rudyard and Kipling.

1 Henry Adams, *The Education of Henry Adams*, Carrington.
2 'In Sight of Monadnock', *From Tideway to Tideway*, 1892-95, *Letters of Travel.*
3 Ralph Waldo Emerson, *Monadnoc.*
4 'The Edge of the East', *From Tideway to Tideway.*
5 *ibid.*
6 *Kipling's Japan.*
7 'The Edge of the East', *Letters of Travel.*
8 'Some Earthquakes', *From Tideway to Tideway.*
9 'Half-a-Dozen Pictures', *From Tideway to Tideway.*
10 *As a Tale that is Told.*
11 RK to WE Henley, September 1892, *Letters*, Vol 2.
12 *SoM.*
13 *ibid.*
14 RK to Margaret Mackail, January 1893, *Letters*, Vol 2.
15 RK to SB, 1895, *Letters*, Vol 2.
16 *SoM.*
17 *Penguin Book of Interviews*, ed, Christopher Silvester, Viking 1993.
18 Wilson.
19 Penelope Fitzgerald, *Edward Burne-Jones*, Michael Joseph 1975.
20 RK to Gore-Gillon, 1894, *Letters*, Vol 2.
21 JLK to CE Norton, 1895, KP.
22 RK to Charles Stoddard, Orel, *Kipling Interviews & Recollections*, Vol 2.
23 RK to James Pond, lecture-manager, 1895, *Letters*, Vol 2.
24 RK to Rev John Gillespie, 1895, *Letters*, Vol 2.
25 Carrington.
26 RK to M Mackail, *Letters*, Vol 2.
27 RK to Norton, 1895, *Letters*, Vol 2.
28 Howard C Rice Jnr, 'Kipling's Winters in Vermont', article in *Upcountry*, 1974.
29 *SoM.*
30 RK to Henry James, June, 1894, *Letters*, Vol 2.
31 Henry James to Grace Norton, 1897, *Critical Heritage.*
32 H A Tapp, *United Services College*, 1874-1911.
33 RK to Stoddard, 1894, *Letters*, Vol 2.
34 RK to Robert Barr, 1894, *Letters*, Vol 2.
35 EL White, American novelist.
36 CK's Diary, KP.
37 *SoM.*
38 RK to Dunsterville, 1917, KP.
39 RK to Henley, 1893, *Letters*, Vol 2.
40 Arthur Conan Doyle, 1924, Orel 2.
41 E L White.
42 In answer to an American enquirer KJ.
43 Saintsbury, 1895.
44 RK to Norton, 1895, Carrington.
45 *SoM.*
46 *Captains Courageous*, excerpts, 1897.
47 *SoM.*
48 RK to Barr, 1896, *Letters*, Vol 2.

49 RK to Norton, 1896, *Letters,* Vol 2.
50 Paul Theroux, *Sunrise with Seamonsters,* Hamish Hamilton, 1985.
51 *ibid.*
52 RK to Mrs Holbrook and Mary Cabot, Carrington.
53 RK to Dr Conland, 1896, *Letters,* Vol 2.
54 RK to W D Howells, Carrington.

CHAPTER SIX

'We must begin again...' in England

Men make them fires on the hearth
Each under his roof-tree,
And the Four Winds that rule the earth
They blow the smoke to me....

With every shift of every wind
The Homesick memories come,
From every quarter of mankind
Where I have made me a home.

'The Fires'

In September 1896 Kipling returned to England – with wife, two children and temporarily, an American accent – to a rented house near Torquay and more letter-writing. 'Imagine...a big stone and stucco Naulakha, long, low with two stories, stuck on the side of a steep hill falling away...to a hundred-foot cliff of pure red soil. [He had forgotten how red was the Devon soil.] Below that is the sea, about two hundred yards from the window...I look straight from my work table on to the decks of the fishing craft who come in to look after their lobster pots.'[1]

He explored the deserted beach, a tiny cove reached by an almost perpendicular lane that would have been 'just the place for smuggling in the old days'. The cliffs had fallen away in great boulders making it impossible to reach the sea without clambering over them. No-one seemed to go there except for himself and the fishermen. Occasionally he found footprints in the sand and the mark of a rowing-boat's keel. And sometimes after a heavy gale there would be blackened tree stumps cast up on the beach; from an underwater burnt forest, it was said.

Before they had been in Rock House a month the weather turned rough and they felt the full force of a sou'-westerly equinoctial. The wind uprooted a huge elm in the adjacent field and took the top out of a poplar tree on their lawn. Altogether the weather was 'Bloody British'.

As for the local residents: 'We are a rummy breed – and O Lord the ponderous wealthy society. Torquay is such a place as I do desire to upset by dancing through it with nothing on but my spectacles...'² As he was put up for the Athenaeum shortly afterwards we must assume that he did not give in to the temptation. But it took time to settle down to work again after the tribulations of the past months, and as he had done on previous occasions he found solace in a day's fishing. According to Carrie they were both sore and bruised by the year's events and it took them longer than the others to forget; which showed her, at least, that they were wrong to feel it so keenly.

Rudyard's way of forgetting followed the usual pattern: he would not talk about Brattleboro, or read a letter bearing an American stamp (apart from those of business and personal friends such as Doubleday and Conland) or do anything that might remind him of the last year's sorrows. Carrie had to save up all the news from her mother country, good or bad, until he was ready to lower his defences and open his mind to the world again; in his own time.

Alice and John came to stay at Rock House and found their son still trying to come to terms with a succession of 'mildewed days with pale blobs of yellow wash on the ground, that they trustfully call sunlight'.³ While Rudyard at his work-table overlooking the sea, put the finishing touches to a new American edition of his works, his father was getting down to the artwork in the coach-house. It was through this edition, suggested by Scribner's while they were still living in Vermont, that Rudyard and Carrie had met Frank Doubleday, the 'large young man' who was to become a life-long friend of the family; and a much-needed one, before the century was out.

John Kipling's illustrations were to take the unusual form of low relief plaques modelled in clay and then photographed. The business was altogether too intriguing to miss, and soon Rudyard had deserted his own work table for his father's in order to have a hand in the fun. The resulting 'illustrations in the solid' delightfully complemented Kipling's Indian stories, bringing the characters to three-dimensional life. In all they were to appear in seventeen out of the eventual thirty-six volumes. The Outward Bound edition was unique in other ways too: it was the first time Kipling used the swastika, the Hindu symbol of well-being, in conjunction with the elephant's head (Ganesh) and lotus flower as his 'trade mark' (dropping the swastika only in 1933 after Hitler annexed it to symbolise Nazi Germany); and it was the first and only time that he arranged the stories in three distinct groups – 'military, Asiatic and ghostly or ghastly'.⁴

For his Outward Bound edition Kipling wrote a rather special Introduction. It was in the form of a Letter or Bill of Instruction from the Owner to the Nakhoda or Skipper of the Venture. Never was there such a Letter before, its language veering from the seamanlike to the beguiling to describe the setting out of this trading vessel on a new voyage. '...The cargo is all in new mats, stowed like by like, to be reached more easily; and I have painted her before and behind, and I have put a new plank deck in place of the old bamboo one, and the tiller-ropes are new as well....The road is West and by South from England, where she will not touch, for the cargo is all for the Western ports, and these, if Allah please, you will find upon the other side of the sea.' As to the trading: 'The men of those ports...come down to trade early in the day, and their hours are longer than we use in the East. Do not, then, sleep in the forenoon or sling a hammock under the stern-awnings; neither unroll the sleeping-mats at sundown...When...the little children come down to the beaches hide away that which is uncomely; let down the gang-plank with the railing on either hand; and spare nothing of the painted clay figures, the talking apes, the dancing bears, the coloured lights, or the sweetmeats to give them pleasure. Thus they will first plague their parents to buy, and later – for a child's memory is very long – will bring down their own babes when we return...'[5]

He had lost no time in taking to two wheels along the Devon lanes, 'tied to a fishing rod'. It was the best possible way of re-discovering his native land which was more full of beauty than he had ever imagined. 'England after all, is literature. One can't believe that the whole landscape hasn't come out of a novel – people houses and all.'[6] He fished for pike and salmon in rivers and lakes over a wide area, discovered a 'perfectly lovely old pub' a few miles down the road where he would sit on a sofa in the parlour – it doubled as the private bar – drinking hot whisky and water to restore his circulation. But the searching winds gave him neuralgia as they had done three years earlier in Vermont, 'played the cat and banjo'[7] with all his teeth and delivered him into the arms of the local dentist for a month on end with raging toothache. Was this his come-uppance for all the tuck he had consumed at school? According to their grocery list, Study Five got through thirty pounds of sugar, six tins of condensed milk and seven pounds of biscuits a month; while in Vermont he had nourished a weakness for maple syrup and was open to any amount of it, maintaining there was no 'sweetenin' ' in the world better than maple-sugar. (More than thirty years later [1932] he would write to thank a friend[8] in Toronto for sending him some McIntosh Red apples and maple syrup, noting how scandalously the price had gone up since the days when he used to assist 'sugaring off'.)

In Drake's own county and within sight of the English Channel it was inevitable that he would soon renew contact with the Royal Navy.

He was invited to the training ship *Britannia* at Dartmouth and spent several happy days aboard the old three-decker with the cadets, absorbing naval techniques and jargon. With the recent publication of *The Seven Seas* the author of 'M'Andrew's Hymn' had been given another unofficial title: 'Poet of the Engine-room' and wherever sailors foregathered he was made welcome. The navy had made a successful take-over bid for his affections, and in doing so Petty-Officer Pyecroft and his mate, 'wot-'e-can't-drive-'e-can-coax' Hinchcliffe were on their way into print, and into the hearts of sailors and civilians the world over.

(*The Seven Seas* was selling 'mighty well' on this side of the Atlantic, he wrote to Conland, although to his amazement some of the verses were considered improper and there had been howls of outraged virtue and no end of a discussion going on, in which he refused to take part. A year later he reported that *Captains Courageous* had sold 16,000 copies in six weeks. 'Not bad for a book they had given up trying to understand in England.'[9] But he was still talking of returning to Vermont sometime.)

He renewed acquaintance with the Captain Bayly from Simonstown who had promised him a trip in a warship and during the next couple of years would twice be the honoured guest of the Channel Squadron, 'playing at being a sailor all across the salt seas'. The average landlubber might not have considered it in those terms; and certainly not under the conditions prevailing when he joined a new thirty-knot destroyer on her test run. She had to do thirty knots for three consecutive hours. '...on and on and on till we all turned white with fatigue.' In this 'devil's darning needle' he felt his (new?) false teeth shaking in his head, and it took him two days to get the jumps out of his legs.[10] He said afterwards that he would not have missed it for anything – but it was an experience he would never forget.

The Devonshire writer Eden Philpotts (also Indian born and Devon educated) sent Kipling his latest book. It gave Rudyard an idea, or perhaps crystallised one that had been at the back of his mind since writing 'The Brushwood Boy' at Naulakha. This was the story in which the hero has the same recurring dream throughout his childhood, ten years of which are spent at an English public school, not dissimilar to the USC, which does not encourage dreaming. Early in the New Year Kipling wrote to an editor friend: 'The notion of writing a Devonshire tale is new to me but, now I come to think of it, I was educated at Westward Ho! nigh Bideford and for six puppy years [four, in fact] talked the vernacular with the natives whose apples I stole. What will EP give me to buy me off?'[11] In fact he was already 'deep in a school tale', he wrote to Crom Price on 18th December. 'But come down and you shall hear it read.' And he baited his line with: 'There's a lovely scene with you in your study.'[12] The bait was taken and Price spent a couple of days at Rock House after Christmas. Later his erstwhile pupil wrote to ask him for reminiscences of the old school, and in particular examination paper mistakes and copies of mathematical, Latin and English Literature papers ' – same as you used to set us.'

Meanwhile Carrie's diary recorded that Rudyard began writing 'Slaves of the Lamp' (the first to be published) on 14th January. One way or the other, by the time cousin Florence came to stay for two weeks towards the end of February Rudyard was about to start a second schoolboy yarn.

The cousins had always got on well together and Florence was one of a select few allowed to sit in the room while he was writing. On this occasion she reported that Rud would write and write, then put down his pen and roar with laughter, read the passage out to her until she too roared with laughter. 'Come on, Florence! What shall we make them do next?' So how much of *Stalky* was true? And that was precisely the question put to its author in a letter from a young brother and sister. His reply was the model of tact from beginning ('Dear Sir and Madam') to end. '...I can only say that some parts of *Stalky* are too true; some are only true and some are not quite so true: but as for the Corpse of the Rat I will say nothing because I do not wish to corrupt the minds of the young.'[13] He had had enough trouble as it was keeping Raven Hill's illustrations within the bounds of decency for the same reason. *Stalky & Co* was of course founded on fact; just as its beloved head was based on Crom Price, and King, the classics master, was an amalgam of Crofts and his predecessor, Haslam; and so on throughout the staff. As for the anarchic trio in Study Five, with their reputation for more 'variegated insanity' than the rest of the school put together, there was absolutely no disguising who they were: marked men for life after the book's publication. But their 'notoriety' did them no harm in the long run; indeed Beresford and Dunsterville broke into print themselves on the matter of their *'Schooldays with Kipling'* and *'Stalky's Reminiscences'* respectively, in the years to come. But with hindsight it seems remarkable that not one of the masters called Kipling to account for taking liberties with his character or undermining his authority. Perhaps the charms of being written about by a world-famous author outweighed any embarrassment caused, in much the same way that a personal appearance on TV does today, even if it is only in a game show in which the contestants are made to look silly. In fact many Old Boys proudly identified themselves with this or that pupil. The book had a mixed reception at publication and opinions were divided over its merits. Many found it 'odious' or 'distasteful' and Kipling's lack of reverence towards the more conventional public schools, towards games in general and cricket in particular, did not go unnoticed. (Although Kipling would dutifully bowl for his schoolboy son in the nets, towards the end of his life he admitted to the heretical view that he found all cricket about as stimulating to the mind as a glass of laudanum.[14])

Relations and friends came to stay by turns: his parents, aunts Edie and Aggie and cousins Ambo and Hugh, and the Doubledays from America. How good it was to hear the energetic New York accent again! Baby Elsie grew fat in the soft Devonshire air and Josephine shot up into a tall slim girl with a mind of her own. 'We've got a governess to look after Josephine: only Josephine doesn't exactly see it that way. She prefers looking after the governess and that bewilders the governess.'[15] Josephine was invited to lunch with some little girls in Torquay, her first social event, and returned 'inarticulate with delight – a small flushed woman of the world'. The governess was a stolid Scot, with the result that Josephine 'was not in as much danger of over-excitement,' according to her mother.[16]

But at Christmas time as he and Carrie huddled over an inadequate fire they felt homesick all over again for Naulakha and the clear crisp New England air. 'I don't think we can stay out a whole year longer without coming over to have a look at things,' he wrote to a friend. 'It's an uncivilised land (I still maintain it) but how the deuce has it wound itself round my heartstrings in the way it has?'[17] For the first time there was no valediction in Carrie's diary at the end of the year. There was something about Rock House, too, a brooding atmosphere that depressed them both, not only the more-imaginative Rudyard. Despite all their visitors, the large bright rooms and enviable position, they found its Feng-shui (spirit) to be an unhappy one. (Later he was to write a story about a house supposed to be haunted, which is thought to be based on Rock House.[18]) In March they were in the thick of an English spring: primroses, violets, hyacinths, birds and butterflies heralded a warm summer to come for this Jubilee year. Kipling confessed to an American friend that he believed he was the only 'poet', in quotes, who was not writing a Jubilee Ode. But, 'like a fool', as he told the Editor of *The Times*, he had used up his best notions in 'A Song of the English' four years' earlier. In any case it was the Laureate's job to write something suitable and he disliked all the fuss: it made him feel apprehensive of disaster to come. Nevertheless, there was a tinge of regret in his words.

By May they had left Rock House for good. Carrie was now expecting their third child and 'eight months damp, rain, sea fog and mildew were rather more than we could stand.'[19] Aunt and Uncle Burne-Jones offered them the use of their holiday home in the seaside village of Rottingdean, next door to Brighton, to await the birth, while they themselves tactfully withdrew. Rudyard and Carrie moved in on Derby Day. (Kipling's description of Brighton sea-front in 1897 is worth noting: 'a huge wide chalk road cut out of the cliffs and crammed with traffic.'[20])

The day of the Queen's Jubilee (22nd June) dawned, dull and foggy. Rudyard wrote some verses then put them aside. He and his father attended the Spithead Review two days later and a week after that Rudyard was off on his own for a 'blissful fortnight' with the Channel Fleet off Ireland. The time that he had – and what a time it was – is recorded in *A Fleet in Being*, and was originally published as a series of articles in *The Times* and *Morning Post*.

'The Naval man's experience begins early, and by the time he has reached his majority a Sub-Lieutenant should have seen enough to sober Ulysses. But he utterly refuses to be sobered.' As the following account would bear out.

The naval officer is a young – very young – sub-lieutenant who is coming to the end of his watch, while the captain sleeps below. There is some disturbance in the line of ships. The next ahead has reduced speed and now lies on his port bow and – oh horror! – the next astern is alongside. 'Heaven send that the captain may not choose this hour to wake.' They have to reduce speed rapidly – 'and when ships slow too much they lose steerage-way, and what is far worse, they wake the Captain.' The sub extricates himself and the ship from a potentially tricky situation, and when relieved at midnight 'descends the bridge in one light-hearted streak, and three minutes later is beautifully asleep, the ship's kitten purring under his left ear. But the Captain was awake all the time. The change of speed roused him, and he lay watching the tell-tale compass overhead, his mouth at the bridge voice-tube; one eye cocked through the open port, and one leg over the edge of the bunk – in case. The Sub must learn his business by himself – must find confidence in isolation precisely as the Captain did a quarter of a century ago. It is not good for him to know that he is being watched.'[21]

Something that disturbed the prescient Kipling was the inadequate staffing of ships' engine rooms. 'The day is coming when the engine room will govern the ship – and in those days newspapers will know a very great deal about technical terms. They will learn them as the beaver learned to climb – because he had to.'[22]

Returned from the sea, his head full of notions, Rudyard set about clearing his desk, consigning unsatisfactory work to his ever ready waste-paper basket. We are told that Sallie Norton, their young friend over from America, asked permission to rummage through the discarded pages. She retrieved a set of verses headed 'After', whose first stanza ended with the lines: 'Lord God of Hosts, be with us yet, /Lest we forget – lest we forget!' When the assembled family heard Rudyard

read it aloud they were united in protest at its fate. He consulted Aunt
Georgie and her approval settled the matter. The hymn was given a
final polish before his aunt carried it up to London on her return.
Kipling's Jubilee offering was published in *The Times* on 17th July – the
Spithead Review and two weeks at sea later. The editor gave it a leader,
to general acclaim. (Once again, a few readers went off at score over a
single misconstrued line. His 'lesser breeds without the Law' referred
to the rulers, not the ruled, with the Americans and/or Germans the
most likely candidates at that time.) Here was the 'Poet of Empire'
espousing humility, not pride; awe, not arrogance. In the aftermath of
the Queen's Jubilee when all the bells had rung out in celebration, the
'Recessional' sounded a more sombre note: a single toll, like an echo
of the Lutine Bell, warning the boastful, 'Lest we forget', that even the
proudest empire is ephemeral. It was one of many significant 'public'
poems published in *The Times* for which its author never accepted
payment. But how close those resounding words came to never being
published at all; words that were destined to be sung in churches
throughout the land, at memorial services after the war – and at their
author's own funeral in Westminster Abbey.

It was at North End House, overlooking the Green, that 'the beetle-
browed John'[23] was born 'on a warm August night of '97, under what
seemed every good omen.'[24] And once again the proud father's pen
worked overtime announcing the arrival of 'one small craft recently
launched from my own works...The vessel at present needs at least
fifteen yrs for full completion but at the end of that time may be an
efficient addition to the Navy, for which service it is intended.'[25] In the
meantime the poet of the sea was proudly wheeling his new son's pram
up and down across the Green...

The house-hunting continued. He had already visited properties in
Kent and Wiltshire, and around Lewes and Hastings. Now, three weeks
after his son's birth, he went down to Dorset for a few days. He had not
forgotten the magic of the hidden county he had glimpsed through
the haze of a June day three years ago. Together with Thomas Hardy
who lived near Dorchester (and who may have been instrumental in
persuading him to house-hunt in the county of his birth – as he had
been with the Gosses a few years' earlier when he had 'pestered' Gosse
with property advertisements, although nothing came of the search),
they cycled to an isolated house owned by an elderly lady. The story
goes that while Kipling tramped round the house, Hardy was left with
the old lady, to whom he confided that the gentleman he had brought
with him was none other than Mr Rudyard Kipling. His announcement
fell flat; she had never heard of the name. A little later, it happened
that Kipling found himself alone with the old lady, and in the course of

conversation said: 'My sponsor is none other than Mr Thomas Hardy himself.' But the old lady had never heard of him either. As those two celebrated men pedalled homewards marvelling at their own insignificance, I like to think that even Hardy's 'grave and bitter humour'[26] was tickled – and that their wheels wobbled in delight, if not unison. The story bears out the medieval remoteness of Dorset. Almost a century later it was possible for a cottage-hunting kinswoman of Kipling's to lose herself completely when the sign-posts ran out and the brooding hills seemed to join hands around her. But as far as house-hunting was concerned she was more fortunate than Kipling who was not to find a home in Dorset.

Across the Green from Aunt Georgie stood a detached house called The Elms lying empty behind its high flint walls. It was to be the Kiplings' home for the next five years – at a rent of three guineas a week. It had been a depot for smugglers, hence its huge cellars, Kipling told a friend. 'It's old red-tiled, stucco-fronted with worm-eaten stairs but low ceiled and warm which in England is everything.'[27] Or almost everything. The one exception to their happiness was the lack of room for their bicycles, now three in number: two plus a tandem that had been a gift from an American publisher (McClure). '...for sheer pace and excitement a tandem beats a bicycle to pieces,'[28] the new owner reported as he played long and lovingly with it. He had been trying it out with the assistance of an unknown girl while Carrie was otherwise engaged with Master Kipling. It was a different story though when at last they ventured out together – Carrie in front – each of them under the impression that the other liked it. Came the day they skidded and were decanted onto the road where, in a moment of truth, both confessed to hating the devilish thing. And that was the end of the tandem; but not of the bicycles.

He took up horse riding again and 'seemed to like it' – until he was thrown twice in a single day and retired badly shaken. In future his exercise would be taken on his bicycle or his two feet. He was an inveterate walker and enjoyed long tramps over the downs. Soon after moving into The Elms in September he had Burne-Jones, Crom Price and J M Barrie for company on a 'great walk'. Ned Burne-Jones came down frequently that autumn and uncle and nephew were deeply engrossed in the Roman occupation of Britain.

As their first Christmas in Rottingdean approached Kipling prophesied that the Green would be very lively. And so it was, with Stan Baldwin and his young family staying with his in-laws at The Dene opposite and the Kipling parents and Trix at The Elms. There would be meetings of prams and nursemaids on the Green, observed one day by Kipling as they 'hauled alongside like Roman Galleys', the Baldwin pram holding two girl babies and the Kipling pram carrying Elsie, while each child 'solemnly and systematically'[29] tried to pull the other cousin overboard. It was the end of a year that had been 'in all ways the richest' for them both, with the birth of their son, the comings and goings of the numerous cousins – and despite endless visits to the dentist for them all. A year which had seen Kipling on course again after the trauma of the previous twelve months.

What was more, he was now on the register as a house-holder and for the first time in his life would be able to vote. 'Can you imagine me on a parish council agitating for drains?'[30] said the one-time campaigning journalist of the *CMG*.

In January they took ship for South Africa, the first of many such trips to avoid the dreaded cold and damp of a British winter. It was also 'a rest for the wife' and Cape Town a paradise for children. With them went '2 servants, 3 kids, 2 bicycles, unlimited perambulators and 2000 tons of baggage...a rather large contract to move'.[31] His father went too, but not his mother. Nothing would persuade Alice to 'up sticks' any more; particularly not the promise of sunshine. She had endured India's unrelenting climate for too many years to be persuaded by that argument.

In South Africa they settled, though none too comfortably, in a boarding house on the slopes of Table Mountain. But this was the only year they would need to board. Rudyard had already made the acquaintance of Cecil Rhodes who was about to build a house on the Groote Schuur estate for the use of visiting artists and men of letters. When it was completed Rhodes placed it at the disposal of the Kiplings, whenever they wanted to use it. And in the years to come the warm South African climate would bring back memories of Rudyard's own childhood in Bombay.

> We shall go back by the boltless doors,
> To the life unaltered our childhood knew...
> The wayside magic, the threshold spells,
> Shall soon undo what the North has done—
> Because of the sights and the sounds and the smells
> That ran with our youth in the eye of the sun.[32]

> 'Song of the Wise Children'

That first year Rudyard explored Matabeleland on two wheels. There is an amusing story told about those wheels which may or may not be true. One day a 'scruffy little fellow' in khaki trousers entered the Bulawayo cycle shop and asked the owner if he could hire a bicycle.

The owner refused: he only sold bicycles – for cash. And he had never heard the name Rudyard Kipling. There followed this brief dialogue. Kipling, irked, leaving the shop: 'I'll bring a guarantor.' – 'He'll have to be a good one,' retorted the owner. – 'I'll bring two.' – 'They'll have to be two good ones.' Kipling brought Charles (later Sir Charles) Metcalfe and Cecil Rhodes. He got his hired wheels for 7/6 (about thirty-five pence) a day, but by the time he returned the machine he had paid out more than it would have cost him to buy it outright – as the owner had urged him to do.[33] Never mind. With their help he discovered the 'great grey-green greasy Limpopo River, all set about with fever-trees' and the elephant's child with his 'satiable curtiosity'[34] that succeeding generations of children, starting with his own, came to know and love.

Back at home the following June Uncle Ned died suddenly overnight in Aunt Georgie's arms, 'his Avalon unfinished'. His ashes were brought down to Rottingdean church and laid simply on his drawing table in front of the altar beneath his own beautiful stained-glass windows. Throughout the night of midsummer's eve Rudyard and the family kept vigil by turns. Next day the great artist's ashes were buried in the 'cozy place' he had chosen in the churchyard, a buttressed recess facing North End House. Rudyard was devastated at the loss of the uncle who had meant so much to him. Now only Aunt Georgie lived in the house across the Green, channelling her grief into positive action by writing her husband's memorials with the help, when needed, of her nephew and Crom Price, Ned's oldest friend. Her little granddaughter, Angela Mackail, (Thirkell) came several times to stay in Rottingdean and was a regular playmate for the Kipling children. From her ready pen we learn something of life at The Elms.

> 'During those long warm summers Cousin Ruddy used to try out the *Just So Stories* on a nursery audience. Sometimes Josephine and I would be invited into the study, a pleasant bow-windowed room where Cousin Ruddy sat at his work-table…[The stories] are a poor thing in print compared with the fun of hearing them told in [his] deep unhesitating voice. There was a ritual about them, each phrase having its special intonation which had to be exactly the same each time and without which the stories are dried husks.[35]

Kipling was never too busy to write a personal note of thanks in his own hand, and latterly with his own typewriter. Back in Vermont he had written a charming letter to Josephine's nursemaid thanking her for her present of buckles for a child's shoes, in which he mentioned the building of Naulakha going up 'hand over fist', referred to his wife informally as 'Carrie' and signed himself 'Yours entirely'. Now, on his return from South Africa he wrote to Sir Donald Currie, Chairman of the Castle Line to tell him how 'splendidly comfortable' they had been on the *Dunvegan* and the *Norham*; how well they had been looked after in every way, as a family with three children. As an afterthought he enquired, 'if it is a fair question' how they built boats that 'do not complain in a sea way?' They had been rolled about in the Bay and 'the woodwork of the *Norham*, which they tell me is fifteen years old, never so much as creaked. This is a secret they don't seem to have mastered in the Atlantic trade.'[36]

In September he was off to Devonport and Captain Bayly's HMS *Pelorus* for more manoeuvres with the navy. 'Once aboard the lugger the past twelve months rolled up like a chart that one needs no longer.'[37] But the past has a habit of catching up with one, even at sea. Off the coast of Ireland where he was having a 'lovely time with the Channel Fleet' some unexpected work overtook him from his American publishers. His tear-sheet revision of one of the stories for *The Day's Work* had gone 'messing in the mail' and an anxious Doubleday, whose first book for Kipling under his own imprint this was to be, had sent him a typescript for his urgent corrections. So instead of 'larking about Bantry bay with landing-parties' he settled down to work in a muddy cabin surrounded by half a dozen men sorting the mail from the Fleet. During this trip he was carried round the quarter-deck shoulder high after reciting some of his verses at a concert; and he renewed acquaintance with Prince Louis of Battenberg with whom he had dined aboard his flagship the previous year.

The following winter the Kiplings decided to go to America instead of Africa. Carrie had not seen her mother for three years and there was unfinished business regarding copyright problems for Rudyard to settle in New York. So in January 1899, the worst month for crossing the Atlantic, they set out from Liverpool taking all three children with them, against Alice Kipling's advice. The weather was atrocious, they met a full gale in mid-Atlantic and all were ill. Arrived in bitterly cold New York all the children had colds, developed whooping cough and were hotel-bound. To make matters worse Rudyard then went down with pneumonia, becoming seriously ill when the inflammation spread from one lung to the other. For days he was delirious and his life hung in the balance. Outside the hotel the world waited for news; inside it resembled a siege with reporters camped in the lobby. Friends rallied round to do whatever they could to help Carrie, herself getting over a bout of fever. In the middle of all this Josephine had a relapse and developed pneumonia. Carrie took her to a friend's house to be nursed, away from Rudyard's sickroom. Leaving her there was 'a moment of conscious agony'[38] for her mother.

The crisis passed for Rudyard, but the enchanting little Josephine, the light of his life, succumbed to her illness. Carrie was with her daughter when she died, attended her funeral and returned to her husband's bedside with a scarlet shawl flung across her black outfit in order not to draw comment. By then Rudyard was sufficiently recovered to be asking for her, but not yet strong enough to be told of his daughter's death. When and how Carrie eventually broke the news to him no-one ever knew, nor indeed how she had managed to keep going so courageously throughout her terrible ordeal. But if anything had been needed to cement their marriage for life, this surely was it: the bond of mutual grief over the loss of their beloved Josephine, together with Rudyard's utter dependence on his wife, physically and emotionally.

Letters and cables were flooding in from all over the world from friends and strangers, kings and commoners, congratulating Kipling on his recovery. (Even the Kaiser sent a telegram of good wishes. 'Damn his impudence,' said the recipient.) Hard on their heels came other letters, searching for words to express their sorrow at the tragic news about Josephine. What can one say to a father who has himself walked through the valley of the shadow that had claimed his first-born instead?

John Kipling went over to comfort his son; kind friends, like the Doubledays, Conland and Sallie Norton, whose family Rudyard had known since childhood, supported them: 'At first [Rudyard] was too ill to realise it quite, but now every day he feels it more...' And when Sallie was allowed in to see him: '...there he lay changed and thin and ill-looking but his voice very natural except for a slight hoarseness...I sat by his bed with his hand in mine, it was wonderfully pathetic to see the look of extreme sensitiveness in his face, about the mouth and eyes and the look of sadness there, even his smile did not dispel.'[39]

As soon as he was fit enough to leave the New York hotel they were whisked away by private car to a small hotel in Lakewood to begin the deadly weariness of convalescence. After some weeks in the brisk country air he gained fifteen pounds in weight and showed every appearance of having recovered, judging by John Kipling's humorous sketches of his son's cycling and rowing activities. Ruddy laughed till he cried, his father said, over what John referred to as an innocent slip on the part of their host's manservant who had mixed up the trousers of two of the guests while packing: so that the tall Frank Doubleday and the short John Kipling received each other's trousers. For a lark, Doubleday had dined in his. It was just the sort of irreverent schoolboy humour that would tickle the Macdonald sense of the ridiculous, reducing them to tears of laughter – a safety valve for tightly-reined emotions.

In June they left America for the last time. Carrie and her mother, but not Rudyard, had visited Naulakha and found that Howard, their old coachman who was acting as caretaker, had everything in excellent order. They sailed on the *Teutonic*, the ship that had taken the exuberant Ruddy and his bride on honeymoon seven years earlier. The Doubledays travelled with them to lend their support and see the invalid safely home. John noted that his son seemed to improve each day, the sun and the sea giving them all 'that brown varnish they dispense so liberally',[40] although in his opinion it was real health and not mere varnish that shone on Rudyard's face. During the voyage the 'wicked' Doubleday and Rud taught John and Bok (the Editor of the *Ladies Home Journal*) poker, a capital game that John concluded was not a diversion for an honest man; and Rudyard helped to produce *The Teuton Tonic*, a hand-written newspaper compiled by the passengers for their own amusement. Outwardly he had recovered from his illness; but from the loss of Josephine he would never recover. It lay buried deep within him, never to be spoken of except to his wife or parents in private. It was the sort of wound that never heals, he said years later, only skins over...

Returned to The Elms, he found it a place full of memories. He saw Josephine in the house and coming out of every dark corner of the garden, radiant and heartbreaking. In a letter to his old friend Mrs Hill he explained: 'This fool-sickness of mine which had the bad taste to leave me and take my little Maiden (I wish you could have seen her) makes it, I believe, impossible for me to stay in England thro' the winters...I thought I knew something of what grief meant till that came to me...I don't think it likely I shall ever come back to America. My little Maid loved it dearly...and it was in New York that we lost her.'[41]

The last two verses of 'Merrow Down' (1902) were the nearest he came to expressing that grief in a poem.

> In moccasins and deer-skin cloak,
> Unfearing, free and fair she flits,
> And lights her little damp-wood smoke
> To show her Daddy where she flits...
>
> For far – oh, very far behind,
> So far she cannot call to him,
> Comes Tegumai alone to find
> The daughter that was all to him!

Two years later came 'They', a tender and compassionate story which may have been written in an endeavour to exorcise those visions of

Josephine and come to terms with her loss. The narrator loses his way when motoring in the depths of Sussex. He stumbles across an old house where a beautiful blind woman lives. He hears the laughter of children and sees them playing in the garden. On a later visit to the house he glimpses the children again; it is as if they are playing hide and seek with him, always just beyond his reach, or behind a screen beside his chair. 'I felt my relaxed hand taken and turned softly between the soft hands of a child. So at last I had triumphed. In a moment I would turn and acquaint myself with those quick-footed wanderers…The little brushing kiss fell in the centre of my palm – as a gift on which the fingers were, once, expected to close: as the all-faithful half-reproachful signal of a waiting child not used to neglect even when grown-ups were busiest – a fragment of the mute code devised very long ago. Then I knew.'

Then he knew that the house was filled with ghostly children, for that kiss was just such a kiss as his own little Maiden used to give him and on which his fingers would close protectively. He also knew that only those with eyes to see – who had themselves lost a child – could see the children. The blind woman says: '"I—I only hear them…I have no right, you know – no other right. I have neither borne nor lost…" – "Be very glad then," said I, for my soul was torn open within me. – "Forgive me!" – She was still, and I went back to my sorrow and my joy. – "It was because I loved them so," she said at last, brokenly. "They came because I loved them – needed them…Was that wrong, think you?" – "No-no!…Not for you. A thousand times no…For me it would be wrong. For me only…"'[42]

For him it would be wrong – unacceptable – to become involved in anything verging on the psychic, because of his sister. Trix's mental health, always delicate, had been giving great anxiety over the last few years; in the family's opinion it had been exacerbated – if not caused – by her active involvement in certain forms of spiritualism.

During those first difficult weeks after their return to The Elms when Kipling was in sore need of a diversion, Phil Burne-Jones came to stay. Like his father, Phil too was a painter. He took the opportunity to paint his cousin's portrait, the familiar profile of Kipling sitting at his desk, pen in hand and pipe at the ready beside him. 'Phil's portrait of me is a Regular Stunner and shows specially well in the reproduction. I resent the sleek baldness of my head, but the intellectual air and the tummy are beyond dispute.'[43] But he found it mighty hard work resisting the torment of cramp and the temptation to scratch himself. Between sittings the two diverse cousins amused themselves with a hand-printing press recently installed at The Elms. One of their more imaginative – and scurrilous – efforts reflected Rudyard's opinion of the American publishers with whom he had been in dispute in New York just before he was taken ill. It was printed on lavatory paper.

'PUTNAM'

George Haven Putnam was born of poor but most disreputable parents. This was done in the Retail Department without his knowledge.

Nevertheless his life casts a shade compared to which that of the Upas Tree is benignant sunshine. At the age of ten he announced his intention to become that thing called a Publisher. His mother upon hearing this awful instance of early depravity straightway fainted. His father, albeit heavily disguised in liquor, expressed the liveliest satisfaction. From this the Gentle Reader will infer the deep-seated vice of the entire family of Putnam. May God forgive them!

We will now consider the Haven in detail. Shortly after attaining his majority he was arrested for stealing a hymn-book from a dying Missionary. He defended his action on the ground of past labours in behalf of American Copyright.

There is a poetic justice in the final resting place of this priceless piece of paper: with details of its provenance in Kipling's own hand on the back, it resides in the rare books department of a New York State university.[44] But the feverishness of the schoolboy humour tells us to what extent he had not yet come to terms with the dark corners of his life. He was writing – but only letters to old friends: 'I've been lying low and doing nothing except going to sleep in the afternoon and getting to bed by ten p.m.'[45] But his head was full of notions and when he got back from Scotland he would 'have a shot at' doing a little work again. In fact he wrote a *Just So* story, finished off another and wrote the dedication for his *Stalky* book in the five weeks he was in the Highlands – in between walking, fishing and sailing expeditions.

According to Angela Thirkell: 'Much of the beloved Cousin Ruddy of our childhood died with Josephine and I feel that I have never seen him as a real person since that year. There has been the same charm, the same gift of fascinating speech, the same way of making everyone with whom he talks show their most interesting side, but one was only allowed to see these things from the other side of a barrier and it was sad for the child who used to be free of the inner courts of his affection.'[46]

1　RK to Conland, 1896, Carrington.
2　RK to Norton, 1896, Carrington.
3　RK to John Hay, 1896, *Letters*, Vol 2.
4　RK to Doubleday, *Letters*, Vol 2.
5　Introduction to *The Outward Bound Edition*, 1897.
6　RK to Hitchcock, *Letters*, Vol 2.
7　RK to Conland, *Letters*, Vol 2.
8　J W Barry 1932, KP.
9　RK to Conland, 1897, *Letters*, Vol 2.
10　RK to Conland, 1897, Carrington.
11　RK to Barr, 1897, KP.
12　RK to CP, 1896, *Letters*, Vol 2.
13　RK to Arthur & Ethel Knight, KP.
14　RK to CE Hughes, Col War Graves Commission, 1934, KP.
15　RK to Conland, 1896, *Letters*, Vol 2.
16　CK to Miss Cabot, 1896, KP.
17　RK to Norton, Dec, 1896, *Letters*, Vol 2.
18　'The House Surgeon', *Actions and Reactions*, 1909.
19　RK to Conland, 1897, Carrington.
20　RK to Conland, 1897, *Letters*, Vol 2.
21　*A Fleet in Being*, 1898.
22　RK to John St Loe Strachey, 1898, *Letters*, Vol 2.
23　RK to Alfred Baldwin, 1897, KP.
24　*SoM*.
25　RK to WJ Harding, Carrington.
26　*SoM*.
27　RK to Norton, 1897, *Letters*, Vol 2.
28　RK to Henley, 1897, *Letters*, Vol 2.
29　RK to Alfred Baldwin, 1897, KP.
30　RK to Norton, 1897, *Letters*, Vol 2.
31　*ibid.*
32　'Song of the Wise Children', *The Five Nations*, Methuen 1903.
33　Robert Moss, *Rudyard Kipling & the Fiction of Adolescence*, 1982.
34　'The Elephant's Child', *Just So Stories*, 1902.
35　Angela Thirkell, *Three Houses*, OUP 1931.
36　RK to Sir Donald Currie, *Union Castle Chronicle*.
37　*A Fleet in Being*, 1898.
38　CK Diary, KP.
39　Sallie Norton to her father, 1899, KP.
40　JLK to Sallie Norton, 1899, KP.
41　RK to Mrs Hill, 1899, *Letters*, Vol 2.
42　'They', *Traffics & Discoveries*, 1904.
43　RK to Norton, Carrington.
44　Cornell University.
45　RK to Conland, 1899, *Letters*, Vol 2
46　*Three Houses*.

CHAPTER SEVEN

East or West? '...A divided mind'.

My brother kneels, so saith Kabir,
To stone and brass in heathen wise,
But in my brother's voice I hear
My own unanswered agonies.
His God is as his Fates assign,
His prayer is all the world's – and mine.

'The Prayer', Kim

Kipling made it a rule never to criticise other writers (his own family excepted and then only if they asked him to) but he was not averse to the criticism of others; and if it was written with style he would be the first to salute it, as one craftsman to another. Young Beverley Nichols had written a letter to the *Morning Post* while still up at Oxford in which he referred to 'the flamboyant insolence of Rudyard Kipling'. Two years later it happened that they both attended the same luncheon. Kipling made a bee-line for the unfortunate Nichols who was wishing himself elsewhere. Was he not the young man who had been so rude to him in print? Nichols admitted his guilt and started to apologise. 'What for?' said Kipling. 'I used to be much ruder to people when I was your age...Besides,' he added, 'that was a jolly good phrase – flamboyant insolence – I liked it.'[1] And he fell to talking about literary style.

What would have been his reaction to the following comment, written after his death? 'Until Mr T S Eliot caused consternation among the genteel by analysing [Kipling's] virtues as a poet he was safely dismissed by them as a sort of literary bounder who was somehow responsible for the Boer War.'[2] A shout of joy, probably, at the beautiful neatness of a sentence that took a swipe at the 'genteel' on its all-encompassing way.

So what **did** Kipling do in the Boer War – apart from being accountable for it in the eyes of some? Except for the fateful year when they went to New York instead, the Kipling family went to South Africa each winter from 1898 to 1908. The Boer War broke out in October

1899 and covered three of these years. From his first-hand experience in India Kipling knew better than most civilians about the harshness of a Tommy's life abroad, even in peace time; and from talking to the men themselves had learned something of the privations endured by their families, official and otherwise, back home. Now, back home himself, and privy to the unshakeable complacency of the political and military hierarchy where the supremacy of the British Empire was concerned, he was 'absorbed with anxiety'[3] over the inadequacies and amateurism of the British fighting forces that were being shipped to South Africa to fight the Boers.

His immediate reaction to the war was twofold. He set about forming a volunteer corps in Rottingdean, the precursor of many more to follow, and he wrote a set of verses in aid of the Soldiers' Families' Fund. 'The Absent-minded Beggar' was published in the *Daily Mail* in the first month of the war and 'Sir Arthur Sullivan wedded the words to a tune guaranteed to pull teeth out of barrel-organs'.[4] Anybody could do what he liked with it: perform it in public or reproduce it in any way he pleased, provided that all fees and profits went into "The Absent-minded Beggar Fund" organised by the newspaper.

> When you've shouted "Rule Britannia", when you've sung
>   "God save the Queen",
> When you've finished killing Kruger with your mouth,
> Will you kindly drop a shilling in my little tambourine
> For a gentleman in khaki ordered South?...
> There are girls he walked with casual. They'll be sorry now
>   he's gone,
> For an absent-minded beggar they will find him,
> But it ain't the time for sermons with the winter coming on,
> We must help the girl that Tommy's left behind him!...
> Pass the hat for your credit's sake, and pay – pay – pay!'[5]

It was a more realistic, or war-time, version of 'And that's what the girl told the soldier'. And he wrote it the same week that he was engaged in finishing off 'The Elephant's Child' – who was 'full of 'satiable curtiosity' and lived in Africa; a striking contrast.

The British public paid. They paid to the tune of a quarter of a million pounds, a fair return in those days for four verses dedicated to the common soldier and his girl. Later Kipling was to say to Sullivan that the two of them ought to be shot for perpetrating such stuff. But as he remarked to Florence Macdonald, who had been singing the song to him as they walked over the downs, it did the job and brought in the pennies.

The year that had started so disastrously with his illness and the death of Josephine, ended with a rather sad and influenza-ridden Christmas and the offer of a knighthood. The honour, though much appreciated, was refused on the grounds that he could do his work better without it; as were all subsequent offers refused, and there were many, in the years to come. (The only honours he did accept were honorary degrees and the Nobel Prize for Literature in 1907.) On the last day of the old century while he was recovering from influenza he wrote in his wife's diary: 'I owe my life to Carrie.'

On the twentieth day of the new century they sailed once again for the sunshine and warmth of South Africa, this time with only two children. The *Kinfauns Castle* was acting as a freight ship during the Boer War and the boat-load of volunteers aboard, with little to look forward to except seasickness and a sniper's bullet, found an unexpected treat in store: the company of their very own poet to cheer them up and recite to them his 'Song of the Banjo'.

He was given a great send-off by the troops when they docked at Cape Town. And there he fell in with a group of journalists who were to become his fellow war reporters and friends. Nothing could have pleased him more than to be asked by Lord Roberts a few weeks later to assist in the editing of an army newspaper, *The Friend*, possibly the first such journal in military history. (It was actually a daily newspaper that had been temporarily taken over, partly for the entertainment of the troops, but also for the publication of military regulations and notices.) For Kipling it was like old times. In bush jacket and broad-brimmed Boer hat, a pipe clamped between his teeth, he plunged happily into a journalist's life once again, writing copy, correcting proofs, sub-editing and occasionally contributing verses, as though he had never been away from a newspaper office. He enjoyed every minute of his editorial duties, he said afterwards. 'Never again will there be such a paper! Never such fine larks!'[6]

In the intervening weeks he had visited military hospitals up and down the country, his pockets stuffed with the plug tobacco beloved by soldiers and paid for out of the fund he had helped to set up. There were many shortages of 'comforts' that his note-of-hand helped to produce and...'I was *persona gratissima* at certain Wynberg Hospitals where the nurses found I was good for pyjamas.'[7] (Except for the occasion when he mistakenly hailed the wrong nurse and knowing the matter to be urgent, announced loudly: 'Sister, I've got your pyjamas.' After which he was *persona non grata* in the eyes of at least one outraged sister.) He went up to the battle lines in an ambulance train and travelled back with the wounded, comforting the sick and writing letters home for those unable to hold a pen; and sometimes he recited a ballad or two at troop concerts.

On his way by train to Bloemfontein just after its capture he had an encounter with an outspoken Tommy. Kipling's carriage was unlit, but he managed to obtain a pair of three-wicked signal lamp candles from the Tommy, one of the many soldiers to whom he had distributed tobacco earlier in the day. When Kipling wanted to know how he had come by such treasures, the Tommy replied: "'Look 'ere, Guv'nor, I didn't ask *you* 'ow you come by the baccy you dished out just now. *Can't* you bloody well leave me alone?'"[8]

He returned to England at the end of April with first-hand, but depressing knowledge of the lack of physical fitness and training (particularly in respect of their long-range rifle-shooting) of the British soldiers who were losing too many battles to the better-trained Boers. He founded the Drill Hall and Rifle Range in Rottingdean and saw to it that local men received proper instruction and practised regularly; and he took his turn acting as Range Officer, signing the Register of Target Practice in that capacity when on duty. On subsequent visits to South Africa while the war was on, he left a retired sergeant in charge of the range and kept up a brisk correspondence with him *vis à vis* the respective merits of side or central sights on a particular rifle, the whereabouts of a certain Gardner gun, and the possibility of his being able to bring some new rifles back for the range. No detail was too small for his concern; even to corresponding with the village postman who was serving in South Africa and who promised to pass on all he had learned of First Aid when he returned home.

Kipling's next broadside, 'The Islanders', berated the (Tory) government for sending out untrained 'amateur' soldiers to be picked off by the Boers' accurate rifle-fire:

Sons of the sheltered city – unmade, unhandled, unmeet—
Ye pushed them raw to the battle as ye picked them raw from the
  street...
Ere-ye fawned on the Younger Nations for the men who could
  shoot and ride!
Then ye returned to your trinkets; then ye contented your souls
With the flannelled fools at the wicket or the muddied oafs at the
  goals.

Strong words, widely misunderstood and they caused offence in some (obvious) quarters. Afterwards he confided to Haggard that it might have made his meaning clearer if he had written hired and not flannelled fools as he'd had in mind the well-trained professional cricketers currently enjoying £1000-gate money performances. 'But as usual people have gone off on a side issue.'[9] It was becoming a habit.

Kipling was never one to water down strongly-held beliefs or play to any gallery outside of a music-hall. Nor would he ever explain what he meant. Shortly before he had been taken ill in New York, 'The White Man's Burden' was published on both sides of the Atlantic. Now there was a phrase for his critics to get their teeth into, like a terrier with a rat.

> Take up the White Man's Burden—
> Send forth the best ye breed—
> Go bind your sons to exile
> To serve your captives' need...
> Take up the White Man's Burden—
> And reap his old reward:
> The blame of those ye better,
> The hate of those ye guard...

The verses were addressed to the American nation who had suddenly found itself with a small empire of its own (Cuba and the Philippines) and seemed uncertain what they should do with it.

In South Africa he met soldiers from one of the Younger Nations, volunteers who had travelled thousands of miles to fight the Boers, and in Lichtenberg he saluted them in five haunting verses.

> ...And I smelt wattle by Lichtenberg—
> Riding in the rain.
>
> It was all Australia to me—
> All I had found or missed:
> Every face I was crazy to see,
> And every woman I'd kissed;
> All that I shouldn't ha' done, God knows!
> (As He knows I'll do it again),
> That smell of the wattle round Lichtenberg,
> Riding in, in the rain!

The Australian poet, 'Banjo' Paterson, (who had also been in South Africa during the war, had in fact been one of Kipling's best contributors to *The Friend*) asked him later if it had been inspiration, that touch about the trooper reminded of home by the familiar scent of the wattle. 'No,' Kipling replied. 'Observation.' He had noticed a trooper pull down a wattle-bough and smell it, and riding alongside, had asked him where he came from. The soldier told him, adding: 'I didn't know they had our wattle over here. It smells like home.'[10]

133

Slotted into and between his yearly visits to the Cape was the continual flow of work that went on regardless of whether he was in his study at home or on the deck of a liner at sea, oblivious to the noise all round him. *Stalky & Co* was published in 1899 to a mixed reception. Schoolboys loved it. Some of their elders thought it distasteful; others, realising it was founded on fact, the characters real, hunted down the originals of Stalky and M'Turk, the headmaster and the school sergeant, while many of the Old Boys proudly revealed themselves as this or that character. In 1900 came the two volumes of *From Sea to Sea*, that inimitable collection of travel pieces on India, the Far East and the USA as seen through the eyes of a globe-trotter extraordinary. We have already seen how these articles were pirated in the USA. To what extent they must have irritated their American readership may be judged by the following two short excerpts. He describes 'the whited sepulchre' that is Calcutta – The City of Dreadful Night and open drains, a city as fascinating to the eye as it is unpleasant to the nose. 'We've got typhoid in Calcutta now...everything seems to be built with a view to its comfort.'[11] No-one would argue with that, but when he then visits Chicago during his eastward-to-England voyage he tactlessly compares it with the city at the mouth of the Hughli River. '(Chicago) stands on the same sort of soil as Calcutta. Having seen it, I urgently desire never to see it again. It is inhabited by savages. Its water is the water of the Hughli, and its air is dirt.'[12]

Towards the end of 1901 *Kim* was published. (The book was actually finished at Rottingdean a week before Rudyard and Carrie saw Bateman's for the first time.) If for no other of his works, Kipling will always be remembered for *Kim*, his farewell to India, with its magical evocation of life on the Grand Trunk Road; the road upon which a young boy and an old man set out together, each in search of a different goal. The book's parentage is an interesting one and its gestation period, even by Kipling's standards, curiously long and peripatetic...Sixteen years earlier in India he had started to write what he semi-seriously called 'his masterpiece'. He was deeply interested in the 'queer ways and works of the people of the land', and he knew Lahore City – 'that wonderful, dirty, mysterious ant hill – blindfold and wandering through it like Haroun-al-Raschid in search of strange things.' How could he have written some of his *Plain Tales* without his nocturnal wanderings to draw upon? But 'the bulk of my notes and references goes to enrich a bruised tin tea-box where lies 350 foolscap pages thick – my "Mother Maturin".' The novel that was always being written but got 'no forrader'.[13]

He had described it in a letter to his (maiden) aunt Edith as not one bit nice or proper, but it tried to deal with the 'unutterable horrors of lower class Eurasian and native life' as they existed outside reports. His mother called it nasty but powerful and he knew it to be in 'large measure true. It's an unfailing delight to me and I'm just in that pleasant stage where the characters are living with me always.'[14]

When he left India he left the unfinished manuscript behind, then had second thoughts and asked his parents to send it on to him in London. His turnover of work there indicated that he might need to plunder it for short stories with an Indian background. (More than forty years later he would be asking his sister to send on her plots as soon as maybe, in spite of already being 'five deep in tales'.[15] If he didn't grab a plot as it passed by, he was afraid he might lose something.) But as it happened his head was already filled with soldier ballads and the rhythm of the music-hall, so nothing came of the idea and the manuscript was locked away in his agent's safe. Six years later in Vermont a notion came to him for a novel set in India about an Indian-born Irish boy, the orphan son of a soldier, who was mixed up in native life. He christened the lad Kim of the Rishti – and once again came to a full stop. He turned instead to a boy from a vastly different background: the spoilt Harvey Cheyne of *Captains Courageous*.

Back in England and living in Rottingdean, Kim came back to him, insistently. Rudyard took him to Tisbury to be smoked over with his father whose judgement, particularly on Indian matters, he respected above all others. 'Under our united tobaccos it grew like the Djinn released from the brass bottle.' There was only one possible form for it, he told his mother, and what was good enough for Cervantes was good enough for him. 'Don't you stand in your wool-boots hiding behind Cervantes with me!' his mother retorted. 'You know you couldn't make a plot to save your soul.' A visit to his parents was always so refreshing. Once again his father would take care of the illustrations in his own way: more of the low-relief plaques that he had worked on at Rock House in such infinite and loving detail. When at last the book was finished his father asked: 'Did it stop, or you?' (This was important, as both men knew, and in his autobiography Kipling tells us why. 'My Daemon was with me in the *Jungle Books*, *Kim* and both Puck books, and good care I took to walk delicately, lest he should withdraw. I know that he did not, because when those books were finished they said so themselves with, almost, the water-hammer click of a tap turned off.') When told *it* had stopped, his father replied: 'Then it oughtn't to be too bad.'[16] It wasn't; nor were his father's illustrations.

The thirteen-year old Kim, brought up by a half-caste woman, lives by his wits in the bazaars. He gets involved in The Great Game (spying for the British Secret Service) and otherwise does nothing 'with an immense success'. He speaks 'the vernacular by preference, and his mother-tongue in a clipped uncertain sing-song' and is unrecognisable as a white boy. He meets a Lama who is seeking the River of the Arrow (where 'who so bathes in it washes away all taint and speckle of sin') and becomes the old man's faithful *chela* (disciple), begging for him on their journey together along the Grand Trunk Road. They come across Kim's father's old regiment and when the necessity of the boy's education is stressed by the two padres (and it is noticeably the Catholic priest who shows most concern for his welfare, but then it was an Irish regiment), the Lama offers to pay for Kim to go to St Xavier's at Lucknow, 'the best school in India'. There for three years Kim learns to be a sahib in term-time, while reverting to The Game and Life on the Road during the holidays. It seems inevitable that he will have to choose between the ways of the East and the West, between contemplation and action, when he reaches manhood. He tries repeating his own name over and over again: 'Who is Kim – Kim – Kim?' like one seeking to free his mind in meditation.

> He squatted in a corner of the clanging waiting-room, rapt from all other thoughts; hands folded in lap, and pupils contracted to pin-points. In a minute – in another half second – he felt he would arrive at the solution of the tremendous puzzle; but here, as always happens, his mind dropped away from those heights with the rush of a wounded bird, and passing his hand before his eyes, he shook his head.

The question remains unanswered until the last chapter, and even then it is not explicit. Kim is exhausted in body and mind from his long journey to the Hills with the Lama and his dual role of *chela* and messenger in the Great Game. He felt unconnected, out of tune with his surroundings…'just like the idle cog-wheel of a cheap Beheea sugar-crusher laid by in a corner…"I am Kim. I am Kim. And what is Kim?"

'He did not want to cry…but of a sudden easy, stupid tears trickled down his nose, and with an almost audible click he felt the wheels of his being lock up anew on the world without. Things that rode meaningless on the eyeball an instant before slid into proper proportion. Roads were meant to be walked upon, houses to be lived in, cattle to be driven, fields to be tilled, and men and women to be talked to.' He falls into a deep, reviving sleep. The Lama's Search is over too; he has found his River and tells Kim that now they are both assured of Salvation.[17]

Kipling, like Kim, faced a similar dichotomy between East and West, and he spelt it out in the verses, 'The Two-sided Man'.

Something I owe to the soil that grew—
More to the life that fed—
But most to Allah Who gave me two
Separate sides to my head…

Were his roots in the East: the Bombay of his early childhood, his 'Mother of Cities', with its vivid memories of light and shade, of early morning walks to the fruit market? Returning home, his sister's pram would be piled high with the golden and purple produce. Sometimes they would stop at a wayside cross where the ayah (a Portuguese Catholic) prayed – 'I beside her' – or, and this time it would be Meeta, the bearer's, hand he held, they would enter a dimly-lit Hindu temple to gaze at their friendly Gods…

Or were his roots in the West: the land of his people – but also of 'Auntie Rosa', of beatings and isolation and darkness and all the jagged misery of the House of Desolation? I do not believe he ever entirely resolved the conundrum for himself, which is perhaps why Kim's future is blurred, unstated. It could be argued that Kipling understood the Indian people better than he did his own countrymen. Had he not spoken, thought and dreamed in the vernacular from babyhood? Like Kim – who would have been about the same age as his creator – his native tongue did not come naturally to him.

If ever a man was a prisoner of his childhood memories it was Rudyard Kipling. And it was in Bombay, where his childhood began and ended that he had been happiest ('You will find a key to a good many things in some verses called "The Two-sided Man,"' he wrote to Chevrillon in 1919. 'One does not outgrow the first six years of one's life.'[18])

Undoubtedly he had deep emotional ties with the land of his birth; which, I believe, was why he would never return to the sub-continent for a visit – even when invited to do so at the highest level. Viceroys were not much in his line, he said; any more than viceregal lodges were his place in India. He wanted to remember the land as he had known it through his senses. Twice before when nearing her coast he had been 'wrought upon' through the nose; had smelt home – all India – even before he stepped ashore. As the smell of wattle in South Africa had meant 'all Australia' to the soldier far from home; and as centuries earlier 'the scent of hawthorn in the sun, or bracken in the wet'[19] would remind the Roman centurion, ordered back to his native land after forty years in Britain, of the country he had come to love as home.

In a speech on 'Some Aspects of Travel' (to the Royal Geographical Society in 1914) Kipling had suggested there were 'only two elementary smells of universal appeal – the smell of burning fuel and the smell of melting grease. The smell, that is, of what man cooks his food over and what he cooks his food in.' And of them all he ranked wood-smoke first. 'A whiff of it can take us back to forgotten marches over unnamed mountains with disreputable companions; to day-long halts beside flooded rivers in the rain; wonderful mornings of youth in brilliantly lighted lands where everything was possible – and generally done; to uneasy wakings under the low desert moon and on top of cruel, hard pebbles; and, above all, to that God's own hour, all the world over, when the stars have gone out and it is too dark to see clear, and one lies with the fumes of last night's embers in one's nostrils – lies and waits for a new horizon to heave itself up against a new dawn.'[20]

Then, too, for an artist like Kipling there were the delights of the eye: 'colour that rejoices, light that cheers, and line that satisfies the innermost deeps of the heart.'[21] Should he, dare he, return a third time to India when all that he held most dear now lay in the West? No. It were better not.

For Kipling his lack of identity and its inheritance, a divided mind, was to be celebrated as a gift from Allah, relentlessly driving him onward. Together with his Celtic insight it meant that he could yearn to be where he was not, long for his home across the sea, whichever sea he was facing at the time. He could long to live in Brattleboro or Bombay, knowing that, practically speaking, he could live in neither. It was the stuff of which words could be made to sing and shout.

But it did nothing for his fundamental need to put down roots.

---

1 Beverley Nichols, *A Young Man's Candid Recollections of his Elders and Betters*, 1926.
2 Frank Swinnerton, Foreword to *Rudyard Kipling, A New Appreciation* by Hilton Brown, 1945.
3 CK Diary.
4 *SoM.*
5 'The Absent-minded Beggar', 1899.
6 KJ.
7 *SoM.*
8 *ibid.*
9 Morton Cohen, *Rudyard Kipling to H Rider Haggard*, Hutchinson, 1965.
10 AB Paterson, *Happy Dispatches*, Angus & Robertson Ltd, 1935.
11 *From Sea to Sea*, Vol 1.
12 *From Sea to Sea*, Vol 2.
13 RK to Kay Robinson, 1886, *Letters*, Vol 1.
14 RK to Edie Macdonald, 1885, Carrington.
15 RK to Trix, 1932, KP.
16 *SoM.*
17 *Kim*, 1901.
18 RK to Chevrillon, 1919, KP.
19 'The Roman Centurion's Song', *Puck of Pook's Hill*, 1906.
20 'Some Aspects of Travel', 1914, *A Book of Words*, 1928.
21 *Kipling's Japan.*

CHAPTER EIGHT

'...the discovery of England' on four wheels

...Sith she is silent, nimble, unnoisome,
Lordly of leather, gaudily gilded,
Burgeoning brightly in a brass bonnet,
Certain to steer well between wains.

'The Advertisement'
(in the manner of the Earlier English)

When the *Daily Mail's* Alfred Harmsworth (later Lord Northcliffe) called on Kipling one autumn day in 1899 to discuss his newspaper's Comforts for the Troops fund, he rolled up to The Elms 'in one of those motor car things'[1] – it may have been his yellow 6 hp Panhard – and changed the course of Kipling's life. Suddenly there it stood, vibrating, outside his front door, this noisy 'thing' that attended to all the senses at once while demanding one hundred and one per cent attention in return – like a new mistress. Kipling needed no second invitation when asked would he like to go for a spin. 'The poison worked from that hour,' he declared after only a twenty-minute drive.

It was just the kind of diversion he needed, little more than six months after Josephine's death, with his sister's health causing much anxiety and the privacy of his home being threatened by inquisitive sightseers.

While he had been learning the art of balancing on two wheels in America, a minor revolution on four was taking place on this side of the Atlantic. In the summer of 1895 (about the time Rudyard and Carrie were embarking for a month's stay in England) a little French Panhard slipped across the Channel upon a crusading mission. She was the first automobile ever to appear on English roads and was greeted with open-mouthed wonder as she made her law-defying run through half a dozen English counties. Her aristocratic British driver was being deliberately provocative in order to draw attention to the absurdities of the Highway Act, drawn up by country gentlemen who despised the riding of 'ironmongery' instead of horses and who were prepared to go to almost any lengths to prevent the nasty habit spreading.

Whatever she did, the Panhard was bound to be breaking the law in some way. Either by 'emitting vapour', by 'furious driving' (anything in excess of four mph) or by frightening the horses – the most heinous crime of all, of course. Would the police regard her as a carriage (a classification that included bicycles) or as a locomotive? Or as neither? In the event the authorities were taken by surprise and sat on their hands. But it is fair to say that if Kipling had been in England at that time, if he had seen the Panhard in motion, heard the rhythmic *teuf-teuf, teuf-teuf* of her two-cylinder engine, he would have joined the ranks of the 'mad' automobilists four years' sooner than he did. For here was Romance all over again, hand in hand with a Cause.[2]

But there was another and more practical reason. A motor car would give him the freedom of movement – in theory, anyway – that he needed. Freedom to explore England, 'the most marvellous of all foreign countries', as he was discovering, and freedom from the hordes of trippers who daily bowled into Rottingdean by horse-bus from Brighton. With little else to do in the village except try and catch a glimpse of 'the world's most famous living author', they would peer through the gates or over the garden wall of The Elms – artfully pointed out to them by the bus driver. While in the nearby pub Kipling's letters of protest to the landlord, who happened to be the proprietor of the horse-bus, were being sold to customers over the counter, unanswered, at a pound apiece. Business, it seemed, was booming again in the one-time smugglers' village, with The Elms as its reluctant pivot. (In smuggling times the house had been linked by underground passages to others in the business of supplying 'Brandy for the Parson, 'Baccy for the Clerk...'[3]) Rudyard recognised that their days in Rottingdean were numbered so perhaps it was just as well they had not been allowed to 'make an honest woman' of the house when they wanted to buy her – as their friend Henry James was in the throes of doing with his rented house in Rye. But they would be sad to move away from Aunt Georgie who, intrepid soul that she was, would often go with them on their motor drives.

By December Kipling was hiring a 'Victoria-hooded, carriage-sprung, carriage-braked, single-cylinder, belt-driven, fixed ignition Embryo which, at times, could cover eight miles an hour.'[4] Together with the services of the young engineer/driver this 'old hired thing' cost him three and a half guineas (£3.67½) a week. Two or three times a week in the summer Rudyard and Carrie would go out in the motor after breakfast to explore the beautiful Sussex countryside, returning in the cool of the evening. Once at least they achieved a round trip of sixty miles in the same ten-hour day. Motoring was somewhere between 'steering a boat and driving an engine', he wrote to Conland back in New England. It was just the kind of 'play' that would delight his old friend. All the same, there had been one or two narrow shaves with startled cart-horses.

Kipling's first 'Very-Own' motor arrived in June 1901. Decisions and motor cars were made slowly in those early days. She was an American steam-car, a Locomobile by name that ran, when she ran at all, on a diabolical mixture of petrol, steam and water. Her only virtue seems to have been her (comparative) silence. 'She reduced us to the limits of fatigue and hysteria, all up and down Sussex,'[5] he recalled over thirty years later. The boiler (beneath the seat – imagine it!) was heated by petrol burners that 'never lit the same way twice', and when they were lit would blow out again in the next cross-wind. Once when she broke down only fifty yards from home, Rudyard was heard to say: 'American girls are the best in the world – but American cars – damn 'em!'[6] A restrained and tactful comment under the circumstances. Five months after the motor's arrival Carrie noted in her diary the advent of an American driver 'to see if he can make the car go'. Things were getting serious.

Not a horn but a bell warned of the Locomobile's noiseless approach behind weaving farm carts. And if the warning fell on deaf ears, which it often did, there was always the 'vociferous' steam air pump to fall back on, guaranteed to produce a response – if only a rude one. Another of her idiosyncrasies was her thirst for water. She needed a refill every twenty miles or so. In moments of crisis when the tank was as empty as the horizon, they would have to push it – half an inanimate ton – to the next water source, which might be 'a cottage, sparsely inhabited by one child who wept'.[7] The appalling road surfaces of those days only added to motorists' problems. They were mostly unmade and consisted of three ruts: the two outer from carriage wheels and the inner from horse's hooves. In summer there would be choking dust, in winter oozing mud. On the other hand the owners of horses had to contend with all the belching smoke, fumes and noise emanating from the 'ironmongery', while trying to calm their terrified animals. The countryside would never be the same again, and did they but realise it, neither would the towns and cities.

The Locomobile soon earned her nickname, the Holy Terror, laid upon her by her exasperated owner. (To his American mother-in-law he referred to her, tactfully, as Coughing Jane.[8]) All Kipling's motor cars had characters – not always desirable ones – or else developed them upon further acquaintance and were christened accordingly. The Holy Terror did have her good points, however, even if they were not immediately obvious. She was the model for the capricious steam car in 'Steam Tactics' (the first of several boisterous motoring tales in which Pyecroft and Hinchcliffe play leading parts), and she was occasionally persuaded to take the Kiplings on the now serious business of house-hunting, while 'the County of Sussex slid by in slow time'.[9]

True to form, the motor broke down the second time they went to look at Bateman's so that yet again they arrived at its gate, horse-drawn. But for once the Holy Terror was doing them a good turn. They had first visited the Jacobean ironmaster's house on a hot summer's day nearly two years' earlier when they had gone by train to Etchingham and from there by hired fly. Both Rudyard and Carrie had fallen in love with the house, had explored every room and found no disturbing shades of the past, no menacing atmosphere. House, garden, mill and brook: the ambience was perfect. Even so, they did not make up their minds immediately, and when they had, found they were too late. The property had just been let. Hiding their intense disappointment they told each other that 'no sensible person would be found dead in the stuffy little valley where she stood'[10] – and continued their search. It was while they were away staying with friends at Crowborough that Kipling saw Bateman's advertised again. He wrote to Leslie Cope Cornford, a friend who lived in Brighton. 'If I know a photo when I see one the Eternal Bateman's at Burwash has coughed up once more for sale! It looks like the hand of fate. I've given myself away too hopelessly over it. Will you, like the best of good fellows tackle [a firm of London estate agents] and get at the price of the house with the twelve or ten acres...His last demand was £10,000. Please get an order to view...in the name of Smith or anything that isn't Yours ever...'[11]

With the contract for the house (including thirty-three acres it cost them £9,300) safely signed, the owner enquired how they intended to travel the four miles to the nearest railway station. The hill had been the death of two pairs of his horses.

'By motor car!' said Kipling.

'Oh, those things haven't come to stay!' replied the owner, and confessed years later that had he thought otherwise, he would have asked twice the price for the house.

At the top of Kipling's next letter to Cope Cornford 'The Elms Rottingdean' is crossed out – and 'Bateman's Burwash' substituted. It was written shortly after the move on the 3rd September and begins with schoolboyish glee: 'Nous sommes ici.' And then: 'We came in over the bodies of two and twenty "leaders of revolts in Faenza."' Once again he is borrowing from Browning (it was a key-phrase in his obscure play, A Soul's Tragedy) to refer to the army of plumbers and whitewashers about the place, and it is an example of how he would 'air' a particular word or phrase in his correspondence that would emerge later in the piece of writing he was engaged upon at that time. In this case the 'revolting' leaders of Faenza appeared in print twice that very month in 'Below the Mill-Dam' (he had only started to write the story in June) – uttered by the erudite mill cat. The phrase occurred again the following year in 'The Files', where the 'leaders' were of the newspaper variety. Kipling never had any problem about re-using a good quotation if he thought it worked to his purpose.

They had survived the traumas of moving house yet again, Rudyard rather better than Carrie who naturally bore the brunt of the exercise, as women usually do, and to whom life was always a serious business anyway. It was different for Rudyard, and not just because he was a man. He felt instinctively that this was the end of the search for the Very-Own-House that had occupied so much of their energies since returning to England. Now at last – at last – he could settle: put down roots and become part of established country life.

The diary entry for removal day reveals that the foreman of the removers was drunk and that 'chaos and black night' awaited them at Bateman's. But the entry is in Rudyard's hand which explains the quotation, presumably from *Paradise Lost*. His pen continues to stand in for his wife's for another nine or ten days, until Carrie felt sufficiently in charge of things in her new home to resume her diary duties. By which time Rudyard's pen was poised over the first entries in the new Bateman's Visitors Book. All the family came by turns in the first few weeks, and all were delighted with the house. By the end of the year Carrie and Rudyard had welcomed and duly recorded forty-two visitors including sixteen family. In the years to come they entertained an average of fifty visitors a year, about a third or a quarter of whom would be relations. Occasionally a visitor's name would be followed by 'f.i.p.' – Kipling's shorthand for 'fell in pond.' The first to take the plunge before the year was out was his austere uncle Edward (Poynter). It must have made his nephew's day. At irregular intervals others followed suit, including at 6.30 p.m. of an August evening in 1920: MOTHER (Carrie) F.I.P. Capital letters were used in honour of that occasion and the entry was tastefully framed – with what glee we can only imagine – with the outline of a 'dip' pen.

Kipling wanted Cope Cornford to design him a couch for his study because 'The old thing from The Elms is a blister and an offence and besides I want something bigger and broader.' (Cope Cornford was an architect. He was also naval correspondent on the *Morning Post* and a writer of historical novels.) Kipling had found some suitable timber, a log of full-bodied Jacobean oak that must have 'surprised and delighted' the carpenter's chisels when they made contact with it. But he would have no truck with Leslie's original idea. 'Who am I to have monograms and gilding and pink morocco? It is too gorgeous.' There followed a rough sketch of what he had in mind, with a broad top rail for books and pipes and two sides open for legs to kick over. 'Your sketch is lovely but lascivious – sorry I am to have to write such a word!' And when the couch duly arrived, in time for Christmas: 'It's a great – an unqualified success! C. is lying down on it even now…It is perniciously lazy and I've been wallowing on it all this afternoon. Best of all it suits the room to a hair, in tone and texture and temper…'[12]

It was through Cope Cornford that Kipling found his next motor. Or did the motor find him? It so happened that Mrs Cope Cornford's brother, one Max Lawrence, had recently joined the Lanchester Engine Company as Works Manager, and their eldest sister was headmistress of Roedean School in Brighton. In the autumn of 1901 Max paid his sisters a visit driving a demonstration Lanchester. From Brighton it was only a short run to Rottingdean and a fellow motorist still struggling with the temperamental Locomobile.

> …I suppose she will settle down some day to her conception of duty but just now her record is one of eternal and continuous breakdown. She disgraced us on June 26th when…the pumps failed to lift and we had to pump dolefully every few miles…We overhauled her on June 27th (all the day). On June 29th we laid out a trip of 19 miles out and back. I took the wife. She (the Loco) betrayed us foully 12 miles out – blew through her cylinders, leaked and laid down. It was a devil of a day…July 3rd, I went out for an evening trip – a few miles along the road. Her steam was beautiful, but she shut down her fire automatically, and amid the jeers of Brighton we crawled to the repair shop where we left her…It is true that she is noiseless, but so is a corpse and one does not get much fun out of a corpse!…Her lines are lovely; her form is elegant; the curves of her buggy-top are alone worth the price of admission. But, as a means of propulsion she is a nickel-plated fraud…

The tale of woe was signed 'Yours Locomobiliously…'[13] The journalist in him was already considering a 5000-word story (to be called 'Locoed') on her performance – or lack of – for the past ten days, to reimburse him for her repairs. No story of that name was ever written, but I think 'Steam Tactics' would have answered the description here – and met the need.

Kipling had another visitor the day Lawrence called to take him out for a trial run: the Australian poet, 'Banjo' Paterson, best known for that immortal refrain, 'Waltzing Matilda'. Paterson recalled piling into the back of the car with Kipling '...the great man as excited as a child with a new toy'. They headed for the Downs 'scattering tourists right and left'. (It had become necessary to bring the car inside the garden at The Elms and right up to the front door to avoid sightseers waiting outside.) The Lanchester climbed a hill of about one in five with nothing much below it but the English Channel. It was at this point that Kipling rashly enquired after the car's braking powers. Lawrence stopped the engine and let the car run backwards towards the edge. Paterson looked anxiously over his shoulder at the sheer drop and was preparing to bail out when the driver 'dropped a sprag and pulled her up all standing'.

As they resumed their forward journey Kipling admitted to Paterson that yes, he had been frightened. 'But I thought what a bad advertisement it would be for the Lanchester company if they killed me, so I sat tight.'[14]

It was not until the following June (1902) that Kipling acquired his first Lanchester, a 2-cylinder 10 hp air-cooled model and Number Sixteen off the assembly line. By which time he must have been heartily glad to see the last of that 'gay and meretricious swindle' of a Locomobile and her 'steam for steam's sake'. Capricious to the last, she nearly caught fire when the asbestos lagging fell off as she was being driven to her new home at Cowdray Park.

A garage bill addressed to Rudyard Kipling Esq from the Brighton Motor Works that month reveals what the present-day motorist would rather not know: that petrol cost one shilling and twopence a gallon – or three shillings for a two-gallon can. The cost of sending someone especially 'to Rottingdean in the evening to remove old tyre, refit new one – repairs to old cover at Works – adjustment of brakes and brazing brake bands etc etc' cost all of eight shillings and ten pence (about 45p).[15]

Such was the intimate size of the motor industry in those days that Kipling's new motor was delivered to the door by its inventor, Frederick Lanchester, in person. Lanchester became a regular visitor and friend-in-need to the Kiplings. The two men would speculate for hours on the reasons for the latest breakdown and swap yarns about their adventures on the road and the 'book-'em-or-bust' habits of the local constabulary. With his 'layman's delight in the expert' Kipling would have looked forward to Lanchester's visits as much for his conversation as for his expertise in getting his brain-child to *go*, where neither coaxing nor bad words had any effect. The Emancipation Act of 1896 had brought a temporary easing of motorists' problems in that a 'light locomotive' was now permitted to travel at up to fourteen mph – in practice this was reduced to twelve mph – and no longer required a man with a red flag to walk in front. On the day of its repeal thirty cars celebrated by driving in procession from London to Brighton – and it has been an annual event ever since for what are now known as veteran cars. The French with true Gallic and onomatopoeic flair, call them '*teuf-teufs*'. The Prince of Wales' evident interest in motoring had helped to get the Bill passed, if only by offsetting his mother's equally evident 'we are not amused' attitude towards those 'horrible machines...I am told that they smell exceedingly nasty and are very shaky and disagreeable conveyances altogether.' And Queen Victoria never did ride in one.

By the time Kipling joined the ranks of automobilists, the police had got their second wind and organised speed traps on the Brighton Road. They consisted of a measured distance with a hidden policeman at either end, and a third policeman stationed further down the road ready to stop and book the offending vehicle. In answer to this latest indignity, unofficial bicycle patrols, recruited from greasy-palmed locals, acted as scouts. They would peddle up and down the road on the look-out for police ambushes and warn the approaching motorist. In the fullness of time their activities were to be regulated, a yellow uniform provided – and *voilà*, the Automobile Association was born.

Cartoonists of the day made the most of what was, for them, a gift from the gods. Sketches of fat-bellied constables clutching primitive timing-equipment while trying to hide behind slim-line trees, or peering over the top of unsavoury pigsties at an approaching vehicle, poked fun at an increasingly serious situation. Even the Motor Car Act of 1903 failed to address the problem realistically when it raised the speed limit, but only to twenty mph. Many drivers were caught exceeding thirty – for the very good reason that they had no accurate means of gauging the speed of their vehicle. The anti-car lobby was still very strong. As *The Times* put it sententiously: '...the number of drivers of motor-cars who are not gentlemen would seem to be unduly large. There is no turning a cad into a gentleman, but there is such a thing as making even cads fear the law.'

Kipling, in the manner of Byron, put it rather differently.

> Thirteen as twelve my Murray always took—
> He was a publisher. The new Police
> Have neater ways of bringing men to book,
> So Juan found himself before J.P's
> Accused of storming through that placid nook
> At practically any pace you please.
> The Dogberry, and the Waterbury, made
> It fifty mile – five pounds. And Juan paid!
>
> 'The Tour'

(A Waterbury was the stop-watch used by the policeman or 'Dogberry', the blundering constable in *Much Ado About Nothing*.[16])

One way and another the owners of horseless carriages were being discriminated against and the Law's impartiality was openly questioned. Kipling took every opportunity to nail his colours to the motorists' mast by ridiculing the officious police and the quick-to-fine magistrates. ('We're making quite a lot out o' you motor gentry,' gloats the policeman in 'Steam Tactics'.) For once in his life Kipling was in conflict with the Law which previously he had admonished us to keep. 'Keep ye the Law – be swift in all obedience' ('A Song of the English'). And in the *Jungle Books*:

> Now these are the Laws of the Jungle, and many and mighty are
>   they;
> But the head and the hoof of the Law and the haunch and the
>   hump is – Obey!

Unless, that is, you were a motorist on the King's Highway...

Kipling, gamekeeper turned poacher, could not cap Lanchester's best motoring story, but he could – and did – use it. And the true tale of how Lanchester abducted a policeman, drove him for many miles through the countryside and got away with it later in court, is now recorded for all time in motoring history; and with fictional adjustments, in 'Steam Tactics'.

His first Lanchester appears in the tale as 'the big, black, black-dashed, tonneaued twenty-four-horse Octopod that sang like a six-inch shell' across the Sussex Downs, her driver steering by 'a careless knee over the tiller that the ordinary expert puts under his arm-pit' – a favourite trick of the youngest Lanchester brother, George – and at a speed that made the captive policeman feel sick and Pyecroft religious: well in excess of the twelve mph speed limit.

"'He's steering with 'is little hind-legs," said Pyecroft. "Stand up and look at him, Robert. You'll never see such a sight again.!"

"Nor don't want to," was our guest's reply. "Five 'undred pounds wouldn't begin to cover 'is fines even since I've been with him.'"

'Robert', the policeman who has apprehended them for exceeding the speed limit over a measured quarter-mile – at a speed the vehicle was not even capable of – is in gleeful mood. He is also in plain clothes – without badge or authority; which is why he is persuaded to take a lift, first in the steam car and then in the Octopod. After a wild drive all up and down Sussex he is eventually dumped in a local landowner's private zoo, surrounded by kangaroos, zebras and beavers, unable to believe his eyes. When last seen the poor man is on his knees, praying for deliverance. (This was written long before wildlife parks had become the preserve of our impoverished aristocracy. But, as it happened, there was just such a private zoo in Sussex and shortly before Kipling started writing 'Steam Tactics' he drove over to Leonardslee in his new motor to take a look at it.)

When they were not talking about motor cars, Lanchester and Kipling would have enjoyed discovering the many parallels in their lives. Lanchester, a brilliant inventor, engineer and designer was also born of artistic parents with little money to spare. Like Kipling he had shown an early aptitude for what was to be his life's work and all-consuming passion; in Lanchester's case by excelling in maths and the sciences, whereas the stringing together of words, even to the obligatory letters home, was an ordeal requiring assistance. In much the same way that Kipling and figures had never enjoyed a close relationship. Like Kipling, too, he responded to excellence in his teachers, but delighted in playing up the less competent. Sent out of the form one day, Lanchester plunged the whole building into darkness by closing the main gas cock – just as Stalky had done in 'The Last Term'. (Why these taps were not kept safely under lock and key remains a mystery, given their irresistible attraction for suggestible boys seeking a little light – or in this case, dark – relief from their studies.) And when Lanchester as a young man was living frugally in London, he too had patronised Harris's sausage shops for twopenny-worth of sausage and mash.

His first love was aeronautical research and he had met and admired Professor Langley (the man who had so nearly beaten the Wright Brothers into the history books) at the Smithsonian Institute in America. As had Kipling. But it was early days for aerodynamics and Lanchester turned to the designing of automobiles instead. One of his experimental cars had won a Gold Medal and the Lanchester Engine Company was formed when his two younger brothers, Frank and George joined him. They had been dubbed 'The Unholy Trinity' – how Kipling would have delighted in the sobriquet – by their God-fearing Birmingham neighbours, because of their habit of working on their experiments instead of going to church on Sundays. Kipling, no church-goer himself, had his own way of setting the Sabbath apart, reading from the Bible (usually St Paul, with Ecclesiasticus as his 'refuge'[17]) and sometimes composing hymns whose 'Amen' might be the waste-paper basket – unless, like the 'Recessional', rescued by other hands.

(So too, I realise in retrospect, did my father set Sundays apart in his own way and for similar deep-rooted beliefs. And both men shared a common Wesleyan ancestry. My father's Sunday morning ritual was always the same: to play the organ that had been his father's – a gift from the Ladies of the local Bible Class – filling the house with glorious swelling chords that would set the little brass ornaments trembling on the mantelpiece, and our neighbours opening their windows in order to share the 'recital' with us. I regret to say that as a child I did not appreciate organ music, as I do today.)

From its superb springing and pre-selector mechanism right down to its foot bulb horn, the Lanchester was both innovative and comfortable, its designer the largely unsung father of the British motor car. An intriguing plus was its detachable and interchangeable body, a godsend to a storyteller like Kipling. And sure enough, in 'The Horse Marines' and 'A Tour of Inspection' the narrator, with Pyecroft's connivance, makes full and comical use of its potential for disguise.

Another guest at Bateman's during those early motoring days when everything was 'a guess or an experiment' was the Punch cartoonist L Raven-Hill who had been the original illustrator of *Stalky & Co*. He too was introduced to the 'joys' of the open road. Shortly afterwards there appeared in *Punch* a cartoon depicting two motor cars, one of them obviously a Lanchester. Beneath it was the caption: 'Friend: "Going about thirty, are we? But don't you run some risk of being pulled up for exceeding the legal pace?"

'Owner of Lanchester: "Not in a sober, respectable-looking car like this. Of course, if you go about in a blatant, brass-bound, scarlet-padded, snorting, foreign affair, like that, you are bound to be dropped on, no matter how slow you go!"'

Both the car and the caption were Kipling's. The Lanchester chairman, recognising the car, lost no time in writing to thank *Punch's* editor for the splendid free advertisement on his centre pages. The editor was not impressed, but honour was satisfied when the chairman offered to buy the original sketch for £25.

From time to time Lanchester would send Kipling, non-driver though he was, an experimental model for his valued comments. For true to form he had acquired as much technical know-how about the internal combustion engine and its four-stroke cycle (induction, compression, explosion, exhaust), as half-a-dozen chauffeur/mechanics put together. According to George Lanchester, Kipling sent them many constructive and amusing reports on their new cars. One of these 'experiments' was an 18 hp, faster but less tractable model than its predecessors. Kipling called her Jane Cakebread, after a notorious Cockney character of the day who had ninety-three convictions for being drunk and disorderly in a single year. The motor lived up to her nickname. One day a wire arrived at the Birmingham works: 'Jane disembowelled on village green Ditchling. Pray remove your disorderly experiment.'[18] Later, the same Jane, put together again, although not for long, was driven by her designer, Kipling beside him, on a trial run to Worthing. And there, in the words of the poet, she fainted. Not until the two men had littered the roadside with almost every removable part under the scornful eyes of the locals, could they get at the trouble and put it right. In the early days every repair had to be done from below, which often meant that the driver was under the car as much as he was in it.

When the next summons from Kipling arrived at the works, Archie Millership was sent down to investigate. Millership was the consummate driver who delighted in thinking up new ways of showing off the Lanchester's versatility. He was the first to drive to the top of Great Orme's Head, and the first – and one would hope, the last – to drive up the steps of the Crystal Palace. There had been no indication of the nature of the trouble in this latest summons, and at dinner on the night of Millership's arrival at Bateman's there appeared to be an embargo on the subject of motors and their ailments.

It was arranged that he would present himself at ten the next morning, when they would try out the car together. And still nothing had been said. Millership, by now more than a little perturbed, decided to arrive half an hour early in the hopes of a quiet word with the chauffeur. But there was no sign of chauffeur or motor and the coach-house doors were securely locked. Millership kicked his heels until the appointed hour when he presented himself at the front door. As he did so the familiar sound of the motor was heard, the front door opened and Mr and Mrs Kipling appeared dressed in all-enveloping macintoshes and hoods which they proceeded to pull over their heads. The mystery deepened for it was a beautiful summer's day. Millership drove to the special test hill with the chauffeur beside him and the hooded pair seated in the tonneau. They ascended the hill, the car climbing well. There were surprised sounds from the tonneau, followed by a request for a repeat run. Something was going to happen, but *what?* Halfway up the hill the second time there were shouts from behind: 'Here it is!' Two heads were ducked as a cascade of boiling water and steam burst out of the water tank amidships, drenching the passengers...And that was the end of Kipling's disorderly experiment.

Writing to Millership thirty years later Kipling reminded him of the occasion 'when the old car erupted like Krakatoa in the middle, and you took off your macintosh and stuffed it into the crater. It was beautiful "salesmanship"'.[19]

And then came 'Amelia' Lanchester. Now Amelia, we are told, was a virgin. Although why she was, or indeed how she could be, given basic engineering principles, is not made clear. But we do know why he called her '...the petrol-piddling descendant of untold she-dogs'. Amelia had let her owner down badly and in front of Henry James, to whom all things mechanical were highly suspect and the 'song of steam' incomprehensible. To make matters worse the proud owner had dared to boast about Amelia, '...how we would drive him [James] all over Sussex in two hours...' And now there she was, 'took with a cataleptic trance...stark and motionless' outside James' house in Rye where Rudyard and Carrie had gone over for lunch. Henry James was in his element and according to Kipling, his 'monologue over her immobile carcase – with all the machinery exposed and our engineer underneath growing progressively blacker – would have been cheap at the price of several wrecked cars.'[20]

Writing from South Africa two years later when time and distance had worked their enchantment – and an innocuous bicycle was his number one form of transport – Kipling set down his thoughts on motoring and England. By then the two were inextricably linked.

'I like motoring because I have suffered for its sake.' He recalls his 'agonies, shames, delays, rages, chills...' and so on over the last 'seven' years on the road [four would be nearer the mark]. 'Any fool can invent anything, as any fool can wait to buy the invention when it is thoroughly perfected; but the men to reverence, to admire, to write odes and erect statues to, are those Prometheuses and Ixions (maniacs, you used to call us) who chase the inchoate idea to fixity up and down the King's Highway with their red right shoulders to the wheel. Yes, I love because I have suffered...in the cause of Humanity.' He touches on the Moral Aspect of Things – how a car demands absolute sobriety, not just from the driver of the motor car but from every other road-user, from the coachman and carrier to the pedestrian.

> I have seen men walking on the road suddenly and accurately distinguish between their left hand and their right, and this not for political reasons...

> But the chief end of my car...is the discovery of England. To me it is a land full of stupefying marvels and mysteries; and a day in the car in an English county is a day in some fairy museum where all the exhibits are alive and real...Horses, after all, are only horses; but the car is a time-machine on which one can slide from one century to another at no more trouble than the pushing forward of a lever. On a morning I have seen the Assizes, javelin-men and all, come into a cathedral town; by noon I was skirting a new-built convent for expelled French nuns; before sundown I was watching the Channel Fleet off Selsea Bill, and after dark I nearly broke a fox's back on a Roman road. You who were born and bred

in the land naturally take such trifles for granted, but to me it is still miraculous that if I want petrol in a hurry I must either pass the place where Sir John Lade lived, or the garden where Jack Cade was killed. In Africa one has only to put the miles under and go on; but in England the dead, twelve coffin deep, clutch hold of my wheels at every turn, till I sometimes wonder that the very road does not bleed. *That* is the real joy of motoring – the exploration of this amazing England...[21]

At the beginning of that year, 1904, the *Daily Mail* had published a set of his verse parodies: 'The Muse among the Motors'. What fun he must have had in writing them, combining a literary form that had been a favourite pastime since childhood with what had undoubtedly become the favourite non-literary pastime of his adult years.

The Muse takes him via Chaucer ('The Justice's Tale') and Ben Jonson ('To a Lady, Persuading her to a Car'), to Donne ('The Progress of the Spark'), and so on through Wordsworth, Tennyson, Browning and Others.

Later he was to return to the parodies for some more fun with words, more gilding of brass bonnets. One of them was a short play, *The Marrèd Drives of Windsor*, in which Falstaff is 'habited as a motorist', Prince Henry is up before the Lord Chief Justice for exceeding the speed-limit and leaving his car unattended in the street, Shylock's bond is a Third Party Risks Policy – and a motorised Ariel sings a song that begins:

Where the car slips there slip I—
In a sunbeam's path I lie!...

---

1 *SoM.*
2 Meryl Macdonald, *Kipling the Motoring Man*, National Trust, 1983.
3 'A Smuggler's Song', *Puck of Pook's Hill*, 1906.
4 *SoM.*
5 *ibid.*
6 Michael Smith (Personal Information).
7 'Steam Tactics', 1902, *Traffics & Discoveries*, 1904.
8 Pinney.
9 'Steam Tactics'.
10 *SoM.*
11 RK to Leslie Cope Cornford, 1902, LCC (Personal file).
12 *ibid.*
13 RK letter published in American magazine, *The Steam Automobile*, nd KJ.
14 Paterson.
15 KJ.

16 'The Tour' (Byron), 'The Muse Among the Motors', 1904.
17 Cohen, RK to HRH.
18 P W Kingsford, *F W Lanchester, A Life of an Engineer*, Edward Arnold, 1960, Anthony Bird & F W Hutton-Stott, *Lanchester Motor Cars*, Cassell 1965.
19 Millership Papers, Birmingham Museums and Art Gallery.
20 RK to Norton, 1902, *Letters*, Vol 3.
21 RK, published letter in *The Complete Motorist*, Filson Young, 1904.

CHAPTER NINE

Haunted landscapes;
and a Viking galley 'beyond the world's end'

Though all the rest were all my share,
With equal soul I'd see
Her nine-and-thirty sisters fair,
Yet none more fair than she.
Choose ye your need from Thames to Tweed,
And I will choose instead
Such lands as lie 'twixt Rake and Rye,
Black Down and Beachy Head.

'Sussex'

More from insight than optimism Kipling had started to write his 'Sussex' verses early in 1902 – and in South Africa – before the property that was to be his home for the rest of his life came on the market again.

Bateman's, an ironmaster's house, was built by 1634 at a time when the Wealden iron industry was at its height and the Weald echoed to the roar of iron forges and mills. It is difficult to believe today that the peaceful East Sussex countryside was once one of England's earliest 'black countries'; at least until the end of the eighteenth century when the discovery of cheap coal in the Midlands brought about its demise.

In the first great survey of England in 1586 the Weald was 'full of iron in sundry places where for the making and fining where of there bee furnaces on every side and a huge deale of wood is yearly spent, to which purpose divers brookes in many places are brought to runne in one chanell and sundry medowes turned into pooles and waters, that they might bee of power sufficient to drive hammer milles which beating upon the iron resound all over the places adjoining.' (sic)[1]

With Bateman's surrounded by several thriving forges, it is unlikely that the privacy-loving Kipling would have even considered living there when it was new, however impressive its modern (Jacobean) architecture and gleaming local sandstone. Apart from anything else the consumption of oak trees would have distressed him; even more than it had Elizabeth 1. The Virgin Queen could not stop the alarming depredations of the dense woodlands that once covered three-quarters of Sussex. The great trees were being felled in their thousands to furnish her navy, or coppiced for charcoal for smelting its weaponry. (Three thousand mature oak trees were needed to build one man-o-war: it does not bear thinking about.) It was a repetition of Roman times when the local industry had first peaked in order to meet the demands of the Roman legions and their fleet.

Bateman's was 'a good and peaceable place standing in terraced lawns nigh to a walled garden of old red brick, and two fat-headed oast-houses with red brick stomachs, and an aged silver-grey dovecot on top. There is what they call a river at the bottom of the lawn. It appears on all maps and that, except after very heavy rains, is the only place where it puts in any appearance...'[2] But there Kipling spoke too soon. He was to be 'up to the neck in the Noah's Ark trade'[3] more than once in the years ahead. (In 1909 for instance they had the biggest flood since 1852: the dynamo was flooded, water came up to the south hall door and was waist deep on the tennis court, all Kipling's beehives were swept away and a pig was floated out of his stye at Dudwell.[4])

'What do you find to do in the country?' puzzled town-dwellers often ask their country cousins. 'Everything except time to do it,'[5] was Kipling's reply. It had not taken him long to come to that conclusion, for now he was not only a house-holder but a landowner too. He had a neglected farm and a water mill on his hands; and he had unsatisfactory tenants. Ten years' earlier in New England he had observed that 'a farm, like an arch, is never at rest'[6] Or shouldn't be. From now on, whether he liked it or not, agricultural matters were to play an important part in his daily life. And he did like it, this link with the land – of which a few Sussex acres were now his responsibility, 'his fraction of England'.

Shortly before Christmas Kipling wrote to Rider Haggard to congratulate him on his just-published 'magnum opus', which he and Carrie had found altogether fascinating and chock-full of instruction. He was not referring to Haggard's latest adventure story, but to a massive two-volume work, *Rural England*, a subject close to Haggard's heart and one that he had been researching up and down the country for the past two years. It presented a disturbing picture of rural decay at a time of agricultural crisis, when imported foodstuffs were cheaper to buy than the home-produced, and when the best of the young men were leaving their villages for the dubious advantages of life in the towns. By now Kipling was at the leading edge of the problem himself and acutely aware of its implications.

Andrew Lang had introduced the two writers soon after Kipling's arrival in London in 1889. They struck up a friendship that was to last until Haggard's death (1925); years during which they corresponded, met at irregular intervals and even worked together, each man genuinely admiring the other's writing. (Kipling had made several references to Haggard's stories in his own work, and attributed the germ of his Mowgli tales to a 'chance sentence' in Haggard's *Nada the Lily*.[7])

They had much in common apart from each possessing odd-sounding names. So odd were they that the brother of one of Kipling's new friends at the Savile Club, (J K Stephen) peeved at all the fuss made of their owners, composed some light verse which ended looking forward to a time...

> When the world shall cease to wonder
> At the genius of an ass,
> And a boy's eccentric blunder
> Shall not bring success to pass...
> When there stands a muzzled stripling,
> Mute, beside a muzzled bore:
> When the Rudyards cease from kipling
> And the Haggards Ride no more.

Far from taking offence at the rhyme, both men wished they had thought of it first.

Going to university had not been an option for either of them. Where Rudyard had returned to India to work when his schooldays were over, Haggard had been sent out to South Africa – whence the background for his hugely-popular African novels. He returned to England to study law, but gave it up in favour of rural life on the small family estate in Norfolk, on the strength of the success of *King Solomon's Mines*. When he was not writing adventure stories he was researching and writing about his consuming passion, English agriculture and the rural economy. 1902 saw the publication of his magnum opus that had kept Rudyard and Carrie reading its eleven hundred odd pages for more than a week '...with deep joy...and admiration.'

But, Kipling chided his old friend: '...I am exceedingly disappointed and wrath...that you did not devote at least 200 pp. to my own county. Sussex, Sir, has been badly treated by you.'[8] Sussex was covered in thirty-three pages which would have been a fair division had all forty counties been included. But Haggard investigated only twenty-six, of which two were Jersey and Guernsey, and the number of pages devoted to each county varied considerably: from a scant seven for Cornwall to a magnificent 101 for Lincolnshire. So Kipling, with all the enthusiasm of the new landowner, could be said to have a point. He had, of course, lived in the county for five years before buying Bateman's; long enough in his eyes, if not in the locals', to account for the proprietorial air.

Hops were grown in East Sussex and Bateman's farm was no exception. Within a week of moving in he had taken Elsie and John to see how they were roasted. Haggard's comment that they were a very expensive crop to grow provoked a rueful reply. With bad tenants on his good hop land he 'might as well keep a small Monte Carlo for hops are a demoralizing gamble'. On the other hand if he grubbed them out altogether there would be no more tenants.

Then there was the 'blessed' mill that was useful for grinding pig food, which meant that any tenant taking it would want a few acres of land to go with it. In the meantime he was spending over two hundred pounds making neglected cottages 'like filthy dog-kennels' habitable.

Over the years Haggard visited Bateman's from time to time and gave 'of his ample land wisdom…His comings were always a joy to us and the children, who followed him like hounds in the hope of "more South African stories."'[9] Kipling envied Haggard's gift for inspiring affection at short notice, particularly with children. 'It must be nice,' he told him years later. He hadn't that gift. '…like olives and caviare and asafoetida, I'm an acquired taste, stealing slowly on the senses.'[10]

Discovering Sussex for Kipling meant not just familiarising himself with the landscape between the whale-backed downs and the zinc-blue Channel, but unravelling its restless history of invasion and counter-invasion, from Roman to Norman. And here 'Allah the Dispenser of Events' dealt kindly with him. When he sank a well on his land (for those cottages) the bronze cheek of a Roman horse-bit was unearthed, a Jacobean tobacco-pipe and a worn Cromwellian latten spoon found. When an old pond that might once have been a marl-pit or even a mine-head, was cleaned out they dredged up 'two intact Elizabethan "sealed quarts"…all pearly with the patina of centuries…[and] a perfectly polished Neolithic axe-head with but one chip on its still venomous edge.'[11]

Kipling was in his element. It was as if the long-dead past had been waiting for him alone before revealing its hidden treasures. Had not Ambrose on one of his visits suggested he write a yarn about Roman times in Sussex? The idea intrigued him and he had demanded to know more. Write about an old Centurion telling his experiences to his children, said his cousin. What was the Centurion's name? (Names – the right names – were as gold in the Kipling household.) Parnesius, said Ambrose. And the name stuck in his head.

Not far off was a little valley running from 'Nowhere to Nothing-at-all' where stood the overgrown slag-heap of an ancient forge that was said to have been worked by the Phoenicians and Romans, and since then until the mid-eighteenth century. 'The ghost of a road climbed up out of this arena, and crossed our fields, where it was known as "The Gunway", and popularly connected with Armada times. Every foot of that little corner was alive with ghosts and shadows.'[12] He was deeply interested in haunted landscapes and the possibility of travelling back into past events which remained suspended in time and space.

> See you the dimpled track that runs,
> All hollow through the wheat?
> O that was where they hauled the guns
> That smote King Philip's fleet.[13]

But there were other and domestic matters demanding his attention. As he admitted in his autobiography: 'The House was not of a type to present to servants by lamp or candle-light.' Or anyone else of a sensitive disposition for that matter. He contemplated harnessing the millpond to run a turbine to generate electricity for the house, and (according to his autobiography), happening to meet the designer of the Aswan Dam, put the idea to him. The result was a foregone conclusion. The new owner of Bateman's was politely elbowed out of the driving seat: '"Dam?" said he. "*You* don't know anything about dams or turbines. *I'll* come and look."' And so he did, accurately foretelling the exact horsepower they would get out of their turbine – '"Four and a half and no more"',[14] while advising them not to run their light cable on poles, but to bury it. On 5th August 1903 Kipling spent the day with a gang of workmen while the cable was laid connecting the dynamo with the stables. By now he knew a thing or two about turbines that would not come amiss. (However, memory plays tricks on us all, and not for the first time Kipling had telescoped two separate happenings into one. He actually met Sir William Willcocks, 'one of the most interesting chaps I have ever met,'[15] at a weekend house-party in 1912, following which the great irrigation expert lunched at Bateman's and gave his host good advice on how to manage the brook.)

During these absorbing operations he got to know the locals who came of a smuggling, sheep-stealing stock – according to the guide-books. But most of them were artists or craftsmen, whether in stone or timber, or wood-cutting, or drain-laying.

> The only thing that ever shook them was when we cut a little
> under the Mill foundations to fix the turbine; and found that
> she sat on a crib or raft of two-foot-square elm logs. What we
> took came out, to all appearance, as untouched as when it

had been put under water. Yet, in an hour, the great baulk, exposed to air, became silver dust, and the men stood round marvelling. There was one among them, close upon seventy when we first met, a poacher by heredity and instinct, a gentleman who, when his need to drink was on him, which was not too often, absented himself and had it out alone; and he was more 'one with nature' than whole parlours full of poets.[16]

This wonderful character was of course the original of old Hobden the hedger, the 'Have it as you're minded. I dunno as I should if I was you' Hobden, of whom the world was to hear more; together with the 'fairly long-lived' Puck and the magic of Oak, Ash and Thorn.

The trail was getting warmer even while he was engaged on other and very different work for his next book, *Traffics and Discoveries*. (The title is taken from Hakluyt's *The Principal Navigations, Voyages, Traffics and Discoveries of the English Nation, 1589-1600* that had so fascinated him as a schoolboy and volumes of which are to be found on his study bookshelves at Bateman's.) This is the book in which 'Steam Tactics', 'They' and 'Wireless' are collected, in which Petty Officer Pyecroft makes his first appearance in tales of the Senior Service, and the unfathomable 'Mrs Bathurst' turns her 'blindish' look on the world through a cinematograph screen. 'Mrs Bathurst' had been at the back of his mind for three years, finally coming away while he was in South Africa early in 1904. It is not surprising he stuck to his maxim, 'so long as you have breath on no provocation explain',[17] because I am not at all sure he could have explained Mrs Bathurst. The story has mystified scholars, readers and fellow writers (see P G Wodehouse's *Performing Flea*, for instance) since the day it was published. He would often keep stories by him which shortened themselves yearly with the help of a camel hair brush and some Indian ink. It is generally agreed that he overdid the brushwork in this tale, but not whether this was done deliberately. What is certain is the amount of ink that has been expended on so-called solutions to the mystery ever since its publication over ninety years ago.

Let us take a look at 'Wireless', a story based on scientific fact and therefore easier to fathom. At least it should be.

Marconi's experiments with radio telegraphy had first come to Kipling's attention when he sailed with the Channel Squadron and saw how Morse-messages were exchanged between the ships in convoy. Then one day the inventor himself came to lunch at The Elms. His host encouraged Marconi to talk about his work and after an hour Kipling felt he knew as much about radio telegraphy as it was possible for a layman to understand. 'Wireless', first published in August 1902, was in part the outcome of that meeting.

The narrator is invited to be present in the back room of his local chemist's shop where Mr Cashell's nephew is preparing to receive a wireless communication from Poole. If everything was in order it was due about midnight via an installation-pole on the roof.

'For reasons of my own,' says the narrator, 'I was deeply interested in Marconi experiments at their outset in England.' Young Mr Cashell, who is an electrician, explains how it works...'He picked up a glass tube not much thicker than a thermometer, in which, almost touching were two tiny silver plugs, and between them an infinitesimal pinch of metallic dust.

"That's all," he said proudly..."That is the thing that will reveal to us the Powers – whatever the Powers may be – at work – through space – a long distance away."' A little later young Mr Cashell adjusts some wire 'that crackled from time to time with the tense, knuckle-stretching sound of the electric spark..."The pinch of dust, you see, is nickel-filings. The Hertzian waves...come out of space from the station that despatches 'em, and all these little particles are attracted together – cohere, we call it – for just so long as the current passes through them. Now, it's important to remember that the current is an induced current. There are a good many kinds of induction..."'

When asked to explain what induction is, untechnically: "...when a current of electricity passes through a wire there's a lot of magnetism present round that wire; and if you put another wire parallel to, and within what we call its magnetic field – why then the second wire will also become charged with electricity...on its own account."'

Why is Kipling going into such technical detail for the benefit of his largely untechnical readers? We have only to move into the front of the shop again to realise that there is more than one layer to this story. We discover the chemist's new assistant, Mr Shaynor, talking to a young woman with 'a rich and promising voice that well matched her outline'. She is determined to drag him out for a walk 'round by St Agnes', in spite of the bitter cold night and his cough. Shaynor is a consumptive, but he is also obsessed with Fanny Brand, and so goes out with her.

When Shaynor returns, chilled through, the narrator (who is obviously familiar with his surroundings) mixes him a warming potion from the apothecary's store. It sends Shaynor into a kind of trance, during which he writes down lines from Keats, at first experimentally, as if searching for the right word or phrase – as if he were the poet himself. (Keats also was a consumptive, had studied medicine and was obsessed with a girl called Fanny Brawne. He wrote 'The Eve of St Agnes', the poem Shaynor was quoting – and Kipling knew something about spirit writing through his sister's activities.) Out of his trance again, Shaynor does not recognise the lines the narrator quotes back at him; nor has he ever read Keats.

While all this has been going on, young Cashell in the back room has been listening in to two men-o-war off the Isle of Wight trying without much success to talk to each other over their Marconis.

'Neither can read the other's messages, but all their messages are being taken in by our receiver here.'

'How wonderful!' I said. 'Do you mean we're overhearing Portsmouth ships trying to talk to each other – that we're eavesdropping across half South England?'

'Just that. Their transmitters are all right, but their receivers are out of order…Nothing clear.'

'Why is that?'

'God knows – and Science will know tomorrow. Perhaps the induction is faulty; perhaps the receivers aren't tuned to receive just the number of vibrations per second that the transmitter sends. Only a word here and there. Just enough to tantalise.'

Again the Morse sprang to life.

'That's one of 'em complaining now. Listen: "Disheartening – most disheartening." It's quite pathetic. Have you ever seen a spiritualistic seance? It reminds me of that sometimes – odds and ends of messages coming out of nowhere – a word here and there – no good at all.'

'But mediums are all impostors,' said Mr Shaynor, in the doorway…'They only do it for the money they can make. I've seen 'em.'

'Here's Poole, at last – clear as a bell. Now we shan't be long.' Mr Cashell rattled the keys merrily. 'Anything you'd like to tell 'em?'

'No, I don't think so,' I said. 'I'll go home and get to bed. I'm feeling a little tired.'

Suddenly the narrator has heard enough. But Kipling is drawing a parallel between the way wireless works, the power of magnetic fields that cause electrical currents to pass from one wire to another, and the power of one mind, given the crucial wavelength, to pick up the thoughts of another across space and time. (As in 'The Finest Story in the World'?) While confirming its truth he cannot condone its practice.

––––––––––

We first meet Petty-officer Emanuel Pyecroft in 'The Bonds of Discipline' and 'Their Lawful Occasions'. He is 'a square man with remarkable eyes' who when asked by the narrator what he drinks, replies: '"Only water. Warm water, with a little whisky an' sugar an' per'aps a lemon."' Clearly a man of original thought. His friend and shipmate, Hinchcliffe, a first-class engine-room artificer, is unique in other ways. 'If you hand 'im a drum of oil an' leave 'im alone, he can coax a stolen bicycle to do typewritin'.' Kipling sat down to write 'Their Lawful Occasions' a few days after spending two memorable weeks at sea on manoeuvres with the fleet.

The narrator travels down to Portland to join Blue Fleet, is delayed *en route*, finds Blue Fleet has already sailed, and falls in with an intriguingly-spurred Pyecroft who is second in command of torpedo-boat No 267, also heavily disguised; and with war between Blue and Red Fleets due to start at midnight.

> The wind went down with the sunset—
> The fog came up with the tide,
> When the Witch of the North took an Egg-shell
> With a little Blue Devil inside.

Pyecroft suggests the narrator should 'buy an 'am an' see life,' which being translated, is an invitation to join them – with porcine provisions – in the torpedo-boat rather than accept the offered berth in a high-and-mighty ship of the line with all mod con.

'It was a clear dark summer night, and from time to time I laughed happily to myself. The adventure was pre-ordained on the face of it. Pyecroft alone, spurred or barefoot, would have drawn me very far from the paths of circumspection. His advice to buy a ham and see life clinched it.'

He sees life: hanging limply over the rail at dawn ('This lop is what fetches it up'); consorting with Hinchcliffe in the 'packed and dancing engine-room, when Moorshed (the nineteen-year old Number One) suggested "whacking her up" to eighteen knots, to see if she would stand it' – the floor was already ankle-deep in a creamy batter of oil and water; and the next night in thick fog and a collapsible dinghy, feeling their way round the iron flanks of two Red Fleet cruisers discovered at anchor in Torbay – to witness the stencilling thereon of the tell-tale 'torpedo' marks. This marking of the enemy was not achieved without the diversionary tactics of the crew of a Brixham trawler with which 267 had earlier been in slight collision and who, subsequently primed with service rum, were now trying to sell the navy fish.

> The wind got up with the morning,
> And the fog blew off with the rain,
> When the Witch of the North saw the Egg-shell
> And the little Blue Devil again.
> 'Did you swim?' she said. 'Did you sink?' she said,
> And the little Blue Devil replied:
> 'For myself I swam, but I *think*,' he said,
> 'There's somebody sinking outside.'
>
> 'The Egg-Shell'

In between the farce there are moments of pure description, and once again it is the seascape that provides the inspiration.

> The sky behind us whitened…and the first dawn drove down the Channel, tipping the wave-tops with a chill glare. To me that round wind which runs before the true day has ever been fortunate and of good omen. It cleared the trouble from my body, and set my soul dancing to 267's heel and toe across the northerly set of the waves – such waves as I had often watched contemptuously from the deck of a ten-thousand-ton liner. They shouldered our little hull sideways and passed, scalloped and splayed out, towards the coast, carrying our white wake in loops along their hollow backs. In succession we looked down a lead-gray cutting of water for half a clear mile, were flung up on its ridge, beheld the Channel traffic – full-sailed to that fair breeze – all about us, and swung slantwise, light as a bladder, elastic as a basket, into the next furrow. Then the sun found us, struck the wet gray bows to living, leaping opal, the colourless deep to hard sapphire, the many sails to pearl, and the little steam-plume of our escape to an inconstant rainbow.

A month after their move to Bateman's the *Just So Stories* was published; those enchanting tales written to be read aloud, 'O Best Beloved', to the very young. The first three, 'How the Whale got his Throat', 'the Camel got his Hump' and 'the Rhinoceros got his Skin', had been published in an American magazine a few years earlier when Josephine was still alive and the doting father had two little 'girl-daughters' to read them to.

Why 'Just So'? He explained why in the introductory paragraph. '...in the evening there were stories meant to put Effie to sleep, and you were not allowed to alter those by one single little word. They had to be told just so, or Effie would wake up and put back the missing sentence. So at last they came to be like charms, all three of them...Of course little people are not alike, but I think if you catch some Effie rather tired and rather sleepy at the end of the day, and if you begin in a low voice and tell the tales precisely as I have written them down, you will find that Effie will presently curl up and go to sleep.'

Was this why he had an unusual dread of his children learning to read too early – because it would exclude him from their bedtime ritual? Those wonderful incantatory phrases just *had* to be read aloud.

Kipling illustrated the *Just So Stories* himself, the only one of his books to get this treatment; and although as we have seen, he never resented criticism of his writing, he could be quite touchy about criticism of his art-work. He took enormous pains over the Indian ink drawings and derived the greatest pleasure from his task. (Over some of them, however, he was 'grieved to the guts' when he saw them and told Cornford he would do some new ones for the next edition. I do not believe he did, but he certainly altered The Animal's head *in situ* in the copy handed down to me.) A detailed study of the illustrations reveals a treasure trove for all ages; in their comic ingenuity some of them are stories in themselves, offering cryptograms, hieroglyphs, runic writing and so on that cry out to be deciphered. But first you need good eyesight and a strong magnifying glass, and for some of them, the help of an expert too. How he managed to execute them at all with his poor eyesight is hard to imagine, although much of the drawing was done during their South African winters when the light would have been on his side. And it was there in the Cape that he first read the stories to Elsie and John and demanded to know what they thought of them.

In the years to come he was to have problems with illustrators, as many authors do, and he commiserated with Haggard over the 'foul' illustrations to his 'Ayesha'. 'Pity one can't sprinkle lime over illustrators – same as slugs.'[18] Even so, the only drawings Kipling indulged in after the *Just So Stories* were the lightning pen and ink sketches that decorated much of his personal correspondence, particularly his letters to the children. It had become a family tradition, like his father and uncle Ned before him.

In 1903, the year that saw the Wright Brothers taking to the air for the first time in a heavier-than-air machine, Kipling finally sold

Naulakha, at a loss. It was the end of a chapter of his life which had brought him great happiness and an abiding sorrow. (Life was arranged, he said towards the end of his span, that the greater the happiness the greater the pain.[19]) He would never set foot in North America again, although he crossed the Atlantic several times in the years ahead; and once in his imagination – in the air.

'With the Night Mail' took him only five weeks to write (in 1904) and was a 'keen pleasure' to him. The story concerns a crossing of the Atlantic on a regular Postal Packet airliner flight in 2000 AD when navigation is by cloud-piercing light beams. In it Kipling predicts the use of gas-turbines, radio-telephony, wide-ranging weather forecasts and, something else we take for granted today, world-wide flying control. Technical detail throughout is stunning; in particular the description of an electric storm.

> The only warning is the electric skin-tension (I feel as though I were a lace-maker's pillow) and an irritability which the gibbering of the General Communicator increases almost to hysteria...The pits of gloom about us begin to fill with very faintly luminous films – wreathing and uneasy shapes. One forms itself into a globe of pale flame that waits shivering with eagerness till we sweep by. It leaps monstrously across the blackness, alights on the precise tip of our nose, pirouettes there an instant, and swings off. Our roaring bow sinks as though that light were lead – sinks and recovers to lurch and stumble again beneath the next blow-out...Our bow clothes itself in blue flame and falls like a sword. No human skill can keep pace with the changing tensions. A vortex has us by the beak and we dive down a two-thousand foot slant at an angle (the dip-dial and my bouncing body record it) of thirty-five. Our turbines scream shrilly; the propellers cannot bite on the thin air; Tim shunts the lift out of five tanks at once and by sheer weight drives her bulletwise through the maelstrom till she cushions with a jar on an up-gust, three thousand feet below.

When the storm is over so too is the night...

> 'Come to the after-colloid. I'll show you something.'...Tim slides open the aft colloid and reveals the curve of the world – the ocean's deepest purple – edged with fuming and intolerable gold. Then the Sun rises and through the colloid strikes out our lamps. Tim scowls in his face.

'Squirrels in a cage,' he mutters. 'That's all we are. He's going twice as fast as us. Just you wait a few years, my shining friend and we'll take steps that will amaze you. We'll Joshua you!'

Kipling was not the only one to derive pleasure from its writing: so too did the crew of the R34 (the British airship) when they made the first double crossing of the Atlantic fifteen years later. A pocket edition of *Actions and Reactions* (the volume in which the story is collected) was the one book the crew took with them on the voyage, and 'With the Night Mail' the one story they all read over and over again, astonished at its technical accuracy. Their Log Book for the westward-bound journey shows that they too first sighted land at Trinity Bay, as had Kipling's fictional crew. To celebrate this 'coincidence' Kipling presented the senior officer on the flight with a signed copy of the book. In return he received the actual pocket edition they had carried with them, inscribed with the signatures of all the crew 'as a memento of the first double crossing of the Atlantic'. (There was a stowaway on the outward journey; it would be interesting to know what became of him.) Kipling felt doubly proud: for the gift of the book and all that that meant to him – and for the special medal which the R34 had brought back to be presented to him from New York's President of the Joan of Arc Statue Committee. A great admirer of Joan, Kipling was deeply touched and honoured to receive it.

(Three years after writing 'With the Night Mail' he was to return to the same theme, but the story, 'As Easy as ABC', would take much longer to write, being re-drafted almost yearly until its publication in 1912. The year is now 2065 AD when 'easy communications nowadays, and lack of privacy in the past, have killed all curiosity among mankind...' and where 'Democracy is Disease'. It reflects his own increasing pessimism as an unheeding world rushes headlong towards the abyss of war.)

In the autumn of 1904, within a week of finishing his first piece of science fiction, Kipling was turning his thoughts towards the past. He wrote urgently to Gwynne (a journalist friend from the Boer War days who later became Editor of the *Morning Post*): 'Now this is Serious. Can you when you come down...on Saturday get for me from some London toy-shop a donkey's head mask, either in paper or cloth sufficiently large to go over a man's head, and also a pair of gauze fairy wings.'[20] He and the children were to perform a play about Puck and Titania in a nearby meadow. (No prizes for guessing who was to be Bottom.) They had found the ideal theatre for the performance, the unmistakable outline of a Fairy Ring at the foot of a grassy slope to the south west of Bateman's.

22 *Above* – Elsie, John and Josephine.

23 *Below* – ss *Majestic*, in which the Kiplings made the ill-fated voyage to New York.

24 *Opposite above* – Bateman's. Its Feng Shui was good and they settled down 'for keeps' in 1902.

5 *Opposite below* – Bateman's front door for which Rudyard begged the iron bell-pull from The Grange.

26 *Above* – Outward bound for the Cape on the *Walmer Castle*, telling the children a *Just So* story.

27 *Above* – How Rudyard altered the Animal's head in a copy of *Just So Stories*.

28 *Opposite above* – Fourteenth century misericord at Chichester Cathedral. Did it inspire 'The Knights of the Joyous Venture'?

29 *Opposite below* – King George V meets his speech-writer on a visit to the War Cemeteries.

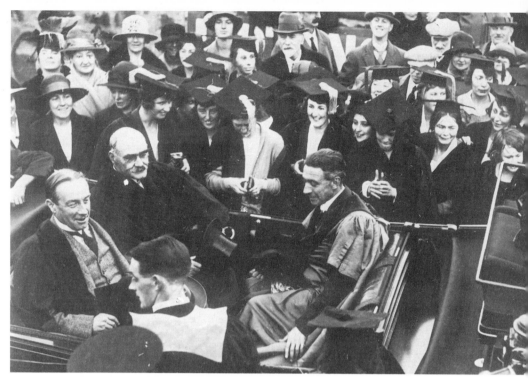

30 *Above* – With cousin Stan Baldwin at Kipling's installation as Rector of St Andrew's University.

31 *Below* – The new Rector signing autographs.

32 *Above* – A peaceful vista in the garden at Bateman's: note the initials RK in the wrought-iron gate.

33 *Below* – Rudyard in later life, happy to be 'dominated' by Aberdeens.

See you our stilly woods of oak,
And the dread ditch beside?
O that was where the Saxons broke,
On the day that Harold died…

And see you, after rain, the trace
Of mound and ditch and wall?
O that was a Legion's camping place,
When Caesar sailed from Gaul.[21]

Pook's Hill, with its mysterious traces of pre-historic earthworks and pathways, had excited him from the moment he first set foot on its springy turf. And now the impulse to express something of the magical element of his very-own haunted landscape could be resisted no longer. In later life he was to say of the Sussex Downs that the hills were full of pure magic and were the true guardians of Time. 'They tell us not to hurry for there is really no past, no future – only Now and Everlasting.' In his own part of Sussex he felt sharp divisions of good and evil in the land. An instance of this was a nearby wood that was full of ill-natured and venomous life: devilishly-contorted tree roots waiting to trip you, clinging brambles that reached out to tear at your eyes and paths that were alive with adders. One evening as he walked through it he had felt something gripping him; some unseen, unknown power pushing against him, until he was compelled to turn round and leave the wood in undignified haste.[22] In later years ghost-hunters had similar experiences and it was discovered that a man had been hanged for murder in the wood a century or so earlier. This man, professing his innocence to the last, vowed he would return to haunt those who had hounded him to his death.

Elsie and John were now aged eight and seven. They were used to a daddy who wrote stories for them and then read them aloud in a special kind of 'howly-growly' voice, who would sometimes steal them away from their lessons in the schoolroom – through the window if necessary – to go in search of ancient tracks or long-gone forges, or just a hatful of mushrooms; a daddy who would look quite as muddy, if not as guilty, as they did when they returned to face Mummy and their governess.

For some time he had been pondering over the importance of teaching history 'in a way which would make it as exciting as a fairy-tale', so that children would never forget it; and now it seemed the most natural thing in the world to turn his hand to the writing of *Puck of Pook's Hill.* But first he must go over to Tisbury to talk it over with his father who at one point said, as though the thought had just occurred to him: 'You'll have to look up your references rather more carefully, won't you?' Both knew that Rudyard had not always done so when working on the *CMG*. It did not, however, stop him taking the occasional liberty with historical fact: he would verify his references first, then ignore them when it suited his purpose to do so. (Hadn't Mark Twain said as much to him that day in Elmira? 'Get your facts first and then you can distort 'em as much as you please.') He placed a well in the wall of Pevensey Castle, where a well was not, because it was vital to his story that there should be one. Almost thirty years later, the year before he died, he had the satisfaction of learning that just such a well had been discovered within the castle's walls. In another tale he quartered the Seventh Cohort of the Thirtieth Legion on the Roman Wall and asserted that Roman soldiers used arrows against the Picts; it was, he said later, a combination of honest research and legitimate inference. Again, years afterwards some Roman-made arrows were discovered on the site and were sent to him, together with a rubbing of a memorial tablet to the Seventh Cohort of the Thirtieth Legion. He suspected a leg-pull here, in spite of being assured that the rubbing was genuine. (Alas, his suspicions were confirmed and it was considered to be a fake, but the arrows were genuine.)

Dan and Una, the children in the book, representing John and Elsie, meet Puck (the oldest Old Thing) who introduces them to Hob of the Dene (old Hobden's ninth great-grandfather), Weland the Smith (who was once a heathen God), Parnesius, the young centurion, a sprinkling of historical characters and a host of others, Saxon, Norman and Dane. All have a tale to tell the children of their adventures by land and sea: but mainly sea, for half the stories are connected with ships, galleys or Vikings.

In 'The Knights of the Joyous Venture' the third Puck story, Sir Richard Dalyngridge tells the children how he and Hugh the Saxon were taken prisoner by Witta the Dane and carried off in his galley. The pirate ship is sailing south in search of gold, guided by the Wise Iron, a box containing a 'magical' needle that always points to the South. (A natural and wishful error which Dan is able to point out to Sir Richard with the aid of his own pocket-compass.) It is 1100 AD and the time of William Rufus's death. On the way south they call in at a small port to trade Baltic amber for 'little wedges of iron and packets of beads in earthen pots'. Also casks of wine, dried meat and fish, beans and dates for the voyage.

'"We were not young," Sir Richard told Dan and Una, "but when we drove out of that secret harbour at sunrise over a still sea, we two rejoiced and sang as did the knights of old...Yet was our leader an heathen pirate...our galley perilously overloaded (there were thirty-five aboard); for guidance we leaned on a pagan sorcerer (the Chinaman whose magic box they steered by); and our port was beyond the world's end."'

After many months' rowing they reach Africa, barter the iron and beads for gold with natives whose chief beats on his chest and gnashes his teeth as if trying to tell them something. Suddenly great 'Devils' taller than a man and covered with reddish hair, leap out on them from the trees. Hugh slays his Devil only after it has left two great gouges in his sword just below the hilt (the wonderful Runic sword which old Weland the Smith had crafted for him when he was a novice), and sunk its teeth into his right arm so that he has to shift his sword into his left hand. When the Devils are finally slain the delighted villagers give them as much gold as they can carry homeward. At long last they reach Pevensey again and the erstwhile prisoners are landed at nightfall. Then Witta, who has come to love the two like brothers, hands them wedge upon wedge and packet upon packet of gold and dust of gold, and only stops when they will take no more. He strips off the gold bracelets on his right arm and places them on Hugh's left and embraces him. By the time the boat pulls out into the darkness, bound for Stavanger, Sir Richard and Hugh on the shore are almost weeping. Although Witta was a heathen and a pirate and had held them by force for many months, Sir Richard told the children: "'I loved that bow-legged, blue-eyed man for his great boldness, his cunning, his skill, and, beyond all, for his simplicity.'"

It has been suggested that Kipling got the idea for this story from two fourteenth century misericord carvings in Chichester Cathedral. The suggestion is appropriate, for wherever he went, at home or abroad, he would always visit the local cathedral. He would soak up its history, glory in its stained-glass windows and examine the carvings in detail. (In the years to come when he was touring in France Chartres Cathedral was to draw him like a magnet again and again, its magnificent windows inspiring a sonnet. As we shall see.)

The first of the Chichester carvings shows a draped figure in mortal combat with a dog-headed, but otherwise lion-like beast whose teeth are clenched on the blade of the broad-sword thrust through its mouth and out at the back of its neck. The drapery suggests the figure is that of a woman, except for the strength in the bent arms as the left hand clutches the beast's mane while the right thrusts the sword home, and for its large protruding feet, which it was not customary to show on female figures at that time.

The second, cruder, carving represents a similar scene but the figure thrusting his broadsword down the throat of an ape-like monster is naked and left-handed. The animal's limbs end convincingly in huge claws, and the carving is flanked by two flat-headed demons.

If the two craftsmen – perhaps master and apprentice – were illustrating the same story, where would they have got their idea from? When working on misericord carvings they were allowed to indulge their artistic fancies in whatever manner their chisels could contrive, from the sacred to the profane. At Chichester they mostly favoured the grotesque and the beastly, their monsters derived, we are told, either from bestiaries or travellers' tales.[23] Perhaps from a story that had been handed down from generation to generation? A story about a Sussex man who had ventured 'beyond the world's end' – whether or not as prisoner of the Vikings like Sir Richard and Hugh – and had seen such a fight between man and 'Devil', otherwise gorilla? It would need only one witness to return to tell the tale…'a masterless man, one who had taken no part in the action of his fellow, who had no special virtues, but who was afflicted…with the magic of the necessary word…a story-teller of the Tribe'.[24] Kipling's words again, but this time he is describing an 'ancient legend' in his speech on 'Literature' at a Royal Academy Dinner just two months after the magazine publication of 'The Knights of the Joyous Venture'. He continued: 'He [the story-teller] saw; he told; he described the merits of the notable deed in such a fashion, we are assured, that the words "became alive and walked up and down in the hearts of all his hearers."' Now Kipling was known as a writer who never wasted anything – especially not a quotation – that came his way; he would re-fashion it to suit his purpose, as we have already observed with his 'revolting' leaders of Faenza. So was the tale of Witta the Viking based on 'honest research and legitimate inference', as were the arrows used by his Roman soldiers on the Wall, or did it arise from a deeper, more intuitive level of thought inspired by two carvings in Chichester Cathedral which were themselves rooted in the words of a story-teller of the tribe?

But what of the women left behind by the Vikings; how did they feel about their menfolk forsaking them year after year? Kipling speaks for them in 'Harp Song of the Dane Women'.

> What is a woman that you forsake her,
> And the hearth-fire and the home-acre,
> To go with the old grey Widow-maker?…
>
> …Yearly you turn from our side, and sicken—
>
> Sicken again for the shouts and the slaughters,—
> You steal away to the lapping waters,
> And look at your ship in her winter quarters…
>
> Then you drive out where the storm-clouds swallow:
> And the sound of your oar-blades falling hollow,
> Is all we have left through the months to follow.

Ah, what is Woman that you forsake her,
And the hearth-fire and the home-acre,
To go with the old grey Widow-maker?

Puck's appeal for Kipling did not end with the completion of the ten stories. Before the year was out he had begun a new set of tales that were to be called – shades of his early, fraught reading at Southsea – *Rewards and Fairies*. By the time they were published four years later, the children were in their teens, the stories more adult and worked in three or four layers, 'since [they] had to be read by children, before people realised that they were meant for grown-ups.'[25] Indeed, some of them would be difficult for children to grasp. But two of them, 'Brother Square Toes' and 'A Priest in Spite of Himself' and their accompanying poem, 'Philadelphia' had a curiously interesting provenance. These are the tales of Pharaoh Lee and his adventures in Philadelphia in 1793. He gets involved with a couple of Seneca Indian chiefs and two French Republican statesmen – one of them the button-peddling Talleyrand – who are trying to persuade the Americans to join them in their fight against the English. All historically accurate, we are told, even to the description of the lilac-scented Philadelphia and its red-brick houses and white stone doorsteps, and with only slight liberties taken regarding Redjacket and Cornplanter, necessary for the action of the plot. So where did Kipling get all this information?

He had first visited the Eastern States in 1889 when he spent much of July and August with the Hills at Beaver, Pennsylvania. From there he paid visits to New York where he met his uncle, to Philadelphia and Boston, and to Lexington and Concord. And it was at Lexington that he had found himself almost choking when he realised he was standing on the first battlefield of the War of Independence (May 1775). He could not explain the emotion, he wrote to Mrs Hill. Not even the graves of Louisa M Alcott or Emerson had touched him so much, and he wondered why. Later he had acquired *A Little History of the Moravian Church in Philadelphia* which supplied him with most of the characters for the two stories. And 'Providence' had sent him an old map of the American colonies of around 1774 which had given him all the old trails and ferries that he needed. Was it providence – or Uncle Harry who was so knowledgeable about the family history? For this is where fact becomes stranger than fiction: 1774 was the year that a kinsman from Sleat in Skye, one Allan MacDonald and his wife, Flora, together with some of their family, had emigrated to North Carolina, there to join hundreds of other Highland settlers who were making a better life for themselves in the American colonies. But first, it seemed, they had to fight and suffer for it: before Allan and his family had been there six months they had to choose which side to fight on, whether as a patriot for the Revolutionaries or as a loyalist for the king. Once again Highlanders were to be divided by their loyalties, as they had been thirty years earlier on their native soil. But there was no hesitation for this couple. Allan had been a young officer in the militia in 1745, had sworn allegiance to King George and for a Highlander to break his oath was unthinkable. As for Flora MacDonald, the Scottish heroine – for it was she who had married Allan of the same surname in 1750 and borne him seven children – as for Flora, she had had enough of lost causes and their painful aftermath of imprisonment. Even so there was to be no peace for her, with a husband and four sons serving their king in America. Allan was taken prisoner himself for eighteen months and one of her sons was wounded *on the battlefield at Lexington*[26] where almost a century later Kipling would find himself near to choking. Was it merely a coincidence, or had he been caught up in the battleground's magnetic field; felt momentarily the charge of an induced current, as from one wire to another?

At Bateman's his work flowed, even as the little brook flowed – and occasionally flooded – at the bottom of his garden.

> See you our little mill that clacks,
> So busy by the brook,
> She has ground her corn and paid her tax
> Ever since Domesday Book.

He felt inordinately proud that 'his' mill was in the Domesday Book. Perhaps above all else it was this that convinced him he was at last part of the very fabric of old Hobden's England; that he had become, as he put it with tongue slightly in cheek, 'one of the gentry'. So now, surely, his wanderings were a thing of his past; surely he could settle for peaceful rustication in his Domesday delight, secure in his own Family Square? Not so. Not while he had two separate sides to his head; and never while every prophetic instinct was warning him of the approach of Armageddon.

---

1 William Camden, *Brittania.*
2 RK to Norton, 1902, Carrington.
3 RK to Sir Percy Bates, 1925, KP.
4 RK to John, 1909 (OBK) see *Notes*, Chapter Ten/1.
5 *SoM.*

6 'In Sight of Monadnock', *Tideway to Tideway, Letters of Travel.*
7 HRH, *SoM.*
8 HRH.
9 *SoM.*
10 HRH.
11 *SoM.*
12 *ibid.*
13 'Puck's Song', 1906.
14 *SoM.*
15 RK to his son John, 1912, KP.
16 *SoM.*
17 ibid.
18 HRH.
19 RK to Mrs Tuite, 1933, KP.
20 RK to Gwynne, 1904, *Letters,* Vol 3.
21 'Puck's Song'.
22 R Thurston Hopkins, *Ghosts over England,* 1953.
23 Francis W Steer, *Misericords in Chichester Cathedral.*
24 *A Book of Words* 1928.
25 *SoM.*
26 Hugh Douglas, *Flora MacDonald,* Alan Sutton, 1993.

CHAPTER TEN

Letters to the children – but meddling in politics

They shall return as strangers,
They shall remain as sons.

'The Recall'

The children were growing up. Young John, destined for the navy and the apple of his father's eye, had long outgrown the days when he would swagger about with a splendid plaited lanyard, and was now ready to start at St Aubyns prep school. On 18th September 1907 Kipling took his son over to Rottingdean in Gunhilda (the Daimler that succeeded Amelia in the Bateman's garage.) After having tea with Aunt Georgie, where John ate so much he had to loosen his waistcoat, father and son explored the school from top to bottom before the dreaded moment of parting. Back at Bateman's again, Kipling found Carrie and Elsie and Miss Blaikie (the governess) waiting in the hall to pelt him with questions. 'I did not sing very much on the road home,' he wrote to John that evening. 'No – it was not a cheerful drive. However I bucked up when I thought of that par-tic-u-larly interesting dormitory of yours and I hoped you had got hold of *The Cruise of the Cachalot* [the recently published account of a voyage around the world in search of sperm whales] and were settling down to read it till the boys came…'[1] Kipling would have arranged to arrive early and get away before the rest of the school turned up, to save any possible embarrassment to the new boy. Had he written plainly enough for John? If not, he could of course 'WRITE LIKE THIS BUT IT TAKES ME EVER SO MUCH LONGER…Just write us a line on Sunday to tell us how you feel. I will send you letters twice a week from Canada and I will also draw you pictures of events on the voyage. They won't be as wild as the events in *The Cruise of the Cachalot* – I hope!'

And so began Kipling's letters to his children: six hundred and forty-three in total, over two hundred of them written to Elsie and John between 1906 and 1915. Exuberant, childlike and frivolling letters they were too, tender and comic by turns, but always with the profound understanding of a child's point of view. Sometimes, and here he took over Carrie's role, they were remindful of duties to be done, like writing thank-you letters to relations, the cleaning of teeth (illustrated) and keeping up with school work. 'There you are, Sir, wallowing – simply wallowing – towards the bottom of the form' when 'your form-master says you've done an excellent week's work. Why? Wherefore?' (Echoes of Kipling's mother here when she wrote to her son's headmaster nearly thirty years earlier on much the same lines. Why was Ruddy bottom of the fifth form, she demanded, if he was so good in Latin, and top of the school in English?) And to Elsie when she went off to finishing school at seventeen, her father wrote: 'Now, my darling, you're in the world for a little bit on your own and (here's the whole secret of life) as you treat the world so will it treat you...If you smile at the world, it grins. If you frown at it, it scowls.'

When Rudyard and Carrie passed through Faenza during an eventful and snow-bound Italian train journey, it was all the excuse Kipling needed to tell John why he had such an affection for Faenza: all because of a quotation. 'Ask Aunt Georgie.' It was good for father and son to know that their aunt was just up the road from the school. As for Georgie, it was like history repeating itself when her great-nephew rang her door bell on his half-holidays. More than once she found herself calling him Ruddy...

1907 was an active year for Kipling the globe-trotter. He received honorary degrees from Durham and Oxford Universities – where Mark Twain also received a doctorate and Crom Price and his young wife joined the Kiplings for the occasion. He had been similarly honoured eight years earlier *in absentia* by McGill University in Montreal; and it was to Canada, 'our Eldest Sister', they went in September to be met by Carrie's mother and the Doubledays. On arrival in the dominion a private railroad car had been put at the Kiplings' disposal. 'Hitch on to any train you choose and stop off where you choose,' they were told. And so they did, from the Atlantic seaboard to the Pacific for a month. But it was not as simple as that, as Kipling reported in a letter to Norton. Things had started to hum while they were still two hundred miles out at sea when '...(May Allah confound Marconi) telegrams burst around us like shells and at Rimouski the strong hordes of the Canadian Clubs took hold of us and literally and absolutely – a thing I did not know was possible – we had not one hour to ourselves unbroken till we were back in the steamer again...I have never worked like it in my life because I have never before been compelled to live and eat, drink etc in public and to prepare speeches in my lack of leisure.'[2] It was a sample of what was to follow. But the maples had 'turned – blood red and splendid as the banners of lost youth. Even the oak is not more of a national tree than the maple...' He wrote a series of travel pieces about his Canadian visit, in which, characteristically, he tackled their immigrant problems head on. He observed that Canada had all the natural resources from timber to fisheries, a superb climate, deep harbours and ice-free ports – 'all the title-deeds to half the trade of Asia', but her weakness was lack of men to work them. And yet they were saying: 'The Japanese Must Go.' Why? Because they worked too hard and were too good at what they did, he was told. So why keep the Chinese – 'the biddable Chinaman'? 'We can get on with the Chinese. We can't get on without the Chinese.' And the English? They did not want English immigrants – 'Remittance-men and loafers' – for precisely the opposite reasons already expressed about the Japanese.

He wrote to a friend who was about to visit Canada, with some down-to-earth advice. '...disconnect your bedroom telephone, so soon as you get to a hotel...Allah knows I have long since ceased to be a virgin, but I cannot help blushing when I am rung-up by women – with nothing on but spectacles and a bath-towel. Moreover I find it interferes with the peristaltic process, and Canada is a constipating land.'[3] (Seven years later Kipling would meet and marvel at the Canadian Army, 'horse, foot, guns, engineers, and all details, fully equipped' camped on Salisbury Plain. Thirty-three thousand volunteers from a population of eight million; and this from a colony that was openly yearning to shake off 'the British yoke'.[4])

The travel pieces were published the following year under the title 'Letters to the Family' (in *Letters of Travel*). But those addressed to his 'Very Dear Family' and signed 'Ever your own Daddo', *and illustrated*, were the letters that gave the most immediate delight to their recipients.

Ten days after their return from Canada came the letter offering Kipling the Nobel Prize for Literature, to be presented to him in Stockholm a month later. It was the first time it had been awarded to an English-speaking author, and naturally not everyone agreed with the choice. What about Hardy, Meredith, Swinburne? 'The goldsmiths are passed by and the literary blacksmith is exalted.'[5] During the Kiplings' journey to Stockholm the King of Sweden died and they had to rush out and buy mourning clothes as soon as they arrived.

They were received at Stockholm station by 'solemn men in top hats of great glory' and escorted to a carriage largely made of plate glass, with silver mountings and lined inside with pearl coloured silk. 'In this glorified bridal-coach Mummy and I sat and behaved beautifully.' They were taken to a suite of stately apartments in a splendid hotel where it was explained to them that owing to the king's death all the ceremonies would be cut down. There would be no banquets or speeches and no large assemblies. 'At this news I looked properly grave and sad but I was very glad to escape from the speeches and the banquets.' He described in words and sketch the half pound of pure gold in the shape of a medal representing poetry listening to the voice of music. 'Never you dare to say that I can't sing again. I thought it was a picture of Mowgli listening to a woman playing on a lyre. He has nothing on to boast of but he is sitting on a bath-towel and saying: – "Now where is the rest of my week's wash." Seriously it is one of the most lovely pieces of work which I have ever seen.'[6] The ceremony was all over in less than an hour. They were then taken into another room to receive the prize money (approximately £7700).

The return voyage across a turbulent and storm-filled North Sea was described in more adult terms to Carrie's sister Josephine.[7] Their cabin was only accessible from the deck, and it soon occurred to him that it would be as much as anyone's life was worth to enter or leave it. He said nothing of this to Carrie as he delivered himself up to the turbulence. But '…I am thankful human beings are not ruminants. One simple little stomach suffices me.' In the middle of a sleepless night he was cheered by the homely sound of the Marconi telegraph office under the bridge sending off messages. If anything did happen at least the latitude and longitude of the funeral would be decently recorded; and the thought consoled him. Much later when the rain had passed he got up and looked at the sea above which 'a panic-stricken piece of moon was running from one flying piece of scud to the next, and the wind was up in earnest. But the extraordinary sight was the sea, snow white, and unable to rise. It reminded me somehow of a nest of serpents wriggling, or of an ermine cloak made of live weasels lying on their backs and squealing because they couldn't rise…I guessed…this could not be open sea any more because…we were simply being jerked about like a corpse being dissected, and as I lifted my eyes…I saw the North Foreland light, and a sparkle of jewels all along the black shore which meant the lights of Margate and Ramsgate.' They were in the mouth of the Thames and the storm pursued them right up to Sheerness as they ran between miles of anchored sailing ships all tossing together. Never was the peace and shelter of Bateman's more welcome to them.

Before the year was out the Kipling family was off to South Africa again, taking John with them, so that he missed the whole of the spring term. The boy shed no tears over that but Mr Stanford, his headmaster, was sorry about it and Aunt Georgie feared it might affect his entrance into the navy, for though a clever lad, she thought, he was backward in his book work.[8] An unforeseen consequence of missing his second term at school was that he had to cope with homesickness all over again at the beginning of the next term. But it was to be the last time they would go to their beloved Woolsack and perhaps this was why the parents allowed the indulgence of taking John with them. Much as Kipling had come to love the country and its beautiful climate where he could work happily surrounded by family and friends, he knew he could never return to South Africa again. It made him sick at heart to see the effects of the Liberal government's policy towards the Afrikaans, and it seemed to him and other Conservatives that the Boer War had been fought and won for nothing. He must hunt about for another country to love, he told a friend sadly. Sooner or later he would go back to the real East, to the people he was brought up with, to the coco-palms and the whispering banana trees.

In the meantime (until the outbreak of WWI) future winter holidays would be spent in Switzerland from where John could easily return to England for the January term. At Engelberg Kipling and the children learned to skate and to ski. And there he found a new brand of the English, some of them determined to give him no peace as they sought him out on the ski slopes. Nevertheless he felt exhilarated by the mountains and lakes and the glittering snow. He loved the air that tasted like 'diamonds and ether mixed' – did it remind him of Vermont? – and the little rack and pinion engine that hauled them up the mountainside.

But still he missed – and needed even more – the warmth of the sun in winter. And in February 1913 he and Carrie 'left Europe for no reason except to discover the Sun, and there were rumours that he was to be found in Egypt'.[9]

Instead, he wrote to the children, they were surprised and annoyed to find that Egypt in February was 'beastly cold'. He found too that even after a quarter of a century he was still hopelessly homesick for the East. Perhaps it was this unexpected discomfiture of mind and body together that produced the magical quality of the last – and best – in his series of *Letters of Travel*: 'Egypt of the Magicians'.

A year later he would have this to say about the *Letters* he had been working on: '...but nothing I could write would give you [Mrs Hill] any idea of the effect of the land which is so like all India in aspect and smell and association: and yet so unlike. I felt as though I was moving in a sort of terrible homesick nightmare and as though at any moment the years would roll away and I should find myself back in India. But it is twenty-six years and twenty-five days since I left it. [He has his sums right for once.] Everything came back as vividly as ever with the bazaar smells and the sight of the sand-banks in the river. I have kept as much of it as I could out of the letters – but you will see that a good deal has got in.'[10]

They were stuck for 'twenty-eight smitten hours' on one of the sandbanks with the thermometer at fifty-five degrees and a wind that cut like a knife. Their boat 'sputters round first with one paddle, then with the other, like a hen in a sand bath,' as it tries unsuccessfully to get off the sand-bank. Four other boats come up and join them on the bank. 'How it would have bored you,' he wrote to Elsie, 'and how it interested us – barring the cold.'[11]

So how much of this did get in to the authorised *Letters*?

From Day One aboard the P & O boat out of Marseilles, an old-fashioned single-screw tub thumping gingerly towards Port Said, Kipling is assailed by memories: in the familiar voices of the lascars, the slap of their bare feet on the deck and the friendly – and familiar – smells from their galley.

People argue as to where the East begins: for him it was 'wherever one sees the lateen sail – that shark's fin of a rig which for hundreds of years has dogged all white bathers round the Mediterranean. There is still a suggestion of menace, a hint of piracy, in the blood whenever the lateen goes by, fishing or fruiting or coasting.

'"This is not my ancestral trade," she whispers to the accomplice sea. "If everybody had their rights I should be doing something quite different; for my father, he was the Junk, and my mother, she was the Dhow, and between the two of 'em they made Asia." Then she tacks, disorderly but deadly quick, and shuffles past the unimaginative steam-packet with her hat over one eye and a knife, as it were, up her baggy sleeves.'[12]

More memories are evoked in the overnight train to Cairo as they pass Zagazig, once a halt in a desert and 'last seen by a very small boy who was lifted out of a railway-carriage and set down beneath a whitewashed wall under naked stars in an illimitable emptiness because, they told him, the train was on fire.' What had stuck in his mind ever since was its absurd name and his father telling him that when he grew up he would come this way in a big steamer.

'So all his life, the word "Zagazig" carried memories of a brick shed, the flicker of an oil-lamp's floating wick, a sky full of eyes, and an engine coughing in a desert at the world's end...'[13] Before the Suez Canal was cut.

It was raining hard in Cairo and they saw the pyramids under a leaden sky that was all too familiarly European. He wandered through the old Arab city where the 'craftsmen and merchants sat on their shop-boards, a rich mystery of darkness behind them, and the narrow gullies were polished to shoulder-height by the mere flux of people...Easterns lean and loll and squat and sidle against things as they daunder along. When the feet are bare, the whole body thinks...

'But I bought nothing. The city thrust more treasure upon me than I could carry away. It came out of dark alleyways on tawny camels loaded with pots; on pattering asses half buried under nets of cut clover; in the exquisitely modelled hands of little children scurrying home from the cookshop with the evening meal, chin pressed against the platter's edge and eyes round with responsibility above the pile...in the slap and slide of the heelless red-and-yellow slippers all around, and, above all, in the mixed delicious smells of frying butter, Mohammedan bread, kababs, leather, cooking-smoke, asafoetida, peppers, and turmeric. Devils cannot abide the smell of burning turmeric, but the right-minded man loves it. It stands for evening that brings all home, the evening meal, the dipping of friendly hands in the dish, the one face, the dropped veil, and the big, guttering pipe afterward.

'Praised be Allah for the diversity of His creatures...Cairo the sorceress...danced before me in the heart-breaking likeness of every city I had known and loved, a little further up the road.

'It was a cruel double-magic. For in the very hour that my homesick soul had surrendered itself to the dream of the shadow that had turned back on the dial, I realised all the desolate days and homesickness of all the men penned in far-off places among the strange sounds and smells.'[14]

With the weight of the desert upon him 'every day and every hour' and the journey up the Nile, 'like running the gauntlet before Eternity', still ahead of him to play havoc with his sensibilities, it is hardly surprising that his pen carried him where he would rather not have ventured. At the turning point of their journey up the Nile he describes the intimate life of the ship after all the tourists (except their two selves) have gone either in boats or on donkeys, to see the second cataract. 'Here we lie at rest under a bank of the Nile just sprinkled with a thin crop of beans and castor oil bushes. The desert begins less than thirty paces away...without a word of apology or compromise and runs without any break for some...three thousand miles...Our native cook – the head scullion – is...along the banks of the river scrubbing out the copper stock-pot with sand. He will bring it back looking like gold...The rest of the crew are a little further away, washing themselves and their clothes in the river. You see, tourists aren't expected to be aboard when they ought to be on donkeys...'[15]

Kipling's sensitivity over the effect of his 'notoriety' on his schoolboy son was only matched by its complete absence in John's schoolmates when they found out whose father had written 'The Children's Song':

Land of our birth, we pledge to thee
Our love and toil in the years to be;
When we are grown and take our place,
As men and women with our race.

Three years after its publication in *Puck of Pook's Hill*, Kipling was apologising for it in a letter to his son. 'All your fault for having a poetical pa!' But the problem did not go away and a few months later he wrote in even more conciliatory tones. 'You know that I didn't write the darn thing with the faintest idea it would be so cruelly used against the young.'[16] (Its fate was to be set to music and sung as a school hymn). Life can be tough for children of the famous and John was still living down an earlier set of verses with which he had the misfortune to be twinned, both having been born within weeks of each other at Rottingdean. The father ruefully acknowledged his son's feelings on the matter when he reported to Haggard John's hopes, on the eve of his first term at Wellington, that there he would hear no more of 'Recessional'. Kipling never talked about his work to his family, apart from Carrie, and the boy was no book-worm so it is more than likely he knew nothing of the offending verses before having them brought to his notice; perhaps by a master in front of the other boys, or by the boys themselves. That must have taken some living down, even though John was not an imaginative child. (Kipling once confided to Haggard that he was thankful neither of his children showed any signs of imagination. He understood better than most what childhood traumas its over-activity could induce – and his little Josephine had been precociously imaginative.[17])

We cannot be sure how John coped when 'If' escaped from *Rewards and Fairies* and ran round the world in twenty-six languages, for there are gaps in the father/son correspondence about this time. But it does not take a great stretch of the imagination to guess the effect of those admonitory lines on a boy like John; immensely likeable though he was and with a ready wit, he had no marked scholastic talents and his only aspirations were on the sports field. Even so, he did rather better at mathematics than his father, as Kipling was the first to acknowledge.

If you can keep your head when all about you
Are losing theirs and blaming it on you...

and so on to the final *coup de grâce*:

If you can fill the unforgiving minute
With sixty seconds' worth of distance run,

Yours is the earth and everything that's in it,
And – which is more – you'll be a Man, my Son![18]

Whatever we may think of the sentiments expressed in 'If' today, they did have a contemporary significance for the public-school boy who, within the space of a few years, would be leading his men into battle in the Great War. However, like the outraged boys at the college when the pink-and-white MP addressed them on '…little matters, like the hope of Honour and the dream of Glory', they were not subjects that boys discussed 'even with their most intimate equals'.[18]

But that did not prevent their being quoted and 'anthologized to weariness', as their author put it. Kipling was careful to point out that the verses were based on the character of Dr Jameson whom he had known and admired in South Africa, but it is unlikely that this would have let his son off the hook at the traditionally military Wellington School.

Puck of Pook's Hill and *Rewards and Fairies* have never been out of print since they first appeared on the bookstalls (1906 and 1910), and yet they were not immediately popular. Why was this? The simple answer is that since the Boer War, Kipling had made himself unpopular by meddling in politics. Art and politics do not make good bedfellows. And when the artist is Rudyard Kipling, the government in power Liberal, and their declared policies to give away India (a trust which, in Kipling's eyes, could not be betrayed) and give Ireland Home Rule (a recipe for civil war in his opinion), the mixture was not so much incompatible as downright explosive.

It was not that he had any political ambitions for himself. Far from it. He disliked politicians as a breed, was often impatient with his own party leaders, and flatly turned down all their suggestions of becoming a parliamentary candidate. This was a good thing, for although he had accrued a fair knowledge of the political world his opinions were formed on the ground – and set in concrete – rather than in the debating chamber and open to discussion. His insight as a writer, although often profound, was of little help to him in making political judgements; and where once the young author of *Plain Tales* had been accused of an irritating 'knowingness', he was now variously described as an 'innocent in politics', a romantic or, as we might say today, 'over the top'. There were never any half measures with Kipling: if he hated something he said so with enthusiasm and much noise, however wrong-headed he appeared to be. Diplomacy was not a word in his vocabulary.

So why get involved at all when he was often at odds with members of his own party? Because the Tories were the party of Order and

Empire, two of his fundamental beliefs. It is important to remember here that to Kipling the word Empire meant service, not exploitation; defence, not conquest. But that did not mean handing back parts of the Empire solely because a sentiment-driven government thought they should – without, it seemed to him, the slightest conception of the consequences of their grand gestures. He might have paraphrased his (mother's) words: What do they know of India, who only England know? How many members of the government had first-hand experience of the sub-continent, had even breathed its air: how many knew anything of the insurmountable divisions between Hindu and Moslem, between princely riches and appalling poverty, between devastating floods and famine? How many of our young men's lives had been lost, even before the regulation insurance age of thirty-three-and-a-half, trying to alleviate some of these problems? As for Ireland, so convinced was he that civil war would be the outcome of the British government's reneging on Ulster (and only the outbreak of the Great War in 1914 did, apparently, prevent this happening, with Germany conveniently waiting in the wings to arm both sides) that by the end of 1913 he and Carrie were involved in schemes for looking after the women and children of Ireland when civil war broke out. So long as he feared these terrible eventualities he could not rest, sometimes could not sleep. All his natural reticence was cast aside, and the man who guarded his privacy more jealously than a dog his bone actually took to making public speeches to assembled thousands. He delivered bitter personal attacks on the government and resurrected the Marconi scandals in which certain cabinet ministers had been suspected, not without reason, of financial involvement. Later he was to write 'Gehazi' (1913) which said it all:

Well done, well done, Gehazi!
Stretch forth thy ready hand.
Thou barely 'scaped from judgment,
Take oath to judge the land
Unswayed by gift of money
Or privy bribe, more base,
Of knowledge where is profit
In any market-place.

These outbursts did his reputation no good. They were immoderate and unrestrained to the point of hysteria and naturally made excellent copy for the press. What was it that compelled him to act in this way, when we recall his repugnance for the unwelcome publicity thrust upon him during the Beatty affair? Three months after the court case he had left his beloved Naulakha for good, virtually driven out by the animosity of the American press. Could it be that, whether he realised it or not, it was the conflict he needed – the medium more than the message – as an essential ingredient of his creativity? There had been little conflict in his life since he had finally settled in Sussex and surrounded by his family and friends, had immersed himself in the history of the land and the creation of the catalytic Puck. His cup was full. But as every artist knows and every art teacher will tell you, a composition needs light and shade to bring it to life – to emphasise life. Further, we must place light against dark, and dark against light in order to create shape and form. For a writer this sometimes means conflict off the page – as well as on it.

Kipling's work pattern seems to point to this need for striking a balance between light and dark: he would often break off in the middle of a dramatic ballad or story in order to play with some light verse – not always for publication – before returning to the drama again. In his autobiography he recalls a certain day at Southsea when the Woman and her son had taken him to visit an elderly relative who lived in the country and where for a few hours he had been entirely happy. But on their return home the 'pleasure that [he] was seen to have taken was *balanced* by punishments and humiliation – above all humiliation. That alternation was quite regular.'[19] (The emphasis is mine.)

Again if we look back to his early childhood in Bombay, it was the strong light and darkness of that tropical climate which epitomised everything that was idyllic for him, and which he recalled so vividly towards the end of his life. Even the shadows beneath the coconut trees held no real fears for him because there was always a hand to hold, a comforting voice to soothe. It was only later in Southsea that his world turned suddenly upside down, when he was surrounded by a darkness where no light entered – and if it did it was a punishable offence – and a loneliness where no comforting hand or voice reached out to him.

It is not surprising then that the adult Kipling was chock-full of contradictory traits: a fierce yet gentle man who was putty in the hands of a child, yet who could write of cruelty and revenge as though he endorsed both; a sensitive philistine who see-sawed between bouts of despair and hilarity, whose compassion for the bereaved was as tender as any woman's while his own unspoken grief remained hidden, or erupted in a political diatribe. It was just such conflicts, arising from the East/West polarity of a riven childhood and to a certain extent from his Celtic/Anglo-Saxon inheritance, which were the basis of 'The Two-Sided Man' – and the bedrock of his genius. These contradictions of temperament might have been why he feared losing his mind as a young man, when he became ill from fever and overwork.

In a speech to doctors at the Middlesex Hospital in October 1908 Kipling said he would resist the temptation to talk about his symptoms. Indeed he had been ordered – on medical advice – to talk about doctors, not patients. It was a little unfortunate, he told them, 'that Death, as the senior practitioner, is bound to win in the long run; but we patients console ourselves...that it will be your business to make the best terms you can with Death on our behalf...Every sane human being is agreed that this long-drawn fight for time that we call life is one of the most important things in the world.'[20]

A week later Bland-Sutton, a surgeon friend of Kipling's, diagnosed his 'trouble' as over-smoking. This may have been the onset of the 'gastric' problems that were to undermine his health – and remain incorrectly diagnosed – for many agonising years. Not smoking meant not working, according to Carrie on hearing the prognosis. Kipling had been a heavy smoker since his schooldays and in spite of everything remained so for the rest of his life. Seven months earlier she had reported in her diary a stiffness on his left side and cramp on the left side of his face with a dropped eyelid: 'the same that he had when we were engaged.'

Carrie's own health had been showing signs of strain at Rottingdean seven years earlier when she had been warned of the need for an operation. This had been followed by the first signs of depression and emotional instability which coincided with Rudyard being away for three weeks in the summer and when she had only her diary to confide in. According to Georgie Carrie had 'collapsed' and was in the hands of a doctor and nurse, but by September was 'gaining strength at last.'[21] And it was Carrie who first consulted Bland-Sutton about her own health problems, three months before he pronounced on Rudyard's smoking. She had been suffering from mysterious pains in her stomach, as we learn from one of Kipling's letters to Elsie, addressed to 'Me che-ild'. ('Ducky Dicky-Bird' was another paternal greeting – quite the lowest title for her that even he had invented. By the time she was sixteen Elsie would retaliate in kind by addressing her father as 'Doodles'.)

'Children could play with me today – and I wish I had one now – or even two kids. You may have noticed that on Saturday and Sunday I was, as your dear French governess says, deestray...This was on account of your Mummy's pains in her inside which grew worse after you left...in addition to pains she sat about and imagined the various diseases that the pain might mean. She counted up ninety-seven of them – or three. I forget which.' Rudyard took her up to London to see Bland-Sutton who said there was nothing wrong with her in the way of the 'five or six terrible diseases she had imagined herself to possess', but what amounted to 'indigestion'. After telling Carrie what she must not eat, to her intense disgust he prescribed that loathsome childhood medicine, *castor oil.* Carrie was not pleased: in fact she was furious, but it made Rudyard want to dance in the puddles in Bond Street. As a result of the relief all round he was able to report that she was now much better – which was why small children could play with him that day.[22]

In 1910 Rudyard's mother died. She had been suffering from Graves's Disease. Within two months his father was taken ill and died suddenly while staying with friends in Wiltshire. Rudyard was devastated by this double loss. He wrote to Mrs Hill: 'Dear as my mother was, my father was more to me than most men are to their sons; and now that I have no one to talk or write to I find myself desolate.'[23] Trix had been living with her parents at Tisbury; they could keep her calm when no-one else could, least of all her husband during her bad times. After their parents' death her mental condition deteriorated alarmingly and for a long time afterwards she was in the care of a nurse or doctor, with Rudyard taking overall responsibility and visiting her whenever he could. For a while in 1917 she was living at Dudwell with a companion and Rudyard would take daily walks with her. But it would be 1930 before the cloud lifted completely.

Cormell Price also died that year. It was with a heavy heart that Kipling set about writing the inscription for his old head's memorial tablet beneath the stained glass window in Westward Ho! church. Price had left a widow and two school-age children, but not much money. Rudyard took care of Ted and Dorothy's education and the children were made welcome at Bateman's during their school holidays. It was the very least he could do for the head who had given his pupil the run of his own library all those years ago. When Kipling had gone to Canada three years earlier he was able in some degree to return the compliment. He invited Crom and his wife and their two children to stay at Bateman's in his absence. And this time it was Crom who was delighted to have the run of Rudyard's library. The host had left a welcoming and instructive note. 'Take a look through my books before letting the boy browse. There aren't more than four he can't look at.' Having just seen his own son off to school the day before Rudyard recalled the misery of his first night at school. 'You were good to me on that dreary occasion about thirty years ago and I bless you for it.' And then, solicitously: 'Avoid the evening chill. We live in a valley by a brook. Bicycle not at all. Sussex is devilish pimply. I am sorry the motor goes to her birthplace to have her innards repaired…Remember that WOOD FIRES are the invention of the Devil…Sit up with them till they die out, rake over the ashes and let no soul leave them a moment without the screen in front of them.' Back at home again ten days later after 'a Heavenly time at Bateman's, Crom noted in his diary: 'Everything in the house looking very diminutive.'[24]

There had been anxiety about John's eyes even before he started school, but by 1910 they were reported to be getting worse. He would not now be going into the navy. What then would he do? The matter exercised the father's mind more than it did his sixteen year old son's during their annual winter holiday in Switzerland. Writing to Gwynne, who would be meeting John in London on his way back to school, Kipling told the editor of the *Morning Post* not to talk to him about journalism which had, briefly, been one of John's ideas. 'I mean to leave him free to choose but I am a little bothered that so far he makes no choice: but I don't want him to lean to letters in any shape.' He suggested that Gwynne tried to draw him out on the subject of a profession and what was in the boy's mind. A year later he agreed with Gwynne that his son was old for his years. '...but what can one do?' When he was only a month older than John he was already earning £10 a month and had whiskers down his face. His son only had a moustache.[25]

John played with the idea of going up to Cambridge but finally settled on the army, which meant passing the entrance exam to Sandhurst. And that meant a crammers.

The war that Kipling had prophesied and in preparation for which he had for years been urging compulsory military training, broke out while they were on holiday in Norfolk. They had rented Kessingland Grange, Haggard's summer house, for occasional use during that year. It was a strange nautical building that had originally been a coastguard station. Perched on the edge of the cliff within sound and smell of the North Sea, its cabin rooms named after English admirals and filled with Haggard's personal collection of souvenirs, it was for all practical purposes like the side of a ship and it delighted Kipling's sense of place and the fitness of things. 'The garden runs about fifteen yards to a cliff – then the sea and all the drama of the skirts of war laid out before us. (This in a letter dated 4th August 1914). Destroyers going up and coming down in twos and fours – then a gunboat or so – then a NYK (Jap boat) all white and disinterested going to London; then a Nelson liner with a sort of "Mike, you're wanted" look on her; then steam trawlers and the usual procession of tows and barges.'[26] The same day Kipling wrote in Carrie's diary – she being possessed by a cold – 'Incidentally Armageddon begins.' On 9th August a seaplane was sighted at seven am and a submarine about nine.

John had joined them at Kessingland at the end of July with a good report from his Bournemouth crammers. He was to go into the territorials as soon as they returned home. It was a bit of a wrench, his father reported, John not being over strong, but he didn't see what else could be done. The boy went up to the War Office on the tenth to apply for a commission in Kitchener's new army and, the family back at Bateman's again, Kipling took him over to Maidstone for his medical on his seventeenth birthday. Although passed as physically fit in every other respect he was turned down because of his eyesight. It was only when John talked of enlisting as a private that Kipling decided to go and see his old friend Lord Roberts who had been C in C in the Boer War. The upshot of their meeting was that John was nominated for a commission in the Irish Guards, Lord Roberts' own regiment, and four days later he reported for duty at Warley Barracks, Brentwood. Within a week of his son's departure Kipling was taken ill, sleeping constantly and restlessly and suffering great pain in his face, and he only recovered when John arrived home on his first weekend leave. It was not the first time that Kipling had suffered partial paralysis of the facial muscles through nervous exhaustion.

But before John went off to barracks, even before he had spoken to Lord Roberts about his commission, Kipling had written and *The Times* had published 'For All We Have and Are', of which the following are part of the first, and the last verse.

> For all we have and are,
> For all our children's fate,
> Stand up and take the war.
> The Hun is at the gate!...
>
> No easy hope or lies
> Shall bring us to our goal,
> But iron sacrifice
> Of body, will, and soul.
> There is but one task for all—
> One life for each to give.
> What stands if Freedom fall?
> Who dies if England live?

During that first winter of the war when it was said that it would all be over in six months he wrote three war stories, 'Swept and Garnished', 'Mary Postgate' and 'Sea Constables'. They were powerful but unpleasant tales – the first two in particular involving the killing of innocent children by the enemy (influenced by news of the atrocities perpetrated on Belgian civilians and the beginning of German air-raids on English towns) – that left a bad taste in the mouth, as if written in an access of bile. Or a presage of what lay ahead? The news from the front was grim but at least John would not be sent to France until his eighteenth birthday next August. While Carrie kept herself busy with Red Cross work, Rudyard visited army camps throughout the south of England. He had been asked to write a series of articles on the New Army.

He met the Canadians on Salisbury Plain, and he met Indian troops in the New Forest and the neighbouring cathedral town. He rejoiced to see the 'solid, large-made men, with...the tan of Indian suns on their faces' who in their turn rejoiced in the keen smells of autumn. He caught the unmistakable whiff of ghee, smelt bazaar-tobacco on a south-country golf-links. Who would have dreamed of it? He visited huge territorial camps where the New Army, still without its proper uniform, was 'maturing itself in the mud,' it being an ordinary English autumn. He saw parade grounds submerged by troops...'rises and skylines were furred with them, and the length of the roads heaved and rippled like bicycle-chains with blocks of men on the move'. It was more difficult to get at the billeted troops: finding a particular battalion was like 'ferreting unstopped burrows'.[27]

When Haggard saw the Kiplings in the spring of '15 he found neither of them looking as well as they had at Kessingland. Rudyard was greyer and seemed to have shrunk in size, although Kipling said it was his stomach that had shrunk. Many of the young men they knew had been killed in action and they were obviously terrified lest the same should happen to John.[28]

It had been a changed boy who came home on leave that first weekend. The laughter had given way to a 'grave and serious John' with many stories to tell of 'his' men. He liked the Irish and got on well with them. 'Not an ounce of vice in 'em even when they are drunk, but quite mad,' he told his father. Which suited John down to the ground, his father said. Fifteen to twenty mile marches apart, one of John's more demanding duties was being sent over to Dublin to bring back a party of recruits on St Patrick's Day, after marching them through the city without an NCO. Fortunately for him he discovered on arrival in Ireland that no troops could be shifted on that day. So at least the powers that be knew better than to attempt the impossible.[29]

On 17th August, his eighteenth birthday, 2nd Lieutenant John Kipling, 2nd Battalion Irish Guards, crossed over to France. As it turned out his father had preceded him across the Channel by a few days; also on war business. Rudyard Kipling had been invited to inspect the French military preparations for a series of articles for the English and American newspapers. And so began an exchange of letters between father and son – between trench and trench as it were – and the rest of the family at home.

1 Rudyard Kipling, *O Beloved Kids*, ed Elliott L Gilbert, Weidenfeld & Nicolson, 1983.
2 RK to Norton, 1908, *Letters*, Vol 3.
3 RK to Lord Milner, 1908, Carrington.
4 'The New Army in Training', 1915.
5 A G Gardiner, *Prophets, Priests and Kings*.
6 *OBK*.
7 Josephine Dunham, *Letters*, Vol 3.
8 Price Papers.
9 'Egypt of the Magicians', 1913, *Letters of Travel*.
10 RK to Mrs Hill, 1914, KP.
11 *OBK*.
12 'Egypt of the Magicians'.
13 *ibid*.
14 *ibid*.
15 RK to GB-J, 1913, KP.
16 *OBK*.
17 HRH 1911.
18 'The Flag of their Country', *Stalky & Co*, 1899.
19 *SoM*.
20 *A Book of Words*.
21 Price Papers.
22 *OBK*.
23 RK to Mrs Hill, 1911, KP.
24 Price Papers.
25 RK to Gwynne, 1913-4, KP.
26 RK to RD Blumenfeld, Carrington.
27 *The New Army in Training*, 1915.
28 HRH.
29 *OBK*.

EXHAUST 1915-1936

CHAPTER ELEVEN

War Correspondent on land and sea; '...a short life'

'Have you news of my boy Jack?'
Not this tide.
'When d'you think that he'll come back?'
Not with this wind blowing, and this tide.

'My Boy Jack'

John's handwriting was inclined to slope backwards although it became noticeably more upright during his year's training in the Guards, as did the young subaltern himself. But he had never quite mastered the rigours of spelling. As a schoolboy some of his more 'vilely spelled' (or 'spelt': Kipling kept his options open here) letters home had moved his father to suggest that his son should walk about chained to at least three dictionaries. 'Why can't you spell? Are you sick? Are you underfed? Do your shoes pinch?...' It was water off a duck's back to John who thought nothing of beginning a sentence without a capital letter. 'It makes it a bit difficult to read as one sentence slides into the other without warning,' his father had mildly complained when John was rising thirteen. But Kipling was not above the occasional misspelling of a proper name himself.

Now that John was in France moving up to the front, he wrote every two or three days to his family in between the long foot-slogging marches and the digging of trenches. And if his spelling was erratic at times, his letters from first to last were always unfailingly cheerful, however grim the conditions. Nor did he forget the thank-you letters to friends and relatives who sent him welcome parcels of foodstuffs.

John's first letter from Somewhere in France was written on his eighteenth birthday and addressed to his 'Dear Old Things'. They had had a good crossing, getting over in seven hours, although he, 'worst luck' had been chosen for 'Picquet [sic] Officer' and so spent the night 'posting & visiting sentries for submarines and on the lifeboats'. They had been escorted by a destroyer on their left flank and finally disembarked at six a.m. Now they were under canvas for the night before moving up the next day – a thirty hour train journey – and he was about to turn in having had only four hours sleep in the last two days. The weather was lovely, 'hot & balmy', and although away from home it had been 'a fine birthday'.

There followed a '*Please Send*' list of requirements which included a pair of 'roomy carpet slippers'; and then simply: '*This is the life.*'

That same day his father wrote to him from Verdun: 'Dear old man, A line of welcome and blessing if you are in France as I suppose you are by now. If you have been one of the disembarkation officers you won't feel like blessing.' He had been with the French army in the trenches and visited Rheims (when it wasn't being bombarded) and was about to see '*your* Colonel [Kitchener, who had succeeded Roberts] review an Army. Odd, isn't it? But it's true.' Like his son, he assured the recipient that he was having a splendid time.

———————

John's next letter was written in the train taking his battalion to the firing line…They had left camp at noon, marched four miles to the station in the 'hotest [sic] weather I have ever known & as I was carrying a very full kit I sweated some.' It took three hours to manoeuvre seventy-three horses, fifty carts and 1100 men into the one single-engined train, whose top speed was fifteen mph. With 140 men to each cattle truck 'the poor men' were packed like flies. The twenty-six officers had three second class compartments between them. 'But it is grand fun we sit here with naked feet out of the window singing and smoking.' At each stop the men would get out and do a step dance to the sound of melodians. 'The French…think us mad.' Hot water for washing was obtained off the engine.

'Am sending enclosed cutting about dad, I follow his movements in the paper…So long old things…'

(Kipling was able to answer this letter six days later, so efficient was the postal service and the Bateman's 'clearing station'.)

———————

'Somewhere in France, Friday 20th August…Here we are billeted in a splendid little village…about the size of Burwash Wield [sic].' He had 'the great luck' to be billeted in the Mayor's house, where he was 'awfully comfortable' with a feather bed and sheets…The mayor couldn't speak a word of English but was the 'kindest chap you ever met…' Moreover he had 'a very pretty daughter – Marcelle – who is awfully nice and we get on very well.'

The one drawback was that food was scarce, the other regiments having 'gutted the place, & one can't get a cigarette for love or money.'

But the men were 'sticking it wonderfully considering they haven't had a square meal since they left England...' Or any letters from home either...'Please remember me to Jerry [the secretary at Bateman's]. Much love to yourself John'

———————

Kipling's next letter to John (incorrectly dated 22nd August) was from the Hotel Brighton in Paris, where Rudyard, Carrie and Elsie had last stayed early in 1914 *en route* for Engelberg. He had got in from Troyes to find 'a batch of Mother's letters with copies of your two letters from S'hampton and Havre. What one hell of a time you must have had hunting pickets round the deck...'

He had been quite close enough to the Boche for his liking, during his 'two hours in the dam trenches' in Alsace. 'The quaintest thing was to watch the NCO gesticulating to his Colonel and me to keep quiet – and to hear a hopefully expectant machine gun putting in five or six shots on the chance and then, as it were, stopping to listen...It's a grand life, though, and does not give you a dull minute.' He had found boric acid in his socks a great comfort; and he reminded his son of 'the beauty of rabbit netting overhead against hand grenades.'

He had not worn his khaki uniform at all. And wouldn't while there was every chance he would be photographed. And he was. But how he wished his son was there with him at the hotel, for 'one good dinner and a jaw'.

———————

Meanwhile from somewhere in France on August 22nd John wrote to thank his parents for the 'splendid parcel of supplies etc' arrived that morning. How 'topping' it was to get parcels & letters from home, and how they all awaited the post from one day to another. Now he had enough kit to last him for a long time. He thought the local crops were a record, and they were being harvested entirely by old women and girls. They all worked 'like horses' to get them in, and an old lady would think nothing 'of cutting a two acre field of wheat with a sickle...I haven't heard from Dad yet; I suppose it is pretty hard to get a letter between the two lines.'

———————

'Paris 24th August Dear old man This morning's post brought in copy of your letter (Jerry typed it I expect) describing your train journey to the music of melodeons. Don't fuss about the French thinking you are mad. They are used to it by now and their own troops on the move make a regular bean-feast of it...I've had to wash in water out of an

195

engine in South Africa. There is a tap just close to the cylinder...if you use it too freely the driver begins to grouse. It's curious to think of you following my movements about France. I am held up in Paris because Joffre [C in C of French Army] wants to see me...so...I am trying to catch up with my account of my journey.'

He described a hair-raising journey from Alsace to Troyes in a Mercedes 'driven by a road-racing Frenchman...I never saw driving to touch his driving...We skidded within half inches of precipices but he whirled us up the hillside and was rather disappointed that he wasn't allowed to bring the car on up to the very crest, where the Boches could have had a mile of fair running shots at her...'

He recounted the tale of how a soldier at Troyes, who knew all about 'me works', came up to him, and when Kipling introduced himself, 'uttered a long and friendly "Ah-haa. God-dam". It was the first time I'd ever heard the oath as a sort of *entente cordiale* greeting: and it fairly winded me for a second...Dear love. I'm going out in a French taxi. They are burning petrol mixed with pee. At least that's how it smells. Daddo.'

While he was kicking his heels in Paris awaiting orders from above Kipling wrote daily letters to John. He described an evening when he and Landon went to a French music-hall and were entertained by an 'English' subaltern in khaki and an English accent who placed his hands on his hips and struck attitudes while the audience howled applause. Then an English naval 'Sub-Lootenant' sang Tipperary with an 'indelicate female in a short green skirt and green holland drawers fastened with red tape bows' who represented the Irish. Kipling was rather shocked that the navy 'Lootenant's' uniform was correct in every detail. 'But as you don't care for the "ceaseless vigillers" you'd have liked it.' This was part of the 'fruity' letter, John told his father, which had been opened by the censor before it reached him. 'It probably cheered him up,' was his father's comment.

'In the train on the way to Boulogne Aug. 26 I shall post this in Boulogne which, when you come to think of it, can't be more than twenty miles from you. I wish I could have a look at you with Marcelle. By the way the best dictionary for French is a dictionary in skirts.'

Back at Bateman's again Rudyard received John's letter of the 26th on the evening of the 28th August. Both in England and France the heat and the flies had been terrible. John reported that all the men were sunburnt and his face was the colour of a 'well smoked briar pipe'.

He didn't think he had ever felt so fit before. They worked like blazes and had eight hours sleep a night with lights out at nine p.m.

More than once Kipling repeated his earnest and illustrated advice about the beauty of a pitched roof of rabbit wire over a trench. But his son in the new army knew better. 'Surely you know it is a standing order never to have anything over the top of a trench, even rabbit wires. If the Bosch comes, he has you like rabbits underneath it.'

The weather changed at the beginning of September: 'It keeps on raining here like old Hades,' John wrote. He asked his parents to send him an oilskin coat, 'the same as those sailor chaps use in the North Sea'...although 'it is a great "comedown" for me to utilise the kit of the Senior Service.' The oilskin duly arrived about eight days later and soon afterwards they began to move up to the front: days, or rather nights, it was so hot, of marching in appalling dust.

Saturday, Sept 25 5.30 p.m.

Dear F—

Just a hurried line as we start off tonight. The front line trenches are nine miles off from here so it wont be a very long march. This is THE great effort to break through & end the war. The guns have been going deafeningly all day, without a single stop.

We have to push through at all costs so we won't have much time in the trenches, which is great luck...this is one of the advantages of a Flying Division; you have to keep moving. We marched eighteen miles last night in the pouring wet. It came down in sheets steadily...

This will be my last letter most likely for some time as we won't get any time for writing this next week, but I will try & send Field post cards.

Well so long old dears. Dear love John. Love to Jerry JK[1]

It was to be John's last letter.

At Bateman's Carrie had been receiving mail regularly from both her menfolk at the front. She would always remember how John had looked as he turned at the top of the stairs for a last goodbye two days before his eighteenth birthday: 'very smart and straight and brave and young'.[2] They had always had a close relationship and the formidable Carrie was putty in the hands of her son. He could tease her out of a mood, however tense she was, where no-one else could; not even Rudyard.

Kipling's letters to Carrie and Elsie described the effects of the war in France in the graphic detail that he had avoided in his letters to John. From the Ritz in Paris he wrote: 'I wish I could give you any idea of this changed Paris…the girls walking (beautifully dressed with the cheapest means) with the wounded soldiers, and the widows with their long black streamers and all the cheery, bright-eyed resolution and smiling patience of it all! Be very proud of your France, my wife and daughter. It makes me humble…The more I look into your marvellous packing, my love, the more touched and grateful I am. The chocolate in the odd spaces nearly moved me to tears…'[3]

———

Kipling was accompanied by Landon[4] and a French captain, Puaux (Pew-oh!) 'We have *only* two cars. He showed us the second which he called a *car de secours* – to follow after us and supply us with bust tyres etc. She is a dull blue, long savage chain-driven 60 Mercedes. We go in a Limousine…So there you are. Two cars – why didn't I bring my library and a portable WC: and a few other trifles…'[5]

From Verdun on 16th August Rudyard described his visit to an almost empty Rheims. He had last seen its cathedral in a spring twilight in '13 when 'the great west window glowed, and the only lights within were those of candles which some penitent English had lit in Joan's honour on those same candlesticks'.[6] Now the shelled cathedral was 'the shame of all the world' with its 'towers smashed, windows little bits of tinkling lacery, the gargoyles maimed and defaced…Inside, there is nothing. The stalls of the choir have been burned out; huge gaps ripped in the side of the chancel; the floor is covered with fine debris of splintered glass and pounded stone…two immense old oak doors opening from the sacristy into the Cathedral have been bent like two pieces of paper and jammed in that position by the mere wind of a shell that fell in the Archbishop's garden…"Put on your hats, Messieurs. This is not consecrated. The Archbishop has declared it desecrated."'[7]

Kipling was impressed, as his son had been, by the way the women were cultivating the countryside to the last inch: like the girl at work with horses in a ploughed field dotted with graves. 'The machine must avoid each sacred spot.' He noticed too how the traffic managed itself without any trace of confusion. 'It is a people settled down to war and all that war may bring.' When they reached Nancy they found a 'glorified' Harrods where he bought a clothes brush and a pirated translation of *The Naulahka* – before they retired to their rooms to '"collect our impressions". I fancy that means a nap.'[8]

Rudyard always addressed his wife in the most loving terms. 'Dearest Heart' from Troyes, 22nd August. 'Just off for Paris and a line to tell you how I love you. This hasn't in the least prevented me from falling in love with a very beautiful VAD (I think) orderly...' And in another letter to his 'dearest dear...Oh those last tearing days. What they must have meant to you! I don't suppose ever was a girl more loved than you by your family and a million-fold more by your Boy!' (He was her Boy.) He confessed that his universal popularity in France was 'unbelievable' to him. It was a case of 'Le grand Rutyar!' up and down the country wherever he went.

On 26th August Carrie met Rudyard at Folkestone with the car. During the two weeks he had been in France he had not once worn the uniform he was entitled to as a war correspondent, in deference to John; and when there was a possibility of meeting his son on his way back to England, he turned it down because John 'wouldn't like to have me tracking him yet'. Later perhaps, when he visited the English lines he might 'accidental like' run across him, he wrote to Carrie. 'Don't you think that would be the most sensible way?' Such sensitivity for his son's feelings deserved better treatment from the fates.

No sooner had Kipling returned from his official visit to the French army than it was the turn of the admiralty to approach him. Would he undertake a similar operation with the British Navy? The Silent Service lived up to its name to the extent that nobody knew what, if anything, it was doing in the war. It was vitally important that the allies should know; and in particular our transatlantic cousins who were still sitting on the fence minding their own business. With Kipling's partiality for the Senior Service he would not have needed much persuading and early in September he set off again. This time to call on the ceaseless vigillers of the Dover Patrol and the Harwich Flotilla.

At Dover he was taken round by an old pensioned able-seaman and introduced to 'those damned trawlers',[9] as the navy affectionately called them when they got in the way. The visit was a great success and at the end of the tour Kipling reported that he had had the time of his life.

The Trawler and Auxiliary Fleet – the descendants of the sloops and cutters, West Country brigs and such-like local craft that fought off the marauding French of an earlier century while His Majesty's ships of the line were busy elsewhere – was chiefly composed of fishermen. But it would take aboard all who had 'maritime tastes – from retired admirals to the sons of the sea-cook' and existed 'for the benefit of the traffic and the annoyance of the enemy'.[10] The 'traffic', that is the steady procession of boats from liners to tramps, six to the hour, going up and down the Channel on their lawful occasions, blessed the fleet wholeheartedly. (Only our submarines – since one periscope is very like another – occasionally had reason to do the other thing…) Most of all did they bless the 'common sweepers' (minesweepers). And it was Kipling's pleasure to write for them a rousing set of verses of which the following is the middle stanza:

> Noon off the Foreland – the first ebb making
> Lumpy and strong in the bight.
> Boom after boom, and the golf-hut shaking
> And the jackdaws wild with fright!
> 'Mines located in the fairway,
> Boats now working up the chain,
> Sweepers – *Unity, Claribel, Assyrian, Stormcock*, and *Golden Gain.*'[11]

'Mine Sweepers'

(*Punch's* version was rather neat. Called 'Lawnsweepers', it began: 'Lawn like a moorland – the young sward caking' and ended with a spot of gardening advice – 'Root up timothy, dandelion, ranunculus, coltsfoot and daisy chain.'[12])

But there was another name topmost in the minds of all sailors at that time. 'You can't look at any water now without seeing "*Lusitania*" sprawlin' all across it.'[13] (She had been torpedoed off Ireland that spring with the loss of over a thousand lives.)

During one of his visits to boats in port he was led across 'many decks from craft to craft to study the various appliances that they specialise in'. The sailors' individual 'uniforms' ranged from a mustard-coloured jersey cleaning a six-pounder on a boat from Hull; a complete blue-serge-suit from Glasgow passing a wire down a hatch supposedly to a lad from the outer Hebrides who instead of attending to it was looking at a girl on the dock-side; an off-white singlet and grey trousers held up by an army belt and hailing from Lowestoft; to the Pullman-car uniform of a nineteen year old wireless operator attached to a flagship. The flagship was all of 120 feet long, under an admiral aged twenty-five who until the other day had been third mate of a North Atlantic tramp.

As for the submarines: they were like cats. They would never tell 'who they were with last night', and they slept as much as they could. He 'was honoured by a glimpse into this veiled life in a boat which was merely practising between trips'. (He had been down in a sub once before the war, with Admiral Fisher at Portsmouth. It would not have made this second visit any easier.) He was struck by the relaxed regulations, men lying about smoking and reading magazines when not on duty, 'calculated to make a man put on flesh. One requires well-padded nerves.' His own would be as taut as piano wires and fighting claustrophobia. He renewed acquaintance with the destroyers whose crews, like the submariners, were a breed apart – 'double-jointed, extra-toed, with brazen bowels and no sort of nerves'. He confessed afterwards to loathing destroyers 'and all the raw, racking, ricocheting life that goes with them...Even at moorings they shiver and sidle like half-backed horses.'

For complete contrast there followed a week with the East Coast patrol when he was the guest of the admiral aboard his flagship and sat at table with him and his staff. At first there was a certain amount of reserve on both sides and Kipling's manner was almost diffident, but all that soon wore off. He came to the conclusion that 'the Navy hasn't the least objection to telling one everything that it is doing. Unfortunately, it speaks its own language, which is incomprehensible to the civilian.' He was in fact severely restricted by the secrecy laws, but who would have guessed it from his lively writing?

After the stresses of life above and beneath the waves, and with his son at the front line never far from his thoughts, it is not surprising that Kipling returned home on Sunday 26th September feeling depressed and chilled and altogether unwell. His doctor diagnosed 'gastritis' and put him on a strict diet, while from France came news of a big attack. This was to be *the* great break-through of the war, for which John and thousands like him had been in training for the past year. The Battle of Loos.

The telegram from the War Office arrived on the second day of October. John had been wounded and was missing. No further details were forthcoming.

During the ensuing bleak months Kipling and his many friends tried every possible channel for news of his son, even getting a message through behind the enemy lines in case he had been taken prisoner. Although, with rumours abounding of German atrocities towards civilians and prisoners, the possibility of his being in enemy hands did not bear thinking about. John's body was never found. He had disappeared on 27th September, the day after Rudyard returned home ill, one of twenty thousand British men lost during that ill-fated and worse-planned battle.

Much later it was established that Second Lieutenant John Kipling had led his men through and beyond Chalk Pit Wood before being wounded. With shells falling all round them the ground gained could not be held and in the general confusion he was not seen again. Writing to 'Stalky' Dunsterville that November, Kipling explained: 'His C.O. and his Company Commander told me how he led 'em and the wounded have confirmed it. He was senior ensign tho' only eighteen yrs and six weeks, and worked like the devil for a year at Warley and knew his Irish to the ground...It was a short life. I'm sorry that all the years' work ended in that one afternoon but – lots of people are in our position – and it's something to have bred a man. The wife...clings to the bare hope of his being a prisoner. I've seen what shells can do, and I don't.'[14]

The matter-of-fact sentences hid his feelings well enough, but when Aunt Georgie saw him for the first time since the news broke she described him as looking as '...if he had all the keys of hell and of death'.[15]

Two years later, he would write 'Mesopotamia', in anger and grief at the continued slaughter of our young men through the sheer bungling inefficiency of those in command, whether politicians or generals.

> They shall not return to us, the resolute, the young,
> The eager and whole-hearted whom we gave;
> But the men who left them thriftily to die in their own dung,
> Shall they come with years and honour to the grave?
>
> Their lives cannot repay us – their death could not undo—
> The shame that they have laid upon our race.
> But the slothfulness that wasted and the arrogance that slew,
> Shall we leave it unabated in its place?

In the meantime he was kept busy with his *Sea Warfare* articles on the navy. The Ministry of Information intended them for the press on both sides of the Atlantic. With the author's blessing and a few pertinent questions in verse, the still-neutral USA was once again the chief target. (America finally came in to the war in April 1917.)

> If it be found, when the battle clears,
> Their death has set me free,
> Then how shall I live with myself through the years
> Which they have bought for me?

'The Question'

When Kipling saw Haggard in town that December he had practically given up hope of John being found alive. Haggard had also lost an only son, when the boy was nine, and had never got over it. After the war when the two men were discussing 'all things in Heaven and earth' as was their wont, Haggard observed that their love for their lost sons was a case of what the Prayer Book called 'inordinate affection'. 'Perhaps,' said Kipling, 'but I don't care for "ordinate" affection and nor do you.'[16] The last thing a parent learned, he said, was when not to love their children too much. He had never felt happier than when he knew that John, as a child, was asleep in the next room. But he had agreed with Dunsterville when Stalky maintained that parents were unfit to bring up their own offspring, the reason being, in Kipling's view, that parents were much too interested in their own progeny to give them enough of that judicious letting alone which makes a child's character. He had reached this conclusion, the nub of child-rearing, only after being deprived of Elsie's company for many weeks when she was twelve and needed treatment in London for a weak back. Although he had hated the separation, he saw for himself how being away from home was developing her.[17] Nevertheless, by the time the war had robbed him of his second child and Elsie had grown into a young woman with a social life of her own, he found it difficult not to be obsessive about his only remaining child. When Elsie married in 1924 both parents would feel her loss with something approaching despair.

At the beginning of 1917 he was approached to write the history of the Irish Guards, something he would never have considered doing in the ordinary way – it smacked too much of writing to order. But this was different; it would be his own unique memorial to his son. By the end of March, shortly before the US entered the war, he settled down to the task that would occupy him, in between other work and increasing bouts of pain, for the next five years – and would be done 'with agony and bloody sweat'.[18] The research entailed visits to the wounded men in hospital and frequent conferences with the regiment's officers, many of the younger of whom became regular and welcome visitors to Bateman's. (During weekend visits he would take them fishing along the banks of the Dudwell and marvel how these young veterans of war who apparently had not minded killing the enemy, would blanch at the very idea of putting a worm on a hook. Would he mind doing it for them, please, while they looked the other way.[19])

The resulting two volume work is a painstaking – and often painful – account of the regiment throughout the Great War. But there are moments of humour and others of thinly-disguised irony when, for example, he quotes the general's speech to the officers about to go into the disastrous action which resulted in the loss of so many lives, including his son's; a speech which the battalion's official diary awarded three exclamation points by way of comment.

In the chapter headed 'Loos and the First Autumn', Kipling describes the formation of the new 2nd battalion: John's battalion. Officially it dated from 15th July 1915 to meet the need. 'But those who knew the world in the old days...know that the 2nd Battalion was born in spirit as in substance, long ere the authorities bade it to be. The needs of the War commanded it; the abundance of the reserves then justified it; and, though Warley Barracks had been condemned as unfit for use by the Honourable the East India Company a trifle of fifty odd years ago, this was not the hour to stand on ancient tradition. So the old crazy barracks overflowed; the officers' damp and sweating dog-kennels were double-crammed; and, by sheer goodwill and stark discipline, the work went forward to the creation...A man may join for the sake of "King and Country" but he goes over the top for the honour of his own platoon, Company, and Battalion.'

When the new battalion paraded for its first route-march of sixteen miles in the flat country around Warley, 'the weather was very hot, nor did that Officer who had bethought him to fill his "full pack" with a full-blown air-cushion, take much reward of his ingenuity when his unlucky fraud betrayed him by bursting almost under the Adjutant's eye. Men said that that was their real introduction to the horrors of war.'

And so the story of the battalion, which is the story of his son, unfolds: the embarkation on the eve of John's eighteenth birthday and the advance through France towards their own particular Armageddon: 'On the 5th September, knowing extremely well what they were intended for...Lieut.-General Haking, commanding the Eleventh Corps, addressed all the Officers of the 2nd Guards Brigade...General Haking said that almost everything depended on the platoon leaders, and "he instructed them always to push on boldly whenever an opportunity offered, even at the expense of exposing and leaving unguarded their flanks." Hence, perhaps, the exclamation points. From the civilian point of view the advice seems hardly safe to offer to a battalion of at least average courage a few days before they are to meet singularly well-posted machine-guns, and carefully trained bombers.'

In another speech on the 24th, (the day before John's last letter) the general explained the broad outlines of the "greatest battle in the history of the world" which was about to start. Speed was essential, he said, but as it turned out when they got away early in the morning of the 25th, out of the question: the roads were 'clotted' with Cavalry going forward and the battle wounded being brought back – all on the same road. They billeted (a euphemism if ever there was one) 'very wet and tired' about one the next morning, the 26th, having been on their feet for twenty odd hours...By the time they reached the selected spot it was nearly midnight and the Battalion had 'now been on foot and livelily awake for forty-eight hours; the larger part of that time without any food. It remained for them merely to go into the fight, which they did at half-past two on the morning of the 27th September when they received "verbal instructions to push forward to another line of captured German trenches, some five hundred yards, relieving any troops that might happen to be there." It was nearly broad daylight by the time that disposition was completed, and they were much impressed with the permanence and solidity of the German works in which they found themselves, and remarked jestingly one to another, that "Jerry must have built them with the idea of staying there for ever." As a matter of fact "Jerry" did stay within a mile of that very line for the next three years and six weeks, less one day.'

There followed what has since become known as the battle of Chalk-Pit Wood. John Kipling was one of the officers who led his men forward into machine-gun and shell-fire upon which one hour and a half's preliminary bombardment from our guns had not had the desired effect and – 'Here 2nd Lieutenant Clifford was shot and wounded or killed – the body was found later – and 2nd Lieutenant Kipling was wounded and missing...and the combined Irish and Scots Guards party fell back...into and through Chalk-Pit Wood in some confusion.' The Battalion had lost seven of its officers in the space of forty minutes.[20]

In May Kipling went to Italy to report on the Italian campaign and to write *The War in the Mountains*. Height was everything in this kind of warfare, he discovered, and the Latins were a hard people 'who have had to fight the mountains and all that is in them, metre by metre, and are thankful when their battlefields do not slope at more than forty-five degrees'. The infinite labour imposed on them by their surroundings impressed him. '"Everything you handle seems to end in a two-hundred-pound package taken up the side of a house, and yet you have heavy artillery on the edge of glaciers. It's a new convention."' But occasionally a mountain-slide 'chose to move into action on its own account' and 'as a woman brushes off snow from her skirt,' removes an established battery with guns, mules, barracks and so forth down to the valley below. '"Fifty we found and buried," said the officer, pointing to a row of little crosses just emerging from a snow hollow. "Ninety are down below in the valley with the mules and the rest. Those we shall never find. How did it happen? A very little thing starts an avalanche when the snow is ripe for it. Perhaps a rifle-shot. And yet," he added grimly, "we must go on and shake all this atmosphere with our guns. Listen!"'[21]

A KBE, closely followed by a CH, were offered and refused after his visit to the Italian front. 'It must not be,' he warned the PM after envoys, including his cousin Stanley, now Financial Secretary to Bonar Law, were despatched to Bateman's to try and persuade him to accept an honour, any honour. It was scarcely the moment to try to persuade him: he was writing 'Mesopotamia' and needed all the freedom there was.

> Our dead shall not return to us while Day and Night divide—
> Never while the bars of sunset hold.
> But the idle-minded overlings who quibbled while they died,
> Shall they thrust for high employments as of old?

> Shall we only threaten and be angry for an hour?
> When the storm is ended shall we find
> How softly but how swiftly they have sidled back to power
> By the favour and contrivance of their kind?

It was too strong for the *Daily Telegraph*. But the *Morning Post's* editor, his old friend Gwynne, printed it.

Early in 1918 Lord Beaverbrook (Max Aitken, another old friend) offered Kipling a post in the propaganda service, doubtless because of his experience in reporting from the various war fronts. The offer was declined but the opportunity taken to offer 'lots of advice' instead.

When the War Graves Commission was formed (1917) the chairman said that they must have Rudyard Kipling, the soldiers' poet, as a commissioner. And it was the soldiers' poet who chose the quotation from Ecclesiasticus which would be inscribed on the Stone of Remembrance in every war cemetery: 'Their name liveth for evermore.' The Commission's task was an enormous one, exhuming, identifying and reburying a million British dead in permanent cemeteries, (five hundred on the Western Front alone) set in gardens, with headstones for each grave to take the place of the temporary crosses. Kipling described the Commission's task as the 'biggest single bit of work since any of the Pharaohs – and they only worked in their own country.'[22] He was responsible for every inscription used, including the poignant 'A soldier of the Great War known unto God' for the graves of unidentified soldiers. But for 'my boy Jack' there was not even that dignity. To the parents' infinite sadness, John's body was never found. * (See Note at end of chapter.)

Kipling worked indefatigably for the Commission and after the war visited cemeteries in France and the Holy Land: as we shall see. But he was not a well man. Unsuspected by all except his family and close friends he suffered from periodic bouts of agonising pain. The eminent doctors and specialists he consulted over the years called it either 'gastritis' or 'irritability of the stomach', and treated him with purging and dieting, so that in 1918 he weighed only 123 pounds. (about 8½ stone). And still the pains continued: 'Overwhelmed with depression and return of his pain'; and again: 'more than usually wretched with more than usually severe go of pain', are just two of the entries in Carrie's diary. Three years later it was thought his teeth might be the cause of his problem, so he had them all out. The pains continued. He had always had a great fear of cancer and this made him doubly wretched and depressed when in pain; as well it might. But according to Elsie, he never complained or 'snapped', even when doubled up in agony; all he asked was to be left alone and he would be 'all right soon.' After one particularly bad spasm he said: 'I think this time I'm going to have twins.'[23]

He continued to work as hard as ever, travelling abroad and attending social functions as required of him. But by the time he had finished writing *The Irish Guards*, two months after the King's official visit to the war cemeteries in 1922, he was exhausted, 'yellow and shrunken'.[24] The pains became so severe that he had an X-ray and later an exploratory operation. There was no sign of the dreaded cancer, but an old ulcer was found and a large area of inflammation of the colon. There followed more diets and purgings, more months of pain and listlessness, gloom and depression that lasted over Christmas – always the saddest festival of the year for him. And yet his doctors appeared to be quite satisfied with his condition. 'Doctors are damned easily pleased,'[25] was the patient's comment. It would not be until 1933 – rather late in the day – that a French doctor discovered he had been suffering from a duodenal ulcer for the past fifteen years. No wonder he would call for less thinking and more imagination in medical research...

The fear of cancer which never entirely left him was reflected in many of his later stories. But so too was the theme of healing and compassion. In 'The Wish House' which he wrote in 1924 while 'quite hopeless with depression, nerves and nerves,'[26] a woman takes on the illness of the faithless man she still loves, by supernatural means, in order to make him well again. He is cured without knowing how or why – and without going back to the woman he had abandoned; while she gladly takes on his pain when a bad place on her leg turns cancerous.

He wrote, too, of another sort of pain: the immeasurable pain of men whose nerves had been shattered and their lives haunted by their experiences in the trenches. As he would be haunted to the end of his life by the loss of his son, knowing that it was he who had engineered John's commission in the Guards, glossing over his boy's short-sightedness in order to do so. Just how much strain can a man take before he breaks? It was a subject he would return to again and again in his work. For one thing he did know: the only cure for grief was to go on working.[27]

*Note After seventy-seven years the Commonwealth War Graves Commission finally identified John Kipling's grave; and in June 1992 a headstone engraved 'Lieutenant/ John Kipling/ Irish Guards/ 27th September 1915 aged 18/' replaced that of 'A Lieutenant/ of the Great War/ Irish Guards/ Known Unto God/', in St Mary's Advance Dressing Station cemetery on the Loos battlefield. Apparently the error arose when the body was found and reburied in 1919 with an incorrect map reference number. However, as we approach the millennium, fresh doubts have emerged as to the accuracy of this late identification. John Kipling served and died as a Second Lieutenant, Irish Guards: his promotion to full Lieutenant was not gazetted until 11th November 1915, six weeks after his death. A week before he died he wrote home to request a new identity disc, spelling out his name and rank as 2nd Lieutenant John Kipling/ C of E/ Irish Guards. Nor was there any hint of promotion in his last two letters home, making it even less likely he would have been wearing that second pip on his uniform.[28]

---

1 *OBK.*
2 CK Diary, KP.
3 RK to CK, 1915, KP.
4 Perceval Landon, war correspondent and friend.
5 RK to CK, 1915, KP.
6 'France at War', 1915.
7 RK to CK, 1915, KP.
8 *ibid.*
9 KJ.
10 'The Fringes of the Fleet', *Sea Warfare,* 1916.
11 'Mine Sweepers', 1916.
12 KJ.
13 *Sea Warfare.*
14 RK to Dunsterville, 1915, Carrington.
15 *Rudyard Kipling,* Lord Birkenhead, Weidenfeld & Nicolson 1978.
16 HRH.
17 RK to Dunsterville, 1908, KP.
18 RK to Dorothy Ponton, secretary, Orel 2.
19 *ibid.*
20 *The Irish Guards in the Great War,* 1923.
21 'The War in the Mountains,' 1917.
22 RK to Sir Fabian Ware, Carrington.
23 RK to Julia Taufflieb, Wilson.
24 CK Diary, KP.
25 HRH.
26 CK Diary, KP.
27 RK to Saintsbury, 1925, KP.
28 *My Boy Jack?* T & V Holt, Leo Cooper, 1998.

CHAPTER TWELVE

Motor tours: pilgrimage and pleasure

Once again the Steamer at Calais – the tackles
Easing the car-trays on to the quay. Release her!
Sign – refill, and let me away with my horses.
(Seventy Thundering Horses!)
Slow through the traffic, my horses! It is enough – it is France!

'Song of Seventy Horses'

It was a clear cold March night and the full moon shone 'bluish' on the dockside buildings as Rudyard and Carrie stumbled up the ferry's gangplank. They were hailed by an elderly caretaker who had been a steward on the old *Kinfauns Castle*, a boat they had used regularly on their winter voyages to South Africa. They had a 'curious and rather a touching talk' with him on the empty deck (the Kiplings had arrived well ahead of the boat train) while their car was being slung aboard and dropped into the hold – 'as she might have been an eggshell'. The caretaker remembered how the children used to 'get things' out of the stewards, like escorted visits to forbidden parts of the ship and extra helpings of dessert after the grown-ups' dinner. (Did Kipling recall that it was aboard the *Kinfauns* he had recited his banjo song to the volunteers on their way to war; and the following year, the verses he had written aboard her on Christmas Day? Verses which ended with a typical Kipling sentiment...'In our yearning for our folk across the sea!' Once or twice they had gone out on her sister ship, the *Kildonan*, and then he would particularly ask if they could have their usual cabins – quoting their numbers – off the children's saloon at the foot of the stairs.) And now here he was crossing the Channel twenty-four years later, to be told by the former steward that they would soon be passing the old ship where she lay waiting to be sold somewhere down the river – but *he* couldn't identify steamers in the dark.

As for the *Normannia*, the cross-channel ferry, she had a funny deep-sea smell about her and the 'quaintest mixture of day-trip and deep-sea manners aboard her'. In the last war she had made over a thousand trips across the Channel during which, the purser confided to him, 'I didn't take off me trousers of course…never knowin' what to expect.'[1]

Rudyard and Carrie were on their way south to seek the sun. But the next day was too cold for comfort and the landscape round Le Havre lay under a powdering of snow, so Kipling at least was not optimistic. Sitting beside Taylor in those first few hours of continental driving when even the best of English chauffeurs automatically turns left in traffic, he dutifully barked "Right!" at two minute intervals, 'like a fog-horn'.[2] They reached Rouen in an hour and a half. He left Carrie resting at the hotel and set off immediately for the cemetery (1100 graves) to interview the head gardener and contractors. He would never get over the shock of the 'Dead Sea of arrested lives – from V.C.s and Hospital Nurses to coolies of the Chinese Labour Corps'. He noticed a yellow porcelain crucifix that an old Frenchwoman had left by the grave of one of the coolies. 'Somehow that almost drew tears,' he wrote to Haggard. (Throughout this trip he would be writing long, vivid letters to his old friend confined to his bed in Norfolk, who was to die within two months.) Standing in the market-place, bare-headed, he did penance at the place where Joan of Arc was burned. Later he lit candles to her in the cathedral, as he had done at Rheims during the war when it was being bombarded by the Germans. It was his belief that it was Joan's spirit that had guided France through the war.[3]

Two evenings later in the hotel at Chartres he started to write a story which would give him something to do at the day's end, and ' – please Allah – it may amount to something'. It did. 'The Gardener' was one of Kipling's finest stories to come out of the war: the story of Helen Turrell who travels to France to seek the grave of the boy she had brought up as her nephew. Arrived at the huge cemetery of 21,000 graves 'she went forward, moved to the left and the right hopelessly, wondering by what guidance she should ever come to her own…' A man who was firming a plant into the soft earth asked her who she was looking for. '"Lieutenant Michael Turrell – my nephew," said Helen slowly and word for word, as she had many thousands of times in her life.

'The man lifted his eyes and looked at her with infinite compassion before he turned from the fresh-sown grass toward the naked black crosses.

'"Come with me," he said, "and I will show you where your son lies."

'When Helen left the Cemetery she turned for a last look. In the distance she saw the man bending over his young plants; and she went away, supposing him to be the gardener.'[4]

Kipling's love for France had brought him across the Channel many times since the twelve-year-old schoolboy had accompanied his father to the Paris Exposition of 1878. Looking back on that first visit many years later he recalled returning to England and the Coll with the 'knowledge that there existed a land across the water, where everything was different, and delightful, where one walked among marvels, and all food tasted extremely well'. Later he was 'invited' to study French. 'You'll never be able to talk it, but if I were you, I'd try to read it.' The method was simple enough. 'Give an English boy the first half of *Twenty Thousand Leagues under the Sea* in his native tongue. When he is properly intoxicated, withdraw it and present to him the second half in the original.' Although French was taught in schools at that time – paying proper attention to the assignment of genders and accents – its literature was considered immoral. The ingenious Rudyard saw to it that his calligraphy 'served as a fig-leaf to cover those delicate problems of sex in inanimate objects so dear to the meticulous Gaul', and he made his accents as 'nearly vertical as might be'. Then during the holidays he read all the French books that interested him – and many that should not have – until at sixteen he could deal with them 'almost as with English'.

It was in Cape Town after the Boer War that he became acquainted with the French navy, and it was aboard one of their cruisers open for inspection that he discovered there were two ways of 'inspecting' ships. 'The first is to go round the ship before taking déjeuner on board. The second is to sit quite still after déjeuner on board, and let the ship go round you.'

But it was the age of the automobile and the pioneer motorist which really brought Kipling to France and France to Kipling – and the discovery of another Gallic truism. A good déjeuner was always to be found if one fell in behind the French Army at half-past eleven. Season after season from 1910 onwards, apart from the Great War, the Kiplings toured France in a series of beloved and more or less reliable motors that were met with varying degrees of enthusiasm. 'But, Monsieur, we cannot accommodate *that* 'ere. It will frighten the 'orses!' was the opinion of the old hotel at Avignon in the early days.

From the tourists' point of view March was not the ideal month to visit France; but it was the month above all others for those who loved the land and its people. Of their five pre-war motoring tours, four of them were taken in that month when France begins her spring-cleaning. 'The roadmen are out taking stock of winter damages; the happy, dirty gypsy-vans are out too; the barges along a thousand miles of canals refit and repaint under the eye of the barge-dogs, who allow no liberties; the roads are made interesting by the dung-carts, the huge bundles of new vine-stocks, and the freshly ordered bright-painted agricultural implements. The working year renews its pulse with the roar almost of a tide.'

He discovered a multitude of beautiful things in small out of the way museums and neglected churches. Why were France's treasures richer than ours? He decided it was because 'their rulers in the past, when they felt religious or angry, merely slew men. Ours, more respectable, contented themselves with murdering the irreplaceable work of artists.'[5]

That first March, in 1910, Rudyard and Carrie had gone by train to Vernet-les-Bains to take the waters. There they met Lord Montagu of Beaulieu, the pioneer motorist, who took them for 'rather an interesting little trip', Rudyard wrote to John, in an 'enormous 6 cyl Rolls-Royce'. The upshot of the meeting was that Claude Johnson, the man who became known as the hyphen in Rolls-Royce, lent him his special trials car, The Silver Phantom, complete with chauffeur for the 600 mile (or it might be 700, Kipling was never quite sure) journey back to Paris. It was a shrewd move of Johnson's, an old friend of Kipling, who had been offering to loan him a car, with a view to his custom, for some time. The ensemble worked like a charm: even Carrie was sufficiently impressed to note that it was amusing to race trains. (It is an enchantment that never dies – at least among the stronger sex. More than eighty years later the Orient Express was 'raced' by several drivers of classic cars in a two-day, 1000 mile race from London to Milan. The cars won hands down.) One of the men responsible for demonstrating the Phantom to Kipling said afterwards that the author's thirst for technical information had severely taxed him and his colleagues.

From that moment there was to be no other marque for Kipling. However, it would be many months of deliberation and planning and many thousands of perfectionist man-hours in the workshops – plus an unfortunate fire at the coach-builders – before he would take delivery of his first Rolls-Royce at the end of 1911. In the meantime the company lent him another model: The Spectre, driven by the quintessential Fleck, for his first motor tour in France that spring. He kept notes of the trip, routes, hotels, mileages and so on. It was a modest start to his *Motor Tours Journal* in which he was to confide anecdotes and thumb-nail sketches of people, places and punctures in the years to come.

But why did he call his first Rolls the Green Goblin? Green, a dark green, was his favourite colour for cars, although many motorists would consider it an unlucky choice; but 'Goblin', the name for a mischievous dwarf, scarcely seems compatible with the Silver Ghost ambience. Maybe that was just why he did choose it: as a deflationary exercise, his answer to that image of silent motoring, that tag of being 'the best car in the world', already bestowed on her. (The original Silver Ghost had been given this accolade by a *Times* journalist a year after she had first glided on to the road and into motoring history.) Certainly he never referred to his car as a Rolls or as a Ghost – too ostentatious perhaps for his simple tastes – but once when he had problems with the car's magneto make-and-break and he had to send a wire to the Company in England, he noted in his journal: 'Silver Ghost. Somehow that irritated one at such a crisis.'[6] (One wonders how he would have reacted to Scarlet Pimpernel, Cookie or Beauty Gal, three of the names originally considered for the immortal Ghost.) But as usual, nothing was wasted, and 'that tiny two-inch spring of finest steel, failure of which immobilises any car', also known as a make-and-break, provided the motivation, or lack of, for one of his later stories, 'The Prophet and the Country'.[7]

All Kipling's later models responded to a name more in keeping with their dignity: The Duchess. Although it must be said that 'dignity' is not the first word that comes to mind when confronted with the following unusual definition of a duchess: 'A woman enjoyed with her pattens on, or by a man in boots, is said to be made a duchess.' (*Dictionary of the Vulgar Tongue*, 1st Edition 1785) It was just the kind of private joke that would have tickled the Duchess's owner right down to the soles of his – boots. However, he bestowed an extra name on his fourth Duchess. She is identified in his 1924 *Journal* as Esmeralda: Fourth Duchess of Tours. Did he have the car's colour (emerald green) in mind; or was he thinking of Quasimodo's Notre Dame and how he had discovered it 'on my own account' as a boy of twelve in Paris? Maybe the 'Duchess of Tours' was a play on words. They would sometimes stop over in Tours on their way to or from the South of France; and in 1926 remained there for nearly two weeks when both were ill. Whatever the reason for choosing the name Esmeralda – and like Amelia, it does have a pleasing sound – he would often refer to his subsequent 'Duchesses' by the same name.

All of a sudden matters 'motorious' dominated his letters to John, forging a common bond between father and son which might otherwise have proved elusive, given their disparate interests and abilities. Even throughout their last exchange of letters in France in 1915, it would remain an absorbing topic for both men.

By his sixteenth birthday John had a motor-bike and was able to drive the car. The following year he joined his parents and sister for what was to be their last touring holiday together. It was April 1914. Elsie and John took it in turns to 'con' from the map. 'He made a bad mess at Versailles ably assisted by Elsie,' was their father's resigned comment. Later that day Elsie excelled herself by 'absolutely denying existence of Beauvais and Cathedral as we entered town from S'. After visiting the cathedral they 'bought lollipops and macaroons. John afterwards devastated family by bathing'.[8]

That was to be the last entry in Kipling's motoring journal for six years.

By October John had his own car, a red open Singer, at Warley Barracks. 'What are you going to call her,' demanded his father in the letter containing the all-important cheque. 'Patti? It must be the name of some eminent singer.' And in a postscript. 'Why not call her Car-uso (he's a great singer.) So was Melba. You might christen her "Dépêche Melba" – which is a foul pun…Don't lend her to chaps who can't drive.'

But who listens to advice at seventeen? At least one new back axle was provided by the father who was so proud of his soldier son, and an attempt to play the heavy parent does not quite come off. 'You were talking t'other day about your limited allowance. I was looking over various trifling accounts for motor bikes, Singer cars and such like and I find that I have expended within six months close on £300 for various forms of ironmongery with wheels.'

When John was about to leave for France with his regiment his father offered to have the Singer repaired at his own expense and to allow his son £100 for her as she stood – about what she was worth – either to be paid into his bank account then or put aside towards a new car – 'when you come back'.[9]

Kipling's own car was laid up from 1917 until the beginning of 1919 and they missed it sorely. He never drove himself and there was a shortage of competent chauffeurs because of the war. But in 1920 they resumed their yearly tours of France. For Kipling, by then deeply involved with his work as a war graves commissioner these tours were to be as much a pilgrimage as a pleasure for the rest of his life. For both parents memories of happier days crowded in on them as they took to the familiar routes once more, often staying at the same hotels as they had with the children before the war. And now there was the added poignancy of inspecting the military cemeteries, large and small, throughout the land, each with its own (English) gardener. 'Silent Cities', he called them. At times it 'tore the heart out'. That year he visited thirty, covering 1500 miles between Ypres, Amiens and Rouen. He saw the 'white glaring trenches', the hideous isolation of the battlefields, and sensed the 'almost insupportable sorrow of it all.' And on the 27th September, the anniversary of the battle of Chalk Pit Wood, they found the place where John had last been seen alive – and where they helped other mourners seek their loved ones' graves. But for Rudyard and Carrie there was no such solace, no focal point for their grieving.

'I plough deep,' said the car.
'I plough old wounds afresh—
'What you thought was a scar,
'I will show you is stricken flesh.'[10]

After an absence of six years they stayed once again at their 'own' hotel in Beauvais. Kipling's journal records that 'they were received with cordiality and love and reminiscences of war and tender enquiries after John'. And at Avignon a year later they were made very welcome by the owner of the hotel whom they remembered as a 'shy boy in the uniform of his conscriptage'. Kipling was able to turn up the exact date seven years' earlier when he had noted that the young proprietor of Hotel de l'Europe was doing his military service '…but he comes in of an evening to look at the hotel from barracks'. They were given their old set of rooms, the ones they had used in 1914. It is such small happenings that make up the fabric of our lives, each tiny strand weaving itself into the whole intricate pattern, bringing strength and comfort in its continuity.

A few miles from Verdun they heard the cuckoo 'among the trenches, wire and bones of the dead'. On the way to Rheims they passed 'fields with poor crops and furlongs of heaped barbed wire…and always on our right the skinned chalk hills'. In the city which he had last described in a letter to Carrie in '15, he found the cathedral being 'cleaned and scraped'.

It was on this trip that Kipling crossed the Rhine for the first time while staying in Strasbourg. ('Very comfy rooms at Maison Rouge with bath like sarcophagus.' An improvement on the '*bain de pied* a little larger than a flower pot' at a pre-war French hotel.) After many tedious formalities on the Rhine Bridge 'the Huns on the far side gave us a dirty red ticket for a "*séjour*" and hung revolting tin number over Duchess's radiator knob. Curious how deep and instriking the hate caused by merely seeing them alive when so many were dead…The whole countryside was sleek and prosperous with smoking factory chimneys, ground cultivated to the edge of the road, and fat children, geese oxen and horses…The villages seemed to lack naught. And they were alive!' It was their last tour in this (1913/4) Duchess, but not the last we shall hear of the motor.

Our King went forth on pilgrimage
His prayers and vows to pay
To them that saved our heritage
And cast their own away…

All that they had they gave – they gave; and they shall not return,
For these are those that have no grave where any heart may mourn.

215

Kipling finished writing 'The King's Pilgrimage' just a week before he had to leave for France. And there, in May 1922, he found himself doing 'a lightning change into blacks and a white shirt in bedroom of cottage lent by old lady (not a mirror or chamber visible: simply two wooden boxes for beds and shutters outside in lieu of curtains).' George V was on an official tour of the French cemeteries and Kipling, as his speech-writer, had been commanded to meet him. While he was waiting for their Majesties to arrive in the Indian cemetery near Boulogne he noticed the grave of one Gunga Din, dooly bearer. ('You're a better man than I am, Gunga Din!') Another strand to be woven in...'The King made his speech with splendid delivery and dignified bearing...K. spoke to Mum...about John. Mum's curtseys nice to behold. Then they moved off. Was sent for and K. said to me what was seemly. I praised delivery which was also seemly. He spoke about politicians. (Note: the look in the eye of a decent man who suspects he is being carted. Rather like a frightened horse).' He noted too that the royal party's hired R-Rs were 'nothing very splendid'.

After the ceremonies were over Kipling and some of his fellow commissioners went for a walk in the town to drink chocolate and do a little shopping. Kipling's shopping was minimal and curious; more often than not it was to buy 'the usual butter-spreading knife' for three francs (their turn-over in butter-spreading knives was prodigious) or a 'small aluminium bucketling for butter' – no price quoted – for their wayside picnics. He rarely had enough money on him to buy anything more substantial. This was partly due to the heavy clasp knife he carried which was forever wearing expensive holes in the pockets of his trousers. So if he was out with Elsie, for instance, and she saw something she fancied he would have to return to the fount (Carrie or the bank) for the necessary funds.

Trouble-free though the Rolls was by comparison with other marques, nothing known to man could prevent the frequent punctures, whichever make of tyre he tried; and he tried them all, Russian Provodniks included. He once recorded as many as three punctures in a single 'Devil's Day'. Equally noteworthy was the day without a puncture. And no amount of watering of wheels in hot weather could prevent a tyre bursting. The French roads were the problem, many of them *impropre pour autos* due to the ravages of war – or in words of one syllable, 'Hell's own pot-holes'. In either language the result was the same: an enforced stop for repairs and a late, weary arrival at their destination. The positive side was the Heaven-sent opportunity for him to talk to the local peasants, like the old man and woman and their pet pig leaning over their gate. 'Pig was allowed in house by day – never at night.' Or it might be the chance-met dung-cart whose voluble driver detested motors and said so at some length – while smoking Kipling's cigarettes. He had time to observe the old women knitting by the fountain in an out-of-the-way town whose little hump-backed bridge had temporarily discommoded the motor. Broken springs were another hazard of bad roads, often giving the Duchess an undignified list to port or starboard. But his luck was out that day in Bordeaux when he failed to notice what Carrie and Elsie had seen. 'A woman at street door in a chemise and hat only. Was arrested by police and put into cab. I alas! missed it!'

He found it satisfactory to see things repeating themselves year by year on their travels through France, where even the punctures became part of the pattern. And he never tired of visiting the cathedrals to rejoice in their windows. Arriving in Troyes late one March afternoon before the war he had hurried to the cathedral...'got 30″ impression – darkness and one jewelled eye in the east – ere we were turned out. Very tired and full of impressions.' They had covered 149 miles that day, a fairly average mileage. Sometimes they would log over 200 miles in a single day, but he seldom found motoring wearisome, unless they had been delayed by a breakdown. At the day's end there was usually time for a reconnoitring walk before settling down to write up his journal, work over a story or poem, or write letters.

Of all the cathedrals he visited Chartres for him was the loveliest; as it had been for his Uncle Ned. Although for Burne-Jones it had been the sculptures with 'such lovely folds as can hardly be imagined'[11] which had impressed him most of all, and which he was to reproduce so gloriously in his own work. Once, before the war Kipling had been allowed to go out on its roof and look at 'the backsides' of the windows, a view not given to many. 'We found that every square millimetre of the glass had been microscopically etched by the years: inlaid here with fine lines of dirt blown up from the street; roughened in places to a tooth-like rough drawing-paper or rubbed down to the silky softness of uncut diamond; studded with minute iridescent efflorescences and conchoidal pittings, and everywhere worked into a thousand varying planes to sift and glorify the light. So we saw that it is not Man that makes perfection but the weather which his works must endure.'[12]

In 1921 Kipling sold his second Duchess for £1550. It had cost him £1254 in 1914. No wonder he maintained that a R-R was the only car he could afford. There was another reason too: punctures and broken springs apart, they rarely gave trouble. (The story goes that on one occasion when Kipling enquired of the company why he had not received their bill for coming to his aid when they had broken down in France, the reply came: 'Our cars never break down, sir!') Eighty years on this car is still on the road, handsomely re-bodied and now bearing on her dashboard a plate engraved with her name: The Duchess. In 1984 her then owner shipped her out to Dubai for British Week, where she was the star attraction and caught the attention of the Princess Royal, who proved she knew rather more about Silver Ghosts than did the owner. There is a curious twist to this car's history. She it was who carried an unforgiving Kipling across the Rhine after the first world war. Now I am told that she has crossed the Rhine once again – to be the property of a German author.[13]

That September the Kiplings and the new Duchess motored to Scotland; through 'heavy' Sunday traffic and 'lots of wife-killers' in the Midlands and past Wombwell's menagerie (a dozen horse-drawn beast vans and three camels plodding behind them) in north Yorkshire. Each year they drove north they seemed to encounter Brough Horse Fair and had once seen an elephant pulling one of the vans. The new car had her first real test in Scotland. She negotiated the little stone bridge at the head of Loch Striven, only to find that the road ran up the mountain-side like a wall. 'Rest and Be Thankful was naught to it. The Duchess dropped to her lowest and scrambled up by her teeth and toenails; for there was no surface – nothing but a slither of gravel and stones clicking under her mudguards.' At least it proved that the Duchess was more than up to her job and throughout the tour she ran 'divinely'. Kipling too was in for a first experience – of Campbell country. 'I can't love Campbells...But the beauty of Inverary is beyond words.' And so were the Duke's woods around his 'unspeakable, cock-hatted, mid-Victorian palace'.[14] (Inverary Castle is the seat of the Duke of Argyll, chief of clan Campbell, an ancient enemy of the Macdonalds.)

This was the only reference and an oblique one at that, to his Macdonald ancestry and the infamous massacre of the Glencoe Macdonalds by the Campbells. There was never any suggestion of visiting Skye or the West Highland coast (apart from their 'triple Devil of Curiosity' which led them to look in at the Oban Games) during their Scottish trips, although they motored as far north-east as Dornoch. I believe this was mainly for logistical reasons. Roads were few in the west of Scotland and had a tendency to 'break off like macaroni'[15] when approaching cliff-tops. Hotels were even fewer, and there was no electricity on Skye until the 1950s.

So what did he think of the Scots *vis à vis* the English? Judging from his poem 'The Puzzler' (1909) he thought the Celt predictable and talkative. Whereas the English—

> ...ah, the English! – they are quite a race apart.
> Their psychology is bovine, their outlet crude and raw.
> They abandon vital matters to be tickled with a straw;

and...

> For undemocratic reasons and for motives not of State,
> They arrive at their conclusions – largely inarticulate...
> And while the Celt is talking from Valencia to Kirkwall,
> The English – ah, the English! – don't say anything at all.

In other words there is not a lot to choose between his forebears on either side of Hadrian's Wall.

The Scottish scenery never failed to stir him, even in blinding rain when the mountains looked like 'new-washed pebbles, with enormous breadths of heather in bloom, brawling waters and the undefeated little railways dodging about through it all'. He noticed the war memorials, with long lists of names in the loneliest and smallest villages. And their hearts turned over when they passed the Old Manse at Creich where they had stayed for a month after Josephine's death. They called at the house. The minister was out but his sister was at home with the same maid of twenty-two years before, who looked 'with that all-piercing Scots eye at me and said: – "Ye'll be? Ye'll no be..." and I said I was and we all piled into the hall and time went backward for a bit.'[16] There were more memories when they called at nearby Skibo Castle and renewed acquaintance with the Carnegies who had offered them the use of the Manse all those years ago, and who now showed them 'priceless drawings by Phil and the Pater when our whisky ran out at the Manse'.

On the road to Oban Kipling briefly noted *not* seeing Dunstaffnage Castle because of the mist; no other comment is forthcoming. This was the Campbell-owned castle, built by a descendant of Somerled, in which Flora MacDonald was held prisoner (before being taken to London on a prison-ship) after helping Bonnie Prince Charlie evade capture. Was this laconic note in his journal a reference-by-omission to her: a doffing of his hat to the intrepid young Scotswoman who would marry a Macdonald kinsman?

They arrived at Oban in a full gale. 'The rain looped before the wind in blinding wreaths and sheets: and the passenger steamers dripped and ducked and bobbed at their piers, all ready to take charge of the 1/6d (7½p) teas on the return journey that the Scots lay out on the drenched grass and on the shining wet rocks like so many seals, rejoicing in their native weather...and the Eminent of these parts 'The O'Ban, The Mac'Arriagh Ban, and the rest of 'em, went to and fro through the hurricane in their kilts and plaids and Cairngorms, and the pipers that were more magnificent than coloured illustrations of army uniforms, piped at 'em. There was a profusion of Stewart Tartan thus proving that most of the Hotels were filled with Blood Royal – but they didn't look it: and they wore heather and myrtle and their appropriate Clan Plants in their bonnets...' It was already three p.m. and they could only stay an hour, but they saw an obstacle race and a 'beautiful Reel of Tulloch by four boys of the Dunblane Military School...who danced like goblins rather than humans...the whole show immensely interesting and explanatory of much about the Scots' (what did he mean?). Before they left Oban they bought a 'wondrous cake with cream and ginger nuts'. Later he reflected on all those 'flamboyant kilts and waving plaids', that would by then have turned back into Bank Managers, Divines and Business men in the south for another year. Whereas – 'God help us! – the English are drearily English all the year round, and if you put 'em into kilts – they'd be more English than ever.'[17]

The next day they went shopping in a Tweed Emporium. After a 'spirited hour or so' Carrie and Elsie ordered 'about seven quids' worth' of cloth, jumpers and a shawl for Taylor's (the chauffeur) new baby. 'But I was not allowed to buy me a Graham tartan travelling rug.' (It was the wrong clan, of course – even if, being green, it did match the car rather well.)

On their way to Beaufort Castle they passed the naval base at Invergordon and saw seven battleships lying there 'against the interminable single street that mothers and wives knew so well in the war...Curious how much passion and sorrow could flow through one street and leave no sign or trace.' The castle was found eventually in the heart of a heavily-wooded park. Lord Lovat (an earlier Lord Lovat had been executed as a Jacobite in 1747) was out, but his wife was at home 'with Lady Bonham-Carter (which I didn't remember was Asquith's daughter but said nothing indiscreet)'. After tea he was shown the most wonderful herbaceous borders he had ever imagined, 'in masses of sumptuousest colour...', and all tucked away behind fifteen foot rose-pink brick walls. 'Felt immensely better over what was a new experience.' By the time they reached Inverness at seven that evening (17th September) there was a hint of frost in the air, and an 8.50 a.m. start the next morning under a cloudless sky revealed white frost already melting on the rooftops. There was no mention of the melancholy Culloden Moor a few miles to the east where in April 1746 the Jacobite cause was finally lost and the Highland clans routed by the 'Butcher' Duke of Cumberland's army. If the day had gone the other way it is likely that this book would not have been written, had no tale to tell.

He hated to see the 'suspicious cleanliness' of choir-stalls or rood-screens in church or cathedral and was outspokenly pleased when attempts to restore them were 'mercifully frustrated by lack of funds'. On one of his evening walks while Carrie rested before dinner he explored an ancient belfry tower in the dusk. From it 'there came out a gust of the smell of all the ages – dry-rot, dirt, raw masonry – a most hopeless, lamentable and besetting stink – exactly, I presume, what a Scotch Calvinistic Hell would smell like. A very long time since I have been so wrought upon through the nose.'

Driving through his father's home county two years later he found it 'nice to hear the good meaty Yorkshire tongue again', and to see the gypsy waggons, tilt-two-wheelers and all the other 'wheeled rapareedom of the road' of the now-familiar Brough Horse Fair. Later, the Duchess was passed (at forty-six mph), as if she were standing, by an 'immoral' light-blue two-seater with lots of luggage behind. 'How sinful and wrong it is to do more than forty-five m.p.h. under any circumstances. We got up to fifty but even then we could not see him.' For some reason they had to pass through a system of 'insane' police controls at Grantham where licences were demanded and a 'filthy red-diamond label offered (by a man with a workmanlike pink tongue) to be stuck on the car as a "protection against further inspections."' He declined the offer. Why should the Duchess look like the cattle on the way to market with labels on their rumps – just to save the police trouble?[18] But the incident made good copy and joined the broken make-and-break spring a year later in 'The Prophet and the Country' (referred to earlier in this chapter).

This Duchess too has enjoyed a distinctive 'life after Kipling'. When she was traded in, in 1928, the company shipped her to their Bombay branch; a shrewd move, given her former owner's Indian background. She was bought by a religious sect who have used her once a year ever since to carry several priests and a heavy silver effigy on an eight mile pilgrimage, during which devoted followers shower the car with coins and red powder. She was last seen in 1982, still in use after an extensive overhaul. In motoring circles she is now known as the Holy Ghost – a nice Kipling touch.[19]

But it was to France's poplar-lined roads that he returned year after year with every expression of delight. Never mind what havoc they caused the Duchess, there was always the R-R depot in Paris to make her well again on the road home. He wrote a poem about them ('A Song of French Roads') in the evenings after dinner, in between working over his 'Botanic nonsense'.[20]

> Now praise the Gods of Time and Chance
> That bring a heart's desire,
> And lay the joyous roads of France
> Once more beneath the tyre—
> So numbered by Napoleon,
> The veriest ass can spy
> How Twenty takes to Bourg-Madame
> And Ten is for Hendaye.

1923 was a better year for Rudyard. *The Irish Guards in the Great War* was published to good reviews in April; and in the same month Bland-Sutton pronounced him cured. At the beginning of May they caught the South of France napping, as it were: although it was hot it was barely open. At Digne they took their usual evening stroll up and down a street that was 'all dirty and stale...shops ostensibly open but really shut: the day's work being done and the people perspiring gently at their own doors.' The hotel was very hot and they went to bed early. 'But the town was full of summer night footsteps and voices: as these ceased one heard the water swishing through the streets. At four-five Digne was livelily awake and cleaning itself with the care of a cat...the whole of the town, so dirty the night before, had been redd up, swilled down and swept.'

It was much the same at Aix. The flower beds had been dug over but were empty of flowers. The shops were all on the edge of opening but mostly they too waited to be filled up. 'A few English wandered about in the heat, looking more English than ever, but the overwhelming impression was of waiting for the curtain to rise...' The night 'was bland and balmy and the early part of it furnished with nightingales who sang ferociously outside.' The next night it rained but in no way 'quenched' the nightingales.

It was on a certain 'inauspicious' (and wet) day the following year that they inadvisedly took a short cut over chalky ground between cemeteries – and got stuck in the mud on the crest of a hill. Horse-power of the type which had a leg at each corner was needed to pull the Duchess out. Kipling and Elsie dutifully trekked downhill to the 'shut Sunday village', a twenty minute muddy walk. 'Everyone at Mass and the rest not available...Dogs in reeking farmyards...At last a woman to whom E. with much drama told the tale and – could anyone in the village hire us horses to pull out the auto?' The woman did not know. Her husband and another man were both ill. There was a farm next door with horses but no help, as everyone was at Mass. Up the silent street again, and another woman who said there was a Monsieur Bertrand in the village who had horses. 'He wouldn't be at Mass – not him...E. had only told the tale thrice. It was better told each time...' Then 'a nice fair young man with a carter's whip [who] asked pertinent questions as to weight and position of car, planks, ropes, etc., and for the seventh time E. told her tale of the stuck motor in the mud on the crest of the hill by the five tethered kine. (Oh, they knew that road.)'

The young man promised to be there in half an hour, and with 'profuse farewells we two went back to the wreck but not alone'. The young policeman and a 'weird brown-coloured boy on a bike – with an intellect' went with them. 'We four walked in great amity talking of life, of farming, of cattle, of a French girl the policeman knew who had married an Englishman in the postal department. "And I know all about it as I conducted the correspondence." What would life be like in England? "Oh, very different," said E. "And they don't drink wine?" "No. They drink pellall and stoot," said the boy swiftly.'

Meanwhile Taylor, 'naked of all but English had fairly pantomimed a horse out of a farmer', while from the village the nice young man approached with a brown and a white horse and some planks and chains. But it was the boy who then took over, 'possessed himself of the planks', and so arranged them under the wheels that the car could not slide back into the rut after the horses had jerked her out. Congratulations and francs were exchanged before 'the musing motor, under her own power, pushed and rooted through the last slough of despond and got on to the firm road she should never have left...It was E's triumph from first to last.' It was also one o'clock – 'two hours lost amid kindly and helpful souls.'

The wonderful individuality of character of the three thousand or so cemeteries in France never ceased to astonish Kipling. In a single afternoon in which he saw nine, there was one where;

> A little Cross of Sacrifice keeps watch over not more than sixty of our men, each beneath his own carven headstone...and the flowers have taken them all into their confidence. The moat at their feet divides them from the 'real' world where the motors go. They see nothing except the willows and thorns along its bank, the patches of brambles, and the long red wall pierced with an arch inside which the farm-yard lies golden and brown. It is so utterly still that one can hear the cows tearing the grass fifty yards away – so still and sheltered that not the bell of a flower moves. The white headstones tell that they have settled there in peace for a long, long while – until their loves come for them across the pasture, open the little gate whose latch is broken in advance, steal across the little, level interlude of perfect lawn and – they are happy for ever afterwards![21]

It was the following spring that Rudyard and Carrie crossed the Channel in the *Normannia* and reminisced with the old steward. This time they were not bound for the cemeteries of northern France but were headed south, with any luck, for the sun – and the cathedrals for certain. On the road to Biarritz they visited nine, including Chartres, whose great blue-grey bulk seemed to dominate the French landscape. To their 'immense wrath' they found their old hotel had been modernised – but the glass was all back in the cathedral windows after the war-time bombings and they hastened to see it as the twilight faded. '…The windows were like spirits incarnate, and made sad and proud together: broke up the deeps,' he confided to his journal.

Now, at each day's end he was working at a sonnet on 'Chartres Windows', in tandem with 'The Gardener'.

'Colour fulfils where Music has no power.' It was a bold first line, but for him it was the simple truth. 'Colour and the light of God behind it', as he described it to Haggard, was to Kipling as much an emotional experience as a Mozart concerto for the serious music lover. Colour was all India to him, the India of his golden childhood which he thought he had lost for ever at Southsea; until, miraculously, he found it again – such colour as he only remembered from his dreams – in the Burne-Jones' house each Christmastide. As for music, he used to say that Allah had left all music out of his make-up – 'except the brute instinct for beat'[22] which gave him all the rhythm he needed for his work. For many years its lack had not bothered him, but late in life he confessed that the older he grew the more he felt its handicap. And yet surely there is a truth in the sonnet's opening line for us all. Music alone could not compensate us for the absence of those glorious windows upon which the inward eye may feast – long after their light has been extinguished.

> Colour fulfils where Music has no power:
> By each man's light the unjudging glass betrays
> All men's surrender, each man's holiest hour
> And all the lit confusion of our days—

It was typical of Kipling's scrupulous eye to note the small but significant difference between medieval and 'modern' windows: that the early stained glass casts no colour on the ground.

In the meantime they had been to see the caves of the Dordogne with their inexplicable animal figures; and to an out-of-season Lourdes bereft of miracles. And where for some reason Kipling was consulted by one of the officials about his young daughter's obstinate constipation. 'Advised orange juice and Vichy,' he wrote laconically in his journal.

There was still no sign of spring at Biarritz, overlooking the Bay of Biscay '—not a bloom and hardly a bud'. Only the foreign mimosa trees were out and a single Catalpa, 'all ablaze: but of flowers in the grass and by the way, nothing but a few demented primroses'.[23] Still, he preferred it to the Riviera; the air came fresh from some thousand square miles of pine forest, and worked better than wine. Was he thinking in medicinal terms here?

At last, at the end of March he reported a day of hot sun and blue sky. Not having seen the sun for a year, he told Haggard, he did not quite know what to make of it. So he sat on the beach and grilled. He had sent off 'The Gardener' and a sonnet to be typed. 'A real fourteen-line Sonnet – only it breaks a lot of rules...so you see, tisn't a real Sonnet.'[24] Only in his journal did he admit to having daily headaches now, whether he worked or not; and a problem with vision in his left eye.

Their journey back to Paris was 'chequered' with more 'pot-holing', which meant a spell at the depot for the Duchess to have replacement springs fitted: 'Going with a car is like travelling with a woman in "a certain condition,"' he told Haggard. 'She needs a deuce of a lot of attention...'[25]

As for Carrie, never had she felt so sad, depressed and hopeless than she did on their return to Bateman's towards the end of April. And in May they were both saddened by three deaths in a single week: Lord Milner, Rider Haggard and Aunt Louie Baldwin.

---

1 HRH.
2 *ibid.*
3 RK after being presented with the Joan of Arc Medal, 1919.
4 'The Gardener', *Debits and Credits*, 1926.
5 *Souvenirs of France*, 1933.
6 RK's Motor Tours Journal, 1911-1926, KP.
7 'The Prophet and the Country', 1924, *Debits and Credits*.
8 Motor Tours, 1914, KP.
9 RK to John Kipling, 1915, *OBK*.
10 Motor Tours, 1924, KP.
11 Penelope Fitzgerald, *Edward Burne-Jones*.
12 *Souvenirs of France*.
13 Personal information (Michael Over).
14 RK to Mrs Hussey, 1921, KP.
15 *ibid.*
16 RK to Mrs Hussey, KP.
17 *ibid.*
18 Motor Tours, KP.
19 *Classic and Sportscar Magazine*, June 1982.
20 The study of botany was one of Kipling's hobbies and old English herbals a special delight.
21 Motor Tours, KP.
22 RK to Sir Percy Bates, 1931, KP.
23 HRH.
24 *ibid.*
25 *ibid.*

CHAPTER THIRTEEN

Bateman's 'enormously empty'; the long trail ends

Oh, veiled and secret Power
Whose paths we seek in vain,
Be with us in our hour
Of overthrow and pain;
That we – by which sure token
We know Thy ways are true—
In spite of being broken,
Because of being broken,
May rise and build anew.

'Hymn of Breaking Strain'

Elsie's announcement to her parents the previous spring (1924) that she wanted to marry could not have been unexpected. She was twenty-eight years old and had known George Bambridge, a captain in the Irish Guards and a man much liked by her family, for some time. It should have added up to the sound of wedding bells for anyone attuned to the situation. And yet Rudyard and Carrie had not allowed themselves to think of the day when Elsie would leave home; and worse still, live abroad. George was in the diplomatic service. Carrie was appalled at the change it would make in their lives, while Rudyard, although delighted at his daughter's obvious happiness, felt an unaccustomed jealousy towards the man who wanted to take his daughter away. Since John's death both parents had come to depend upon their only remaining child to lift their spirits and to be a constant companion – particularly to Rudyard. Without perhaps realising it, they had burdened her young shoulders with their unspoken grief.

After Elsie's wedding at St Margaret's, Westminster, that October they returned to Bateman's too weary at first to take in their loss. Ahead lay a long dark winter secluded from the world in their steep valley, in a house which Rudyard suddenly found 'resonant, silent, and enormously empty',[1] and which visitors described variously as chilly, gloomy, uncomfortable and hard-chaired. Elsie herself referred to the furniture, of the same period as the house, as stiff and lacking in comfort. Although it is fair to say that none of those descriptions would have occurred to either Rudyard or Carrie who were made of sterner stuff. (Even Rudyard's custom-made couch in his study was described by a friend as a 'settle', so hard was it.[2])

They went up to London often that winter – too often to please Carrie – to theatres, receptions and official ceremonies which Rudyard appeared to enjoy more than his wife who was now suffering from insomnia and depression. Kipling's enjoyment of London had much to do with the opportunity it gave him for lunching at one of his clubs; not for the delights of its dining-table (he was invariably on a diet of some kind) but for conversation with chance-met dining companions. For increasingly, as chronic ill-health settled on both the Kiplings in the ensuing years, they would be thrown upon each other's company, day in and day out, each worrying about the other's health to the detriment of their own: a vicious circle. So too was Rudyard's increasing dependence on his wife and her obsessive care of him. Alone together at Bateman's their only relief was the welcome weekend visitors. Welcome at least to Rudyard who came to look forward to their visits like a shipwrecked mariner his rescuers; while Carrie's 'eternal servant difficulty' (as Rudyard described it in a letter to Elsie in 1929) caused many a domestic upheaval.

But even when they did have visitors and Rudyard longed to steal away for a quiet smoke with an old friend, Carrie rarely allowed him out of her sight. She dominated his life from the time he got up in the morning to the time he retired in the evening – which, according to some, she also decreed. A guarded flame indeed. And Rudyard deferred to her in all things; even to the extent of allowing her the satisfaction of finishing off a story he was telling, in his compassion for the mother who had borne and lost her only son. For hers was the greater loss, he maintained: the mother who had also given him Josephine and borne her loss alone when he had been too ill to be told. He owed her so much that he subordinated his own grief to hers, whatever it cost him. However difficult she became, and there were times when her impossible behaviour verged on mental instability, his patience was endless, his loyalty unswerving.

Rudyard's way of keeping in touch with Elsie was to write her long letters and interest himself in every detail of her new life. He bombarded her with questions about the house and furniture, her domestic arrangements (even their plans for improving the kitchen), their friends and their social doings; and above all about her health. No domestic detail was too insignificant for his interest; no common cold too trifling for his anxious concern; and his relief on hearing she was better would be almost palpable. In February the Kiplings went over to Brussels for the first of many visits to their daughter and son-in-law when later they moved to Madrid and Paris. Rudyard saw for himself that they were happily settled in the house he had given Elsie. And Carrie 'refound' the daughter who had seemed to her sometimes to be dead. The two men got on well together, swapping stories and jokes in a way that would have been out of the question between him and his brother-in-law, Jack Fleming. But Carrie could never come to terms with losing her daughter, never refrain from trying to interfere in her married life, sometimes to a dangerous extent.

By the end of the year (1925) Rudyard was ill again, seriously ill with pneumonia. There followed seven weeks of acute anxiety and it would be the end of February before they could dispense with a nurse. By which time they were comfortably installed in a villa above Monte Carlo for a two months' stay. But his old gastric pains had returned as soon as he recovered from the pneumonia, and the weather in the South of France was none too warm. He decided that the motor car had made the Riviera 'an Hell – and a noisy smelly one', and referred to Canne's 'seasonal whoredom – very brilliant and crowded.'[3] They motored home in Esmeralda in leisurely fashion, resting for ten days in Tours where they were both ill. In Paris they stayed with friends and Rudyard rallied sufficiently to dress for dinner – for the first time since November. (When he was well he always dressed for dinner – entirely to please Carrie.) But noticeably his journal entries had shrunk, were now as brief and matter-of-fact as they had been when he first started to make notes of their tours fifteen years earlier in the Spectre, when they had also been Paris-bound. And they were to be the last he would make in his red-backed motoring diaries. Somewhere along the road to Paris he had run out of steam, lost the desire to record the journeys that by now he knew off by heart – complete with memories. As he had written two years earlier in his 'Song of French Roads'—

> The crops and houses spring once more
> Where Thirty-seven ran,
> And even ghostly Forty-four
> Is all restored to man.
> Oh, swift as shell-hole poppies pass
> The blurring years go by,
> And Twenty takes to Bourg-Madame,
> And Ten is for Hendaye!

That December Bland-Sutton advised him to go to South America for the winter where he would be assured of the warmth he craved.

The idea appealed to Kipling. It was twenty-five years since he had written: 'Oh, I'd love to roll to Rio, some day before I'm old!' He had just turned sixty-one when they set out for Brazil in the RMSP *Andes*. And they did roll too, in the Bay.

But it did not deter him from taking a deep interest in his fellow travellers, mainly homeward bound Spanish and Portuguese. He had not smelt the tropics for fifty or sixty years,[4] he told Gwynne largely, and was not sure how they would take him after all that time.

> I had some friends – but I dreamed that they were dead—
> Who used to dance with lanterns round a little boy in bed—
> Green and white lanterns that waved to and fro:
> And I haven't seen a Firefly now since ever so long ago!
> I had some friends – their crowns were in the sky—
> Who used to nod and whisper when a little boy went by,
> As the nuts began to tumble and the breeze began to blow:
> And I haven't seen a Coco-palm since ever so long ago!
>
> 'The Friends'

He had no commitments and no plans for the trip and apart from his speech to the Brazilian Academy of Letters in Rio, had resisted all invitations to make it an official visit. And he was not going to do any work. Or so he rashly confided to Gwynne – who then persuaded him to write a series of travel sketches for the *Morning Post*. The vivid descriptive passages of his 'Brazilian Sketches' bring to mind some of his earliest travel pieces, so maybe the smell of the tropics did have something to do with it. (Four years later in Egypt he would find the sight of mosquito curtains in place similarly stirring. 'Curious how that always wakes up memories of the house in Bombay,' he would write to Trix. And watching the light fade in the evening brought back memories of Lahore and the 'hot weather feeling on a May night.'[5])

> The South American boats are a world to themselves…Before our steamer began to shift the sun, all known centres of gravity had shifted, and were spinning on new bearings. As the blessed warmth brought back all the rules of right living – the thin kit, the long drink, and the disregard of what manufactured clocks say up North, men talked…The purple-blue seas pushed under and crowded back behind the ship; the sunrises without a shiver to them, when the day rules at once, full-born; and the instant down-dive of night over the very head of the sunset, had been forgotten too long for the soul's health.[6]

Somewhere in mid-Atlantic, a week before their arrival at Rio, he received a Marconigram announcing the formation of the long-threatened Kipling Society, an event which he regarded with gloomy distaste. 'How would you like to be a subject for dissection before death?' he asked 'Stalky' Dunsterville, the Society's first president. (His attitude towards the society would gradually soften until finally, in 1934, he gave it his blessing.)

He first saw Rio by night, a tropically warm one, lit up 'in constellations and cloud-stars of unbridled electricity...Hats, coats, hurry, time, and the other trifles had been dropped on the far side of the Line. The only trouble that remained was lest this dream-city of shell-white palaces, intensely lighted green foliage, arrogant statuary, silvered waters, and brooding mountains, would vanish if one dared look aside.'

From his eighth-floor hotel window next morning, he could see families – 'Papa, Mama, and some children in gay dressing-gowns' strolling along the 'immaculate embankment' to bathe. 'Never having noticed many English households bathing off, say, the Embankment, this interested me strangely. So did the gentleman in the bathing suit on a motor-bike; and the two girls so wet from their dip...that they were very justly put on either running-board of the family car, where they clung like heraldic supporters and discoursed in their damp dressing gowns across it.'

He went to the Botanical Gardens in search of the Victoria Regia lily 'at home', last seen in a picture-book of his extreme youth. And if possible, 'that bird with the very long toes (Jacara might have been its name) represented in the same picture-book as walking by choice on its leaves'. He found the lily living in a pond, her pads five to six feet across and turned up at the edges in three-inch rims. Her blossom was the size of an 'effective hat-box'. But the only Jacara bird he found was in a cage, for sale in the marketplace.

In his speech to the Brazilian Academy of Letters, given after attending the Carnival in Rio, 'of which we are all, this evening, the exhausted survivors', he reminded his audience that although he lived in 'that temperate world which puts on a thick coat when it looks at the stars', he was born and passed his childhood and early manhood in the tropics – 'who is a mother that never forgets her children however far they travel'.[7]

Under Brazil's own immense skies he is 'hauled up the face of a two-thousand-foot difference in level which occurs rather abruptly on the road between Santos and Sao Paulo'; and is promised that he will be brought down 'respectably by rail,' in a luxurious inspection car, no less. 'Next to travelling through a summer port in an English Admiral's own barge...there is nothing to equal Inspection Cars. You can do everything except run backwards for a second look...' He describes how the coaches, in blocks of three, are apparently pitched over an abyss, up-coaches balancing the down and worked by cable through five separate hauling stations. He mentions three of the engineers who were 'untemperamental Yorkshiremen and Scots; for the reason that all vital bearings in human machinery must run on the hardest jewels in the market' – a rare but even-handed compliment from Kipling towards maternal and paternal ancestors alike.

On the voyage home, while his indigestion returned, he worked on his 'Brazilian Sketches'. They disembarked at Lisbon and went by train to Biarritz to meet Elsie before motoring slowly home through France.

In October they were again in France where Rudyard spoke at the opening of the Indian War Memorial at La Bassée. Our Indian troops were 'of a great simplicity and an utter loyalty', despite their natural bewilderment after crossing oceans of whose existence they had never conceived; to find themselves in strange lands beyond the limits of their imagination, and countries which, for aught they knew, were populated by devils and monsters. But it was not long before...'the sane thrift of France as an agricultural nation soothed their hearts and set their minds at rest'.

One young Indian wrote home to reassure his mother not to be afraid. 'These people are as civilised as ourselves, and, above all the women are as good agriculturists as the men.' He had seen it, and learned that their land passed from father to son precisely as it did with them. 'They buy and sell in the streets, too – portions of fowl and meat, with needles, thread, scissors, and matches, just as we do in our bazaars at home.' Have no more fear, wrote the dutiful son, for they are in all respects like ourselves.[8]

The following February finds the Kiplings motoring in a hired Fiat in Sicily and – 'There is no sound reason why we should not be dead...' is the arresting first line of a long letter to Elsie on the matter. (This was the year that Carrie was warned of incipient cataracts in both eyes, had diabetes diagnosed and was at times almost crippled by rheumatism – and Rudyard was warned to stop smoking. So maybe they felt the time had come to live a little dangerously.) The previous day they had 'frolicked forth' from Palermo at nine o'clock on their 'little jaunt': a sixty-mile trip across the island to Girgenti where they were assured they would find it warmer. They had been told that the road was not very good, but still it was 'some sort of a road'. Until they came to a village called Fratri when it became 'a thing that could give points to the Somme at its palmiest. There was everything in Fratri except road.' Their driver who was becoming 'increasingly interesting' to Kipling, 'magicked her through somehow or other'. On the return journey they met a car on a precipitous section of the mountain where there had been a recent fall of stone, and their man proved his worth by helping the other driver, a boy of about fifteen, to negotiate the pass while his passengers, three women and a lady's maid got out. The latter 'cherished in both arms a square of plate glass about two foot each way. I thought at first she had come away with the inside of the car and looked for the blood. But it was part of their shopping in Palermo. She leaned against the parapet with this cut-throat machine in her arms, and I wondered why we went to Hollywood for films.'

After passing through an 'unexplained town' whose main street was full of men wrapped in shawls, and not a single woman visible, he came to the conclusion that 'Sicilians propagate in ways unknown to the rest of the world'. There were not more than five women per hundred kilometres – he had counted them – but they were all in the family way and all the children were sons and they never had less than seven at a birth. He had counted them too. 'It's the most prolific place outside a rabbit hutch that I have ever paid hotel bills in.' And after all that tortuous journey to Girgenti in search of warmth 'it was of course, quite fresh, not to say cold, with a high S. West wind blowing from the sea'.[9]

Two Mediterranean-based stories about St Paul – one of them aboard wheat-boat galleys – were the outcome of this trip; but not before Rudyard had called upon the expertise of his ship-owner friend, Percy Bates, for technical details of 'lading, bagged wheat and hides' for Paul's ship from Mycenae. Bates was a regular correspondent of Kipling's during the last twelve years of his life, but it took eleven of them before they reached Christian name terms – at Rudyard's postscript suggestion. In the 1930s Cunard was building its latest transatlantic liner (known until her launch as the 534) and, true to form, Kipling was interested in every last detail of her progress. Not that he wanted to sail in her: nothing would make him go to New York again, but he would like to attend her launching. A few years earlier, in a speech to the Chamber of Shipping, he had spoken of the shipping industry as the 'mother of the Old Navy and the sister of the New...the mainstay of our prosperity and our very lives'; had reminded his audience how 'by comparison it was only yesterday that, when a ship was once under the horizon, she passed beyond help or call for, perhaps half a year. To-day a tramp cannot report a cockroach-leg in a slide valve without half the North Atlantic coming to her help.' As for the 'gilt-edged' liners of today, 'every effort is made to persuade passengers that they are not at sea, but in a much safer place'. It did not work for him. He knew he had only to take the lift upstairs from the Tudor grill-room and look out of the window of the 'more or less Perpendicular library on the top floor', to see that 'same old grey wolf, the Ocean that harried our forefathers, waiting outside...a ship is a ship, and you cannot get away from it'.[10]

He had had his own 'ship' – his six-foot paddle-boat – painted green, red and aluminium and christened *534*, he told Bates, ready for 'summer cruises on the pond next spring'. He had even made a miniature Cunard House flag for her.[11]

Unfortunately Kipling was not well enough to attend the launching of the larger vessel – otherwise known as the ss *Queen Mary* – in September 1934. He sent the following telegram instead.

'Ecclesiasticus ch.9 verse 17. Heard it all with deepest contentment in your triumph.' (– For the hand of the artificer the work shall be commended: and the wise ruler of the people for his speech.) It was typical of Kipling to have chosen such an amazingly appropriate quotation, said King George. Since the war and their common interest in the War Graves Commission the two men had come to know and like each other well, and Kipling had written his monarch's Christmas speech to his people in the empire for the past two years.

Afterwards Kipling confessed to Bates that 'that dam launch' of his had been lying across his diaphragm for the last week. But once it was safely over he rejoiced in a 'détente of great happiness' – and had the *Queen Mary*'s length and beam marked out in a field stretched over a meadow and a half. He reckoned it looked more gigantic on land than it would at sea. And not to be outdone, he had sent his *534* for a refit. The numbers were to be scratched through and *Queen Mary* painted below, the house-flag and forward moorings of window-blind cord renewed, and the boat finished with three coats of varnish over all.[12]

Bates asked him to devise a Latin motto for the *Queen Mary* medal. After some thought Kipling delivered a text for consideration and Bates, being a cautious man, had it 'vetted' by the finest Latin scholars in the civil service. In due course they reported back that the text was appropriate but the Latin was indifferent. They recommended a simpler phrase – 'Maria Regina mari me commisit' – which was eventually chosen. Bates had then to write and explain the situation to Kipling. Back came the reply the next day on a postcard. 'Do you suppose I was ass enough to try to compose a Latin motto of my own? Tell your Whitehall pundits they'll find it in Horace's Odes.'[13]

There was always an ecstatic welcome waiting for him on his return to Bateman's, always an unquestioning companion (usually two) on his daily walks. Since 1925 Rudyard had been 'dominated by black Aberdeens'[14] after nearly thirty dogless years. He would brush their coats until they 'shone like bottles' – it was a new system of intensive brushing, he said, which meant they did not waste their lives scratching.[15]

They could be seen devotedly following him about the garden while he half sang, half talked to himself as he tried out some new verses. Sometimes he would take them 'sabbath-breaking' for mushrooms. But it was a different story when he bought himself a bow for exercise: 'which indeed it is,' he wrote to George. 'It makes the whole of your upper works creak – and if you don't take care skins your fingers…the dogs deeply mistrust it and never suggest retrieving the arrows.'[16] A Bateman's secretary once complained that Miki slowed down her walks along the lane because he would stop and sniff every blade of grass – until Kipling gravely explained to her that he was only reading his morning paper.[17]

After dinner in the evening was the dogs' playtime and they would be waiting for their master in the drawing-room. Rugs were rolled back and Kipling would throw himself on the floor in front of the fire for a game of ball. The child in him was never far beneath the surface and an onlooker would be hard put to it to say which side enjoyed the game more: man or dogs. But there would be no question about the state of the room after an hour's play.[18]

Inevitably the dogs begat stories, as well as the occasional litter of pups. The most successful of the former was *Thy Servant a Dog*, a collection of three stories told by Boots (another black Aberdeen) in simplified dog language, indulgently 'edited' by Kipling and with illustrations by G L Stampa. Published in October 1930 it had sold almost 100,000 copies by Christmas: its 'editor' had not been so popular for years.

Early in 1929 they again went to Egypt, his ever-fascinating 'length without breadth' country. At home there was ice on Brighton beach, the inner harbour at Dieppe was frozen up and the old Ostend boat, *Ville de Liege*, sank 'peacefully' in Dover Harbour. These things 'reconciled' Kipling to the jazz in their Cairo hotel and the crowds of tourists. It had been a most 'comfy' ship on the way out and everything possible done for the passengers' comfort. In spite of which, he confided to Elsie, words couldn't begin to convey his boredom. It was as if he had never been away from a ship in all his 'weary' life – but it was, visibly, giving Mother a rest. (According to Carrie's diary they spent the voyage doing their accounts – which could explain Rudyard's boredom.)

He went to Cairo Zoo and to the museum to see the Tutankhamen finds; visited cemeteries and battlefields of the Palestine campaign from Cairo to Haifa; and again sailed up the Nile for warmer weather and the fun of negotiating the shifting sandbanks. He was as interested as ever in the river's boatlife, even if it did turn him into a 'gibbering lounge lizard'[19] who could do no work. But as always his letters filled in the bare outlines with priceless brushstrokes of colour: the three-weeks old baby lions at the zoo playing with the bob on their mummy's tail; roadside Bedouins in their black tents in Palestine, each tent with its poultry which packs up and goes on camelback when they move on; a new-born baby donkey in a pannier on another donkey, 'his mother nuzzling behind him and his ears pinned up above his innocent little head, to give them the proper carriage...Do you know that camels on a string are always led by a little donkey? Wise small persons.'[20]

Writing to a friend of Elsie's (Isabel Sykes) whose brother Charles was buried at Gaza 'with a soldier of his own battalion on either side of him', Kipling describes the cemetery for her, just before sunset as it 'lies down to rest among the hills in the quiet...all one breathing stillness; and the breathing was the noise of the surf along Gaza beach'.[21]

They were taken to see the Greek church's treasure in the Holy City, climbed stairs 'worn to snaily-slimy smoothness and came out on a gallery high above all the congregations and religions...lost in a sort of gigantic stone attic with a steel trap-door over the stairs we had crawled up by.' While the unseen congregation below 'roared' through its psalms they were shown jewelled reliquaries and crosses beyond price and croziers of gold and ivory for an hour on end. It was the same only more so with the Armenians in an 'austere church of perfect peace and silence': jewelled embroideries and stoles the like of which he had never seen; 'books of beauty and perfection beyond anything known to the Greeks – a Gospel of St Luke...with marginal illustrations...that made us gasp.' And so across 'more courts of silence into a sort of papal palace where – one single figure at the end of a hundred foot room – stood His Beatitude the Armenian Patriarch – [who] knew your Dad's works in French'.[22]

That autumn there was a 'drouth' at Bateman's. With ninety thirsty oxen and 150 sheep to water it was no joke. Neither was their new cook who, they discovered, was out dancing every night until two a.m. (leaving the back door open) and furthermore, smoked in the kitchen while cooking. Then it was found that their bailiff had gone off round the world in a boat, having assured them he was going into a nursing-home, leaving the farm papers in a 'ghastly confusion where they aren't missing altogether' plus a lot of his unpaid bills. 'So there's three things – no food, no water and no peace!...And now – damn it! – to go out and get a meal at the Bedford – thirty-two miles down the road. And *this* is civilization.'[23] They were about to go up to town for a few days while their secretary skirmished round for help. Miss Walford, an English graduate, often spent much of her day driving about the countryside looking for staff during the four years she was working at Bateman's and living at Dudwell Farm. After she left them to breed Scotties in the Cotswolds (Kipling bought one or two of them for himself) she would sometimes come and stay with the Kiplings. And in all that time she was never once put in the embarrassing position of having to confess she had not read one of her employer's books![24] (She did read them eventually, at Wimpole, where she stayed with the recently-widowed Elsie Bambridge who herself did not read *Kim* until after her father's death.)

The following year it was Carrie's turn to be ordered abroad by her doctors. Early in February they set out for the West Indies, embarking at Avonmouth in the *Coronado*, a 'primitive' little boat built for the banana trade and carrying fewer than fifty passengers. But the cabins were 'most comfy...the nicest cabins we have ever met.'[25] Although Carrie reckoned that the captain regulated the heating towards the needs of his bananas rather than those of his passengers. Which was probably true.

A month later in Jamaica Carrie was taken ill with something that 'looked like enteritis...I was on duty day and night, fairly continuous and, tho' I say it, made a dash efficient nurse.' But further on in the letter to Elsie he admitted that '...oh, my Bird, I'm so tired'. They continued to Bermuda where Carrie, now seriously ill with appendicitis, went straight into hospital, leaving Rudyard to face the world on his own. In the grand new Bermudan hotel he found himself surrounded by visiting boatloads of Americans fleeing their prohibitionist country at weekends, for what he called 'drunken orgies' and they called making 'whoopee'. Kipling was 'reactionary' enough to feel 'sickish at seeing or talking to drunken women'.[26] Everyone at the hotel was as kind and sympathetic as they could be but the price of fame was high. He dared not linger downstairs when he went for his meals or 'there forms itself a sort of levée'. For the same reason he could not walk in the gardens in peace, when there wasn't much else to do except watch the 'unbelievable' flowers growing, in between visits to Carrie. Settling down to any work was not easy under the circumstances, although as usual he had something 'simmering' in his head. If it wasn't for that he would 'go off his rocker' from sheer boredom. (Much later, following 'the law that all the funny ones are written out of the deeps of dejection,'[27] he would write the comical parrot tale, 'A Naval Mutiny', set in *Ba*muda – as he referred to the island. It made him laugh to read it. This was not unusual. Visitors to Bateman's who enjoyed the privilege of being read to by their host in his study – perhaps one of his latest tales – reported how well he read them. He would lose himself completely in the story, choking over a sad passage and laughing uproariously, as if hearing it for the first time, over the funny parts.)

When Carrie was discharged from hospital with a nurse some days later Rudyard waited on her every whim in their hotel suite. But just as she seemed to be getting stronger she developed a secondary infection and had to return to hospital. Rudyard moved into an adjacent boarding house so as to be on hand to help look after their difficult and demanding patient. Or as he put it, tactfully: his wife responded better to his ministrations than the nurses'. It was to be the end of May, ten weeks after their arrival on the island, before Carrie was fit enough to travel home; via Canada. Nothing would persuade Rudyard to set foot in America again.

But his affection for Canada, coupled with his enthusiasm for things mechanical, had resulted in an unusual request from that country's engineering institute a few years earlier. They wished to establish an oath or creed to which young engineers could subscribe and decided there was no-one who could put it up in better form or have a deeper insight into its meaning than Rudyard Kipling. His reply contained a draft for the entire form of The Ritual of the Calling of an Engineer including the Obligation, and the suggestion that all engineers should wear a steel faceted ring on the little finger of their *working* hand.[28] The first such ceremony of initiation took place in 1925 and included four of his poems. One of these was an early draft of 'Hymn of Breaking Strain', written especially for the purpose which had been at the back of his mind for some time; although it was not finished until late 1933.

The careful text-books measure
(Let all who build beware!)
The load, the shock, the pressure
Material can bear.
So, when the buckled girder
Lets down the grinding span,
The blame of loss, or murder,
Is laid upon the man.
Not on the Stuff – the Man!...

We only of Creation
(Oh luckier bridge and rail!)
Abide the twin-damnation—
To fail and know we fail.
Yet we – by which sole token
We know we once were Gods—
Take shame in being broken
However great the Odds—
The Burden or the Odds.

237

That winter Carrie was ill in bed with rheumatism and his beloved Wop died. 'He had owned me for six years and a few months. It hurts damnably.'[29] At such times, with wife and grieving servants to be sustained, everything fell upon his shoulders. Nor did he enjoy having to sleep without sheets, one of his 'by no means minor objections' to rheumatism. It made him feel like Dartmoor. In the New Year they went to a freezing and fog-bound Bath for Carrie's treatment: it was gout now, not rheumatism. And they went by courtesy of R-R's latest 'close-coupled' demonstration car: 'a revelation!'[30] he told Elsie – and drew her a sketch.

While his wife was being massaged and bathed Rudyard walked about the city seeing literally nothing except swirling fog and steam. And it was too dark to see anything inside Gregory's bookshop. Could he, perhaps, get something pretty for his Bird at Jolly's: bits of ribbons, or groceries – or patent preparations? All orders would be faithfully executed. Otherwise his day was brightened by his annual bargain with the Corona people, where by mistake he was given a machine with 'micro' type. At first he thought it rather neat, but half way through his letter to Elsie decided it was impossible for his 'literary workin's' and fled in a taxi to change it for another. Kipling had a close if erratic relationship with a series of typewriters which, he said, couldn't spell; and one of which, as he explained to an old soldier, was as hard-mouthed as an army mule.[31] When ultimately he reached the heights of owning a noiseless model – she spelt under her breath, so that he couldn't hear what she had put down till he saw it.[32] This year however he was 'seduced' into buying the latest Remington model. It was reckoned to be an extravagance – by Carrie? – although he stoutly maintained that it was a tool of the trade. Either way, he was for the moment 'as happy as a child' with it, and his 'new and shy' typewriter accompanied him to Egypt at the end of February.[33]

While he was in Egypt he bought a tiny charm for a cousin's cat: an amulet representing Pasht the Cat Goddess, which would probably have been worn on the wrist about 1000 BC. It was guaranteed to him 'with many oaths as genuine'. (And so it is.) The hieroglyphs at the base, which could be used as a seal, mean Protection and Truth. 'As a cat has nine lives, she needs less protection than any other beast, and no cat ever knew anything about Truth.'[34]

In the summer a new pup arrived at Bateman's to be a companion for lonely James – who ignored him, except for 'peeing on his head' one day when they were both exploring the same tuft of grass. 'Wish I could do that to people whom I love not,' he confided to George.[35]

September's 'ruinous' budget worried them, and they gave some thought to giving up the car and finding a place for the chauffeur.

Instead they economised with a smaller model: the 'dinkum' new 25 hp similar to the 'revelation' that had taken them to Bath. Not only was she lighter and warmer than his previous Duchess (the 40/50 Phantom) but she '...scuttles like a rabbit; turns like a hansom and doesn't even whisper!'[36]

But the fun was going out of motoring and Kipling was one of the first to see the implications. It was no longer just a few 'wife-killers' among the Sunday drivers that he had noticed ten years earlier on his way north. Now he observed the ever-increasing motor traffic, road surfaces that skidded like soap in the wet – and a new kind of ignorant driver. He suggested there should be a road safety campaign with competitions for rhymes or couplets on the subject, and that the AA should adopt the winning lines. 'It's gone warm here,' he wrote to George that May, 'and all England is out killing each other on the road...We saw five smashes by the roadside between Chelmsford and Colchester. One was a large Rolls copulating with an embarrassed bus.'[37]

The last two lines of his fox-hunting poem, 'The Fox Meditates', spelt it out in words of one-syllable.

> And so began, in skid and stink,
> The real blood-sport of Britain!

To Rudyard's great joy Trix was now her old self again, had 'come clean out of the cloud that lay upon her for so long; and I can't well tell you how cheered I am.'[38] She came to stay at Bateman's and brother and sister went off for long companionable walks together; just like the old days.

By the end of the year he was hesitating between titles for what would be his last collection of tales. *That* was the difficult part of a book, he told his Aunt Edie. And one can see why, with Kipling: the title was usually the only discernible link between the book's contents. *Limits and Renewals* was no exception. As a hen covers a clutch of eggs, including the odd bad one, the title covered fourteen disparate tales.

Five of them deal with the after-effects of war and how each man's recovery is achieved – in one joyous case by the healing power of laughter; in another by a man's love for his black Aberdeen. There is a slight, late Anglo-Indian tale about a six year old boy; the two stories of St Paul in the Mediterranean already mentioned; a late motoring farce and a revenge story-cum-farce in a rural setting. Of the two other revenge stories, the lesser of the two, an early tale needlessly dredged up, shows grown men acting like schoolboys; while the greater (by far) relates how a man of letters plans revenge on a thoroughly unpleasant Chaucer specialist (by successfully forging a Chaucer manuscript) –

until he discovers the man is dying of cancer and has a faithless wife. Typically, Kipling conducted his own piece of Chaucerian forgery, just to prove it could be done. There is a story of the after-life and 'breaking strain'; and there is a medical tale ('Unprofessional') involving a cancer patient in which Kipling explores the concept of the stars' influence on a patient's progress – in this case the 'tides' they cause in human cells – while suggesting that '"Imagination is what we want. This rigid 'thinking' game is hanging up research. You told me yourself, the other night, it was becoming all technique and no advance..."'[39]

Kipling's friend, the surgeon Bland-Sutton was astonished by this tale which he said was as much in advance of the times as its author's flying stories.[40] Kipling was, in fact, anticipating by many years the research into biorhythms.

Whether by chance or design these fourteen uneven tales, together with their elucidatory poems, seem to represent a microcosm of Kipling's life: his joys and despairs, his beliefs and obsessions.

A month after its publication in April 1932, Kipling was 'not a little proud' of being made an honorary Fellow of Pepys' own college at Cambridge. Now he could speak of 'his' college, he told Bates. By July he had settled down to the task of revising, classifying, indexing and arranging in chronological order the proofs of what was to be the last edition of his *Verse (Inclusive Edition, 1885-1932)*. This was the nuts and bolts of the printed word, tedious, eye-straining – and essential. One might think, given his bad eyesight and appalling health, that he would for once delegate the task. But it was not in his nature to give up what was, for him, all part of the job. Perhaps sentiment had something to do with it too, knowing it would be the last collection of verse to be published in his lifetime. And perhaps he recalled the first: that slim volume whose verses had come 'without invitation, unmanneredly, in the nature of things...'[41] and outside office hours; and those 'glorious and sometimes obscene misprints'[42] of the native compositors that used to enliven the day's end for him.

Now forty-six years later he described the way of it in a letter to Trix. '...For the moment I am in a small and pernickety Hell. 'Tis thus.' And he told her about the latest collection with its accumulation of new material since it was last published and how he must read the proofs of the whole thing and 'wheel them into some sort of order. (Now I am *not* orderly) and that has meant a set of proofs the size of a small hayrick...they arrive in duplicate – some in triplicate – in wudges of from two hundred to a hundred pages all neatly tied up with paper-tummy bands (and I am *not* neat!). I cleared my writing table to the bone, and spread 'em out yesterday and they all got mixed as the wanton eels. They are all back again in their belly bands and harnessed with additional ones of red elastic so that they can't get off and "commit poetry" with other wudges. And the whole blessed thing is about 800 pages.'[43] And so it was. He finished the proofs six months later (in between writing *Souvenirs of France* and the occasional story or poem) and it was published in October.

Long voyages were now forbidden him, so it had to be the south of France in future. They rented the Villa L'Enchantement set among vineyards and only five miles from Cannes, but in all other respects a world and a half removed from civilisation. (Nevertheless it boasted three bathrooms and at least five 'rears' that he knew of. They all worked too – until the day the main drain became blocked when he supposed it was tempting the gods to have a house with five of them.) He settled down to doing nothing whatever, except for learning more Horace Odes by heart – 'I can say ten of 'em now as the children say' – and feeding and making fat four or five starving cats. And as always, writing letters. 'The almonds [are] almost crazy with bloom, and the bees, who have come in to plunder, quite so. They are banded, rather savage, ladies who have been losing their tempers over the ragged and frost-bitten rosemary outside our windows.'

One day they strayed into another and warmer world on the other side of the hill and found themselves among 'timeless terrace-works of old orange trees, heavy with fruit, and not a breath to trouble them'. Exploring further they came upon a terrace set with more orange trees, plus 'a loquat and a peach in fullest bloom...' and beneath them 'some brilliant-hued cocks and hens and a Nun pigeon on most vivid grass, adorned with low wild irises in flower! It sounds mad, but under the sunlight and the slashing shadows of the loquat-leaves, it all composed like a most marvellous piece of Jap cloisonné lacquer-work.'[44]

They were invited to lunch with the Duke of Connaught who showed them his two gardens: the 'tame' and the wild. The five or six acres of wild garden was on the edge of a cliff. 'It was a garden! The Duke said that all the things therein had "sown themselves". (But, I fancy gardeners don't quite tell the truth to Dukes.) Among the rosemary, salvia, gentians and daisies was every manner of rare iris (and I'll be damned if an iris sows itself!)'[45]

It was during their stop-over in Paris in 1933, on their way home from the south of France that Kipling was taken ill again – violent pains and haemorrhage – and where at long last a correct diagnosis was made of his trouble. It was a duodenal ulcer, but nothing worse, and he was put on a strict diet of rice, macaroni and one boiled egg a day. 'But one can't work on farinaceous flap-doodle.'[46] Not that he was well enough to work anyway; any more than he was fit enough to return home in time for them to be Elsie's first guests at Wimpole Hall, a magnificent *circa* eighteenth century Cambridgeshire mansion, which she and George had leased for the summer; and which would be the Bambridges' home for the rest of their lives. 'With both wings dynamited it would be a lovely gite...' Kipling teased George. But it cheered him up to hear their descriptions of being introduced to English rural living, English food and English clergy. They would simply have to put up with British cuisine, he warned them: it was a religion, not an art. After five weeks' convalescence and the occasional 'walk-about' in the Paris sunshine he was at last fit enough to make the journey back to Bateman's, full of rebellion, but little else, about a diet that would insult a canary.

At the beginning of 1934, a year in which he did little work and they were both unwell, Kipling noted that the Hun was getting into position for – ''36? or a year later? I don't suppose anything will teach our people anything.'[47] (Hitler was now the German Chancellor and swastikas were much in evidence.) He raged at the pacifism prevailing in English schools and universities in stark contrast to the fanaticism being pumped into the eager Teutonic youth; and he urged the authorities to start planning air raid precautions. For the second time that century his prophecy of the Armageddon to come was ignored. No prophet was without honour more than was Kipling in the last thirty years of his life. He waited until an opportunity arose, in 1935, to address the issue publicly. In a sombre speech to the Royal Society of St George and in a voice suppressed of all emotion he spoke of the generation of Englishmen, three-quarters of a million of them, wiped out by the war; and of the large but unknown number who had since died from their wounds or been permanently incapacitated. He spoke of our 'State-defended defencelessness' that had not borne much fruit – and only in the past year had it been recognised that we had 'walked far enough along the road paved with good intentions. It is now arranged that, in due time, we will take steps to remedy our more obvious deficiencies...but if that time be not given to us...it is possible that before we are aware, our country may have joined those submerged races of history who passed their children through fire to Moloch in order to win credit with their Gods.'[48]

The speech was generally resented as being unsuitable for Jubilee Year and hardly reported in the press. In much the same manner had his prescient verses, 'The Storm Cone', been dubbed 'exaggerated and gloomy' three years earlier.

> This is the midnight – let no star
> Delude us – dawn is very far.

This is the tempest long foretold—
Slow to make head but sure to hold.
Stand by! The lull twixt blast and blast
Signals the storm is near, not past;
And worse than present jeopardy
May our forlorn tomorrow be.

That August Carrie was taken ill and advised to go to Marienbad for the cure. It would be a painful ordeal for both of them to travel through Germany, but go they did. To add to the joy of nations, a German newspaper had recently revived the old chestnut about Kipling being a half-caste – which, it said, explained his super-jingoism and attitude towards their country. The visit to Marienbad brought no improvement to Carrie's health, but against all the odds Rudyard found unexpected happiness in the woods and hills that reminded him of Vermont.

On the first day of August he had started to write his autobiography. He kept at it assiduously over the next few months, allowing nothing to take precedence over it. The time had come to put his affairs in order, clear his work-table of those 'unneeded essentials'[49] and sort out his life into more or less neat piles. Some of those piles would be discarded, others ignored altogether in an autobiography that dealt with his life only from the point of view of his work. There would be no mention of Flo Garrard or Mrs Hill, of Wolcott Balestier or his brother Beatty; nothing at all about the deaths of Josephine and John.

He was still revising the typescript on Boxing Day in the middle of a family Christmas and with his seventieth birthday only days away; an event, he said, that seemed 'to lack charm'.[50]

For all its omissions and occasional inaccuracies *Something of Myself* makes maddening yet compulsive reading; and like so much in Kipling's life, leaves many unanswered questions. In his biography (1978) Lord Birkenhead states that the book's apt title was suggested posthumously by Kipling's friend and surgeon, Webb-Johnson, who also edited it. However, to date no evidence has been found to uphold Birkenhead's statement.[51]

He had no fear of death he told his Aunt Edie who had written to him for his birthday. 'He who put us into this life does not abandon His work for any reason or default at the end of it. That is all I have come to learn out of my life. So there is no fear! I was hoping for your letter, my dear; and it makes me feel better to have got it. Ever your loving Ruddy.'[52]

In a letter to Theo Dunham he touched on the Cosmic Ray and the 'advance-guard of Research...skirmishing along the borders of Matter and Spirit and finding out that that frontier...is "debateable."' It was all set out in 'The Threshold', he said, the verses that followed 'Unprofessional'.

Dunham sent him a book called *Man the Unknown* which set Kipling musing deeply. It re-established the fact for him that man was 'as unknown as the internal combustion engine, every detail of which is explicable except the nature of the spark that causes the mixture to explode. So it may be with us.'[53] It was typical of Kipling to have put his finger on such a brilliant, yet workmanlike, analogy. And to the end of his life he never lost that touch.

The weather was 'steadily beastly', he wrote to Bates from Browns Hotel on 10th January; the brook was in permanent flood at the bottom of the garden, and banks were caving in at the tail-end of a first-class gale. He and Carrie were in town for a few days before embarking for Cannes.

Two days later he was taken violently ill in the night and rushed to the Middlesex Hospital. Webb-Johnson was called to his bedside to operate. 'What's the matter, Rud?' he asked his patient. 'Something has come adrift inside,' explained Rudyard, accurately summarising his condition – a perforated duodenum – in five simple words.[54] But time had almost run out for the consummate wordsmith. Rudyard Kipling died six days later in the early hours of 18th January 1936.

'...Our Wedding Day,' wrote Carrie in her diary. And closed the book.

1 Carrington.
2 Julia Tauffleib, KJ.
3 Motor Tours, KP.
4 RK to Gwynne, 1927, KP.
5 RK to Trix, 1931, KP.
6 'Brazilian Sketches', *Letters of Travel*, 1938 (Sussex and Burwash Editions).
7 'The Spirit of the Latin', 1927, *BoW*.
8 'Our Indian Troops in France', 1927, *BoW*.
9 RK to Elsie, 1928, KP.
10 Shipping, 1925 *BoW*.
11 RK to Bates, 1933, KP.
12 *ibid.*
13 KJ.
14 RK to Trix, 1932, KP.
15 RK to Elsie, 1928, KP.
16 RK to George Bambridge, 1930, KP.

17 Cecily Nicholson, 'Some Recollections of Bateman's', 1978.
18 Taufflieb.
19 RK to Elsie, 1929, KP.
20 *ibid.*
21 RK to Lady Isabel Sykes, 1929, KP.
22 RK to Elsie 1929, KP.
23 *ibid.*
24 Miss Walford (Personal information).
25 RK to Elsie, 1930, KP.
26 RK to C E Hughes, 1930, KP.
27 RK to Elsie, 1931, KP.
28 Documents at Bateman's, Burwash.
29 RK to C S Jarvis, 1930, KP.
30 RK to Elsie, 1930/1, KP.
31 RK to Sgt Stringer, 1935, KP.
32 RK to Edith Macdonald, 1933, KP.
33 RK to Elsie, 1931, KP.
34 Personal Papers.
35 RK to George Bambridge, 1931, KP.
36 RK to Hughes, 1932, KP.
37 RK to George Bambridge, 1931, KP.
38 RK to Elsie, 1931, KP.
39 'Unprofessional', *Limits and Renewals,* 1932.
40 Carrington.
41 'My First Book'.
42 *SoM.*
43 RK to Trix, Birkenhead.
44 RK to Herbert Baker, 1934, KP.
45 RK to Lady Bland-Sutton, 1932, KP.
46 RK to Dr W S Melsome, 1933, KP.
47 Birkenhead.
48 'An Undefended Island', Speech to Royal Society of St George,1935, *BoW,*
   Sussex Edition, 1938.
49 *SoM.*
50 Carrington.
51 Professor Pinney.
52 RK to EM, Carrington.
53 Birkenhead (*Man the Unknown,* by Alexis Carrel, Hamish Hamilton, 1936).
54 Birkenhead.

Epitaph

At the beginning of World War Two a new and powerful destroyer was named after the poet who had foretold the coming of a second world war; the man who had confessed to loathing destroyers – 'half switchback, half water-chute, and Hell continuous'[1] – ever since attending that nightmare trial of an 1890s prototype.

In 1941 HMS *Kipling* – her motto 'Keep On', her crest the familiar elephant's head – took part in a major rescue operation off Crete. Ahead of her two of her sister ships, the *Kashmir* and the *Kelly*, commanded by Lord Mountbatten, were dive-bombed and sunk. HMS *Kipling* steamed to the rescue, dodging Stuka bombs as she wove in and out of the wreckage picking up survivors. Although overladen and with a hole in her side she managed to reach her home port, Alexandria, safely. Later that year she sank a U-boat while on convoy escort duties, but then was herself sunk by the Luftwaffe the following spring.[2] The Voice of the Silent Service would have been proud of his namesake's record.

---

1 *Sea Warfare.*
2 Lecture by Lieut Robinson, DSC, RNR to Kipling Society, 1946.

Index of Kipling's Works

'.007' 103
Abaft the Funnel 49/*n*3, 63/*n*30, 66/*n*41, 73/*n*12
'Absent-minded Beggar, The' 130
Actions & Reactions 166
'Advertisement, The' 139
'American Notes' 53
'Amour de Voyage' 21
'As Easy as ABC' xx, 166
'At the End of the Passage' 69

'Baa Baa Black Sheep' 9, 11,12, 42, 45, 77
'Ballad of East and West, The' 65
'Ballad of the *Bolivar*, The' 89
Barrack-room Ballads 49, 66, 71, 97
'Below the Mill-dam' 143
'Bonds of Discipline, The' 162
'Boots' 234
'Brazilian Sketches' 229, 231
'Brother Square Toes' 171
'Brugglesmith' 65, 101
'Brushwood Boy, The' 115, 135

Captains Courageous xvi, 102, 105-7, 115, 135
'Carolina, The' 13
'Cells' 63/*n*32
'Chartres Windows' 225
'Children's Song, The' 180
'City of Dreadful Night, The' 31/*n*15
'Conundrum of the Workshops, The, 103
'Danny Deever' 66
Day's Work, The 95, 102,123
Departmental Ditties 63, 74
'Devil and the Deep Sea, The' 103
'Disturber of Traffic, The 76

'Dusky Crew, The' 18

Echoes 30
'Edge of the East, The' 89-90
'Egg-Shell, The' 163
'Egypt of the Magicians' 178-80
'Elephant's Child, The' 122/*n*34, 130
'En-Dor' xx
'English Flag, The' 75
'English School, An' 17/*n*32, 18/*n*35, 20/*n*38
'Exiles' Line, The' xiv, 89

'Files, The' 143
'Finest Story in the World, The' 76-7, 162
'Fires, The' 112
Fleet in Being, A 118
'For All We Have and Are' 188
'Fox Meditates, The' 239
'France at War' 198/*n*6
'Friends, The' 229
'Fringes of the Fleet, The', *Sea Warfare* 199-202
From Sea to Sea Vols 1 and 2 xv /*n*7, 53, 134

'Galley-Slave, The' 71
'Gardener, The' 210, 224-5
'Gehazi' 183
'General Summary', *Departmental Ditties* 27, 36
'Gipsy Trail, The' 87-8

'Half-a-Dozen Pictures' 92/*n*9
'Harp Song of the Dane Women' 170
'Home' 82/*n*26
'Horse Marines, The' 149

'House of Shadows By Its Occupant, The' 37, 69

'House Surgeon, The' 117/*n*18

'Hymn of Breaking Strain' 226, 237

'If' 181-2

'In Partibus' 62/*n*28, 68

'In Sight of Monadnock' 88/*n*2

'In Springtime' 44/*n*49

'In the *City of Berlin*' 56

'In the Neolithic Age' (Illustration 16)

Irish Guards in the Great War, The 203-5, 207, 222

'Islanders, The' 132

'It!', *Abaft the Funnel* 49

'Judson and the Empire' 79

Jungle Books, The 100, 102, 104, 107, 135, 147

Just So Stories 122, 127, 163-4

'Justice's Tale, The' 152

Kim 134-5, 236

'King, The' 104

'King's Pilgrimage, The' 216

'Knights of the Joyous Venture, The' 168, 170

'Last Term, The' 148

'L'Envoi' 79

Letters of Marque 41

Letters of Travel 44, 53, 89, 176, 178

'Letters on Leave', *Abaft the Funnel* 73/*n*12

'Letters to the Family' 176

'Lichtenberg' 133

Life's Handicap xiv

Light that Failed, The xvi/*n*11, 61/*n*26, 72, 74, 77-8, 81

Limits and Renewals 239

'Lisbeth' 61

'Literature' 12/*n*9, 170

'Long Trail, The' 78

'M'Andrew's Hymn' 80, 93, 100, 102-4, 115

'Mandalay' 49

Many Inventions 102

'Marrèd Drives of Windsor, The' 152

'Mary Gloster, The' 104

'Mary Postgate' 188

'Mary, Pity Women!' 60

'Menagerie Aboard, A', *Abaft the Funnel* 49/*n*3

'Merrow Down' 125

'Mesopotamia' 202, 206

'Mine Sweepers' 200

'Mrs. Bathurst' 81, 159

'Mother Maturin' 32, 134

'Motor Tours Journal' 212-15, 221, 223, 228

'Mowgli' 156/*n*7

Muse Among the Motors, The 152

'My Boy Jack' 193

'My First Book' 27/*n*2, 36-7

'My Great and Only', *Abaft the Funnel* 66/*n*41

'My Sunday at Home' 101

'Native Born, The' 98

Naulahka, The 73, 75, 78, 92, 199

'Naval Mutiny, A' 236,

'New Army in Training, The' 176/*n*4, 189/*n*27

'New Dispensation, The' *Abaft the Funnel* 63/*n*30

'One Viceroy Resigns' 74

'Our Indian Troops in France' 231/*n*8

Outward Bound Edition, The 113-4/*n*5

'Phantom Rickshaw, The' 30

'Philadelphia' 171

Plain Tales from the Hills 28-9, 37, 40, 44, 61, 63, 81, 134, 182

'Prayer, The' 129

'Priest in Spite of Himself, A' 171

'Progress of the Spark. The' 152

'Prophet and the Country, The' 213, 221

Puck of Pook's Hill xx, 135, 158/*n*13, 167-8, 181-2

'Puzzler, The' 218

Quartette 30
'Question, The' 202

'Recall, The' 174
'Recessional' xvi/*n*12, 119, 148, 181
'Record of Badalia Herodsfoot, The'
    59, 65
Rewards & Fairies 135, 171, 181-2
'Rhyme of the Three Captains, The' 74
'Rhyme of the Three Sealers, The' 91
'Roman Centurion's Song, The'
    137/*n*19

'School Song, A' 16/*n*27
Schoolboy Lyrics 29
'Scribbler, The' 10
'Sea Constables' 188
Sea Warfare 202, 247
'Sestina of the Tramp Royal' 109
Seven Seas, The 102, 115
'Ship that Found Herself, The' 3, 103
'Shipping', *A Book of Words* 232-3/*n*10
'Slaves of the Lamp' 116
'Smuggler's Song, A' 140/*n*3
Soldiers Three 63, 68, 80, 93
'Some Aspects of Travel' 137-8
'Some Earthquakes' 92/*n*8
Something of Myself xv/*n*9, 12, 81, 243
'Song of French Roads, A' 221, 228
'Song of Seventy Horses' 209
'Song of the Banjo, The' 131
'Song of the Cities, The' 81
'Song of the English, A' 117, 147
'Song of the Exiles, The' xxvi/*n*10
'Song of the Wise Children' 121
Souvenirs of France 19/*n*36, 212/*n*5,
    217/*n*12, 241
Stalky & Co 17/*n*31, 116, 127, 134, 149
'Steam Tactics' 142, 144, 147-8, 159
'Storm Cone, The' 242
Story of the Gadsbys, The 43
'Sussex' 154
'Swept and Garnished' 188

'Taking of Lungtungpen, The' 93
'Their Lawful Occasions', *Traffics and
    Discoveries* 162

'They' 125, 159
'Three and – an Extra' 40/*n*40
'Threshold, The' 244
Thy Servant a Dog 234
'To a Lady, Persuading her to a Car',
    The Muse among the Motors 152
'Tommy' 66/*n*42
'Tour, The' 146
'Tour of Inspection, A' 149
Traffics & Discoveries 159
'Two Lives' 20
'Two-sided Man, The' 136-7, 184

'Undefended Island, An' *BoW*
    242/*n*48
'Unprofessional' 240, 244
Verse (Inclusive Edition 1885-1932) 240

'Voyage, A' 1882, 3

'War in the Mountains, The' 205
'White Man's Burden, The' 133
'White Seal, The' 91
'Wireless' 159-161
'Wish House, The' 207
'With the Night Mail' xx, 165-6

General Index

Aitken, Max *see* Beaverbrook, Lord
Allahabad 40-3, 44
Allingham, William xxiii
Australia & New Zealand *see* Globe-
    trotting in
Automobile Association 146, 239
Arundell House, Tisbury 100
Athenaeum Club 113
Austen, Jane 44

Baldwin, Alfred xxiii, 26
Baldwin, Mrs A (Louisa Macdonald)
    xxiii, 5, 84, 225
Baldwin, Stanley 1st Earl of Bewdley
    PM xxiii, 5, 13, 32, 95, 120, 205
Balestier, Beatty 88, 99, 107-9, 183, 243
Balestier, Wolcott 72-5, 79, 82, 95, 243
Bambridge, George 226, 234, 239, 242
Bambridge, Mrs G 1896-1976 (Elsie
    Kipling, RK's daughter) 117, 121,
    167-8, 175, 179, 185, 203, 207, 222-
    3, 226-8, 236, 238, 242
Barr, R ed: 'The Idler' 69/*n*4, 107
Barrie, Sir James 120
Bateman's, Burwash xiii, 142-3, 154-
    5, 157-9, 166, 172, 174, 203, 235,
    239
Bates, Sir Percy 232-3, 240, 244
Bayly, Capt, RN 79, 115, 123
Beardsley, Aubrey 62
Beast and Man in India 71, (illus: 13)
    see Kipling, John Lockwood
Beaverbrook, Lord 206
Beresford, G C ('M'Turk') 15, 18-19,
    116
Bewdley, Worcs 24, 36
Bible, The 71, 148, 206, 233

Birkenhead, Lord 243
Bland-Sutton, Sir John 185, 222, 228,
    240
Bliss Cottage, Vermont 93
Boer War 129-33, 178
Bok, Edward 125
Bombay xxv, 3-4, 6-12, 22, 82, 109, 184,
    229
Branwell, Maria xxiv
Brattleboro, Vermont 88, 109
Brontë, Patrick xxiv
Browning, Robert xxv, 10, 17, 74, 92,
    97, 142, 152, 175
Buchanan, Robert 63/*n*35
Burne-Jones, (Sir) Edward xxiii, 5, 14,
    38, 58, 68, 120, 122, 217, 224
Burne-Jones, Lady (Georgiana
    Macdonald) xxiii, 10-11, 53, 57-8,
    68-9, 117, 119, 174-5, 177, 185, 202
Burne-Jones, Sir Philip (Phil, RK's
    cousin) RK acts 'father-confessor'
    to 58; dines with EB-J & RK
    Christmas 1889 68; paints RK's
    portrait & plays with printing press
    at The Elms 126-7
Burton, Mrs dedicatee of *Plain Tales
    from the Hills*, 40

Cambridge University, made
    Honorary Fellow of Magdalene
    College 240
Canada 96, 174-6, 189, 237
Carnegie, Andrew, Scottish-born
    American steel magnate 219
Chevrillon, André 137
Chichester Cathedral 169-70
China, dislike of 50-1

Civil & Military Gazette, (*CMG*) Lahore 21, 28-9, 32, 36-7, 43, 168
Clan Donald xvi-xx
Conan Doyle, Sir Arthur 62, 102
Conland, Dr James 105, 109, 115, 124, 141
Cope Cornford, Leslie 142-4
Crofts, W ('Mr King') 17, 28
Cunard: ss *Queen Mary* (*534*) 232-3
Currie, Sir Donald 123

Daily Mail, The 139, 152
Daimler motor car, 'Gunhilda' takes John to prep school 174
Dare, William John, general manager *Pioneer* xiv
De Morgan, William 10
Dickens, Charles 53-4, 58-9
Dorset 101, 119-20
Doubleday, F N D 113, 117, 123-5, 175
Dowson, Ernest 62/*n*27
Dufferin, Lord 29-30, 74
Dufferin, Lady 36
Dunham, Dr Theo 243-4
Dunsterville, L C Major-General, ('Stalky') 19, 102, 116, 202-3, 230
Durham University 175

East, Alfred 93
Egypt, Nile and Middle East 178-80, 229, 234-5, 238
Eliot, T S 129
Embryo, the hired motor car 140-1
Emerson, Ralph Waldo 88-9, 171
Engelberg, learning to skate & ski 178
England, discovery of 140-1, 218, 221, 238

Father and Son: see Gosse, Edmund
Fisher, Admiral 200-1
Fleming, John (Jack) 228
Fleming, Mrs John Alice ('Trix') Kipling, RK's sister (1868-1948) birth 5; at Southsea 9-11; in London with mother 14, at Southsea 20; Lahore 30-1, 39; London 70; mental health 126, 139; at Tisbury

186; 229; well again 239; RK describes proof-reading to 240
Forster, John (Dickens' biographer) 58
France, discovery of 19; *see also* motoring in
Fulford, William xxiii
Garrard, Florence xiv, 21-2, 39-40, 70-1, 78
George V, King 216, 233
Globe-trotting in:
    Australia & New Zealand 80-2
    Canada 96, 174-6, 189, 237
    China 50-1
    Egypt, Nile & Middle East 178-80, 229, 234-5, 238
    Japan 51-2, 89-93
    South Africa 79-80, 121-2, 164, 177-8
    South America 229-31
    USA xvi, 50, 52-4, 95, 97, 127
    West Indies 236-7
Gordon, Arthur xxvi/*n*1
Gosse, Edmund 8-9, 63-4, 82, 87, 119
Grange,The, North End Road 5, 11, 38
Great War, the 187-206
Gwynne, H A 166, 187, 206, 229

Haggard, Sir H Rider 62, 132, 155-7, 164, 181, 187, 189, 202-3, 210, 224-5
Hardy, Thomas 62, 74, 119-20
Harmsworth, Alfred (Lord Northcliffe) 139
Haslam F W 81
Heinemann, W 82, 87
Henley, W E 89
Hill, Mrs S A 'Ted' meets RK in Allahabad 42; her impressions of 42-43, 69; RK writes to 44, 51, 54, 56, 62, 69, 125, 178, 186; RK travels with the Hills 46, 57; RK calls onLondon 74; staying with Hills (1889) 171; no mention of in autobiography 243
Hill, Professor, S Alex 42, 46, 48, 51-2, 74

Holloway, Capt , Pryse Agar 'Uncle Harry' 8

Holloway, Mrs P A 'Aunty Rosa' and son Harry, 6-9, 11, 21-22, 71

Horace 17, 233, 241

Hughes, C E 236/*n*26

Hunt, Holman 10

India, as RK knew it 7, 22-46, 136-8
Allahabad 40-43, 44
Bombay xxv, 3-4, 6-12, 22, 82, 109, 184, 229
Lahore 27-40, 43, 45-6, 229
Simla 30, 33

James, Henry 63/*n*36, 82-3, 87, 100, 104, 140, 150-1

Jameson, Dr 182

Japan, enchanted with 51-2, 89-93

Joan of Arc 166, 210

Johnson, Claude (the hyphen in R-R) 212

Keats, John 160

Kincaid, Dennis 31

King Edward's School, Birmingham xxii

Kipling, Alice ('Trix') *see* Fleming, Mrs John

Kipling, Elsie *see* Bambridge, Mrs George

Kipling, H M S 247

Kipling, John 1897-1915 (RK's son) birth 119; St Aubyns school 174; 'living down' father's verse 180-2; eyesight 187; commissioned Irish Guards 188; in France 189; letters home 193-7; motorbike and Singer car, last motor tour with family 213-14; killed in action 201

Kipling, John Lockwood, (RK's father) comments on Alice's family xxii; his parents, schooldays, engagement xxiv-xxv; to Bombay with Alice 4; leave Ruddy at Southsea 7-8; portrait of at V & A Museum 14; takes Ruddy to Paris

Exposition 19; concern for son's future 21; his place in Indian society 29; father and son work together in London 71; comments on Carrie 83; visits Naulakha, comments on 95-7; father and son to Westward Ho! 100; Alice and John at Rock House 113; to New York to comfort Rudyard & Carrie 124-5; death 186

Kipling, Mrs J L (Alice Macdonald, RK's mother) dislike of sea travel xiv; 'table turning' xx; a flirt xxiii; engagement xxv; her influence over son's early years 4-9; removes Ruddy from Lorne Lodge 12-14; arranges education at USC 14-17, 175; unaware of son's treatment at Lorne Lodge 20-21; Rudyard must 'be civil' 42, 44; 'all Celt' 71; her contribution to son's work 75, 135; retires to Tisbury 96; death 186

Kipling, Josephine (RK's daughter) 94, 117, 124, 139, 181, 219

Kipling, Joseph Rudyard (1865-1936)

Aspects of his Life and Work

acting ability 89, 93, 102, 236
ambitions xiii, xiv
ancestry xvi-xxv, 77, 148
ancestral memory 77-8
anxieties 130, 172, 182-3, 233
appearance: at school 15; London 30-1, 63-4; Vermont 99-100
birth Bombay xxv
childhood 4-12; legacy of Southsea 11-12; mother returns 13-15; memories of 137, 179, 181
colour and, 138, 224
conflict, need for 184
copyright problems 52-3, 74
criticism 30, 103-4, 129, 164
Daemon, RK's xx, 96, 107, 135
death London 244
devotion to children 94, 96, 203

East/West dichotomy 136-8

education at USC 15-21

emotions, prey to Southsea 12, 40; over pirated books 52, 54, 127; praise 63; patronage 64; need for emotional ballast 68; at Christmas 69, 207; writing *Irish Guards* 203

eye-sight 9, 12-13

home life with parents 29

homesickness 72, 100-1, 117, 178-80

honours/awards 131, 175-6, 205, 240

ill-health/breakdowns 12, 34, 37-8, 43, 69, 185, 188, 206-7, 225, 241

imagination as child 4-5, 6, 8, 10, 13; Canton 51; London 69; dreaded his children learning to read too soon 164; childhood traumas caused by, 181

inheritance xix, xx, xxii, 77, 138

insomnia 13, 31, 134

journalism:

in India xiv, 27-30, 32-3, 35-7, 39-46

in London 59, 62, 65-6, 69-72, 74-7

in Boer War 131

the Law & RK 117, 147

London *literati* and 62-4, 66, 68, 74, 97

loneliness 53, 62, 66, 68,

marriage & children: Vermont 93-109; John's birth 119; death of Josephine 124-5; letters to his children 174-7; to Carrie 199

memory xv, 179

music, lack of 102, 224

music halls (Gatti's) 61, 65, 135, 196

pets 38-9, 70, 233-4, 238-9

prophetic eye xx, 172, 187, 242; in science fiction 165-6; and medicine 240

sensitivity 31, 157, 180, 199

smell, sense of 22, 82, 137-8, 178, 221

stress/breaking strain 12, 207, 240

temperament xv-xvi, 29, 30-1, 72, 122, 127, 236; contradictory traits in 184

titles, unofficial: Poet of Empire xvi, 119; Poet of the Sea, Voice of the Silent Service 12, 247; Poet of the Engine-room 115; the Soldiers' Poet 206

War Graves Commission 206-8, 210, 214-6, 223, 233

war reporter 189, 194-9, 199-201, 202, 205

women, dependence on xiv, 21-2, 32, 33-4, 39-40, 62, 70-1, 72, 76, 78, 82-3, 96, 226-7

Opinions & beliefs

America and Americans xvi, 50, 52-4, 95, 97, 127

cricket 116-7

foreign missions, 97

life & death 165, 243

politics xxi, 182-3

publishers 74, 127

religion xiii, xvi, xix, xxi, 32, 39, 71, 148-9, 206, 233, 243

revenge 74; theme of, 188-9

Interests/activities

cycling 114, 120, 121-2, 139, 151

expertise of others, the xv, 10-11, 159-60, 212

fishing 105, 113-4, 203

golf 99

kite-flying 45

letter-writing 32, 42-3, 54, 94, 122-3, 210, 222-3, 236, 240-1, 243

motive power 18, 42, 48, 79-80, 99, 102-4, 118, 166, 178, 212, 237, 244

motoring 126, 139-42, 144-52, 174, 212-4, 222-5, 228, 231; thirst for technical information, talking point with John 212-13; fears for future safety on roads 239; *see also* motoring in: England, France, Scotland, Sicily

rifle clubs/shooting 132

sailor, the 90, 93

sea, the xv, xiii, 48-50, 53, 72, 74, 77, 80, 90, 93, 187, 229
ships 49, 56, 77, 90, 102-4, 168, 179, 187, 199-201, 209, 211, 229, 232-3, 247 *see also* ships sailed in 'Tommy', the 49, 66/*n*42, 68, 93, 130

Events

birth & early childhood Bombay xxv, 7; to England (1868) with mother for Trix's birth 3-4; at Lorne Lodge with Mrs Holloway 6-10; 'paradise'at The Grange 10-11; Alice returns, Ruddy near breakdown and almost blind 12-13; long holiday 13-14; school at United Services College 15-21; writes verse & edits school magazine 18-19; visits Paris with father 19; infatuated with Flo Garrard 20; journalism in India 27-46; Family Square complete 30; breakdowns & fever 37-8, 43; meets Mrs Hill 42; voyage Home via USA 48-53; tours USA, calls on Mark Twain and Uncle Harry 54-6; London and rooms in Villiers Street 58; reaction of the *literati* 62-63; engaged to Mrs Hill's sister 62; fever and overwork 69; breaks off engagement, is rejected by Flo 70-71; friendship with Wolcott Balestier 73; meets Wolcott's sister, Caroline 74; told to take long voyage: to Cape Town 78, Antipodes and India 80-2; marries Caroline 82-3; honeymoon voyage to USA and Far East 88-92; Josephine born at Bliss Cottage,Vermont 94; 'M'Andrew's Hymn' 100; Elsie born at Naulakha 105; *Captains Courageous* 105-7; quarrel with Carrie's brother 107-9; leave Naulakha for good 109; at Rock House 112-17; at sea with Royal Navy 114-5, 118, 123; 'Recessional' and John born at North End House 119; they rent The Elms 120; all to South Africa 121; Uncle Ned dies 122; illness of RK & death of Josephine in New York (1899) 123-4; 'They' 125-6; anxiety over Trix 126; Boer War & 'Absent-minded Beggar' 129-33; refuses knighthood 131; *Stalky & Co* and *Kim* published 134; becomes pioneer motorist 139-152; 'Steam Tactics' & conflict with the Law 147; Bateman's & 'his fraction of England' 154-9; two weeks with the Fleet (1901) 162-3; *Just So Stories* published 163-4; receives Joan of Arc medal 166; the *Puck* stories & Viking galleys 167-72; John at St Aubyns 174; RK to Canada & McGill university for degree-giving ceremony, 'Letters to the Family' 175-6; Nobel Prize for Literature 176-7; to Egypt & Nile, 'homesick for East' 178-80; Carrie's health 185; death of parents, Trix in care, death of Price 186; war breaks out; John turned down for territorials because of eyesight 187; Lord Roberts offers him commission in Irish Guards 188; both father and son in France on war businesss (1915) 189; exchange of letters 193-8; with Dover patrol and Harwich Flotilla 199-201; John missing 201; writes history of the Irish Guards 203-205; reports from Italian front 205; offers of 'any honour' turned down 205; becomes War Graves Commissioner 206; suffers periodic agonising pains, fear of cancer 206-7; John's body never found 206; breaking strain 207; post-war pilgrimage to cemeteries; 'The Gardener' 210; discovers France by motor car, pre- and post war 211-18, 221-5; tour Scotland 218-221; Elsie's marriage desolates parents 226-228; RK seriously ill, advised to go to South America for warmth 228; writes travel sketches 229-31; and to Sicily 231-2; corresponds with Bates re new Cunard liner 232-3; and Black Aberdeens 233-4; to Egypt & Palestine 234-5, 238; to West Indies where Carrie is taken ill 236-7; to Bath for Carrie – and new typewriter 238; economise with smaller R-R 239; themes of stories in *Limits and Renewals* 239-40; made honorary Fellow of Cambridge college 240; revising last edition of *Verse* 240-1; his warning of war to come resented (1934) 242; Carrie ill again; they go to Marienbad 243; revising his autobiography as 70th birthday looms 243; taken ill in London & dies 18 January 1936 244

Kipling, Mrs Rudyard 1862-1939 (Caroline Balestier) meets RK 74; understanding with 76, 78; marries RK 82; takes charge 83, 89; protects him 96; row with Beatty 107; Josephine dies 124; revisits Naulakha (1899) 125; move to Bateman's 143; collapses 185-6; mail from the Front 197-8; racing trains in R-R 212; depressed 225; interferes in Elsie's life 228; taken ill in West Indies 236-7; to Marienbad for the cure 243; Rud dies 244

Kipling Society 230

Lahore 27-40, 43, 45-6, 229

Lanchester, Dr Fredk delivers motor to Bateman's 145; becomes regular visitor 147-50

Lanchester cars 145, 147; experimental models 149-51

Landon, Perceval 196, 198

Lang, Andrew 63, 156

Langley, Professor S P 148

Lawrence, Max Lanchester Works Manager, takes RK on trial run 144-5

Leonardslee, Sussex 148

Locomobile steam car in 'Steam Tactics' 141; continual breakdowns 141-2, 144

London, working in 57-66, 68-78, 97

Macdonald of Sleat clan history xvi-xx

Macdonald, Edith 1848-1937 (RK's aunt) never married xxiv; at Bewdley with Ruddy 5; RK corresponds with 34-5, 38, 134-5, 239, 243; at Rock House 117

Macdonald, Florence 1869-1956 (RK's cousin) larks with Ruddy 20; visits Rock House (illus 16) 116; visits The Elms 130

Macdonald, Rev Frederic William 1842-1928 (RK's uncle) birth xxii; gives sisters away in marriage xxiii; meets John Kipling xxiv; gives Alice away xxv; pronounces on young Ruddy 5; to New York with RK to dying brother 75; gift for mimicry & oratory 93

Macdonald, Rev George Browne 1805-1868 (RK's grandfather) in harness to the ministry at twenty xxi; educated at Woodhouse Grove School xxiv; too sick to attend Alice & John's wedding xxv

Macdonald, Mrs G B 1809-1875 (Hannah Jones, RK's grand-mother) marries GBM xxi; unable to attend Alice's wedding xxv; visits Ruddy & Trix at Southsea 11

Macdonald, Henry James 1835-1891 (Harry, RK's uncle) introduces Ned Jones and Crom Price to sisters xxii; emigrates to America xiii; Fred sends news of Alice & children 5; RK calls on him in New York 55; dies before Fred and RK arrive 75

Macdonald, Rev James 1761-1833 (RK's great grandfather) birth, upbringing, itinerant preacher xix, xxi

MacDonald, Alan and Flora 171-2

Mackail, Angela (Mrs G L Thirkell) 94, 122, 127

Mackail, Professor J W 119

Mackail, Mrs J W Margaret Burne-Jones (RK's cousin) 10, 30, 34-5, 43, 70, 83, 94

Maidencombe *see* Rock House

Marconi, G 159-60

Millership, Archie Lanchester trials driver 150

Milner, Lord 225

Montagu, Lord, pioneer motorist; takes the Kiplings for drive in his R-R 212

Morris, William (Uncle Topsy) 10, 14

Mother Maturin 32, 134-5

motor cars, RK's, *see under* Daimler, Embryo, Lanchester, Locomobile, Rolls-Royce

motoring in:
England: discovery of 140-1, 218, 221, 238
France: 210-18, 221-5, 228, 231, 241-2
Scotland: 127, 218-21
Sicily: 231-2

motor tours Journal 212-225

Naulakha, Brattleboro 95-109, 112, 117, 123, 125, 165

Nichols, Beverley 129

Norton, Professor C E 98-9, 107, 175

Norton, Sallie 118, 124

Oxford University 57, 175

Paterson, A B ('Banjo') 81, 133, 144-5

Phillpotts, Eden 115

Pioneer, Allahabad RK star reporter on, 40

Plowden, Edith, a family friend 21/*n*40, 27/*n*1, 32/*n*18

Poynter, Sir Ambrose (RK's cousin Ambo) 58, 82, 101, 117, 157

Poynter, (Sir) Edward John, P R A xxiii, 14, 143

Poynter, Lady (Agnes Macdonald) xxiii, 117

Poynter, Sir Hugh (RK's cousin) 58, 117

Price, Cormell ('Uncle Crom') xxii, 15-19, 21, 28, 100-1, 115-6, 120, 175, 186-7

Raven Hill, L *Stalky* illustrations, 116; *Punch* cartoon, 149 (illus: jacket)

Rhodes, Cecil 121-2

Roberts, Lord 131, 188

Robinson, E Kay (Ed: *CMG*) 29, 35, 37, 39, 42

Rolls-Royce cars, lent RK car & chauffeur 212; no other marque in future 213, 217-8, 221-2, 225, 228, 238-9

Rossetti, Dante Gabriel 93

Rock House, Maidencombe 112-117

Rottingdean
North End House 118-19
The Elms 120-142

Royal Navy 79-80, 114-5, 118, 123, 159, 162-3, 199-201, 247

St James Gazette 89

San Francisco Harbour xv

Savile Club 68, 74, 156

Scotland *see* Motoring in

Scots Observer 66

Ships sailed in
Africa, ss B I 1889 Rangoon-Singapore 49, 66
Aller, ss North German Lloyd 1891 New York
Ancona, P&O 1889 Hong Kong-Yokohama 49, 50
Andes, RMSP 1927 to South America 229
Armadale Castle, Union Castle Line, 1904, 1905 South Africa
Brindisi, ss P&O 1882 to India 21
City of Berlin, Inman Line 1889 New York to Liverpool 56
City of Peking, Pacific Mail Co 1880

Yokohama-San Francisco 53

Coronado, ss 1930 Avonmouth-West Indies 236

Doric, Shaw Savill Line 1891 Cape Town-Wellington 80

Dunvegan Castle, Union Castle 1896 to South Africa 123

Empress of China, C P R 1892 Yokohama-Vancouver 93

Empress of India, C P R 1892 Vancouver-Yokohama 89, 91

Ho-nam, steamer trip 1889 Hong Kong-Canton 50-1

Kildonan Castle, Union Castle 1902, 1904 S Africa and back 209

Kinfauns Castle, Union Castle 1901-1906 S Africa and back 131, 209

Lahn, North German Lloyd 1896 New York-Southampton 108-9

Madura, ss BI 'Mutton Mail' 1889 Calcutta-Rangoon 46, 48

Majestic ss Ocean Steam Navigation Co 1899 Liverpool-New York 123

Mexican, Union Steamship Co 1891 London-Cape Town 78

Nawab, P&O 1889 Singapore-Hong Kong 49

Norham Castle Union Castle 1898 Cape Town-Southampton 123

Normannia, Southern Railway 1925 Southampton-Le Havre 209, 223

Ripon, P&O 1865 & 1868 to and from India 3,4

Talune, Union Steamship Co of NZ 1891 Wellington-Melbourne 81

Teutonic, White Star 1892 Liverpool-New York 88, 92, 125

Walmer Castle Union Castle 1902, 1903 Southampton-Cape Town (illus 26)

Sicily, *see* motoring in

Simla, *see* India

South Africa 79-80, 121-2, 164, 177-8

South African War *see* Boer War

South America 229-31

South Kensington Museum xxiv, 13 *see* Victoria &Albert Museum

Southsea 6-13, 20-1, 29, 184, 224

Stephen, J K 156

Stevenson, R L 63/*n*37, 80, 87, 92, 97

Stoddard, Charles 97

Stoker, Bram 87

Study Five, USC 17-20

Sullivan, Sir Arthur 130

Sussex, discovery of 155-7, 167, 172 *See also* motoring in, England

Swinburne Algernon C 17, 102

Sykes, Lady Isobel 235

Taylor, Caroline, (Mrs Hill's sister) 56, 61-2, 70-1, 74, 78

Tennyson, Alfred 9, 65, 75, 104, 152

Thirkell, Angela (Mrs G L) *see* Mackail, Angela

Thomas Atkins ('Tommy') 66/*n*42, 130

Times, The, Moberly Bell, manager 71, 92, 98, 117, 119, 146, 188, 213

Tisbury, Wiltshire *see* Arundell House

Twain, Mark (S L Clemens) 55, 168, 175

typewriters 238

United Services College (USC), Westward Ho! 14-21

United States of America xvi, 52-3, 54, 95, 97, 127

Victoria & Albert Museum *see* South Kensington Museum

Villiers Street, Strand RK at , 58-9, 61, 69, 76

Walford, Miss Mary, Bateman's secretary 235-6

War Graves Commission 206-8, 210, 214-6, 223

War of Independence, American 171

Webb-Johnson, Sir Alfred, surgeon 243, 244

Wellington School 182

Wesley, John xxi, xxiv, 32

Westward Ho!, N Devon *see* United Services College

West Indies 236-7
Wheeler, Stephen, ed: *CMG*, Lahore
    21, 27-8
White, E L 101/*n*35
Wilde, Oscar 63
Willcocks, Sir William 158
Wimpole Hall 242
Wodehouse, P G 159
Woodhouse Grove School xxiv
Wordsworth, William 9, 152
World War One *see* Great War, the

Younghusband, Sir Francis 30